Marion Ernwein, Franklin Ginn, James Palmer (eds.)
The Work That Plants Do

Marion Ernwein is a lecturer in environmental geography at the Open University. She researches the changing place of plants in contemporary urbanism.

Franklin Ginn is a senior lecturer in cultural geography at the University of Bristol. He is author of *Domestic wild: Memory, nature and gardening in suburbia*, and co-editor of *Environmental Humanities*.

James Palmer is a lecturer in environmental governance at the University of Bristol. His research examines resource-making practices associated with new bioenergy economies and infrastructures.

Marion Ernwein, Franklin Ginn, James Palmer (eds.)

The Work That Plants Do

Life, Labour and the Future of Vegetal Economies

[transcript]

Bibliographic information published by the Deutsche Nationalbibliothek

The Deutsche Nationalbibliothek lists this publication in the Deutsche National-bibliografie; detailed bibliographic data are available in the Internet at http://dnb.d-nb.de

Cover layout: Maria Arndt, Bielefeld
Cover illustration: Jean-Jacques Kissling, jjkphoto.ch

Print-ISBN 978-3-8376-5534-6
PDF-ISBN 978-3-8394-5534-0
https://doi.org/10.14361/9783839455340
ISSN of series: 2703-1640
eISSN of series: 2703-1659

Contents

SECTION I
Planty commodities

SECTION II
Vegetal Labour

SECTION III
Future-making with plants

Acknowledgements

The idea for this book first emerged at the 2018 Annual Meeting of the American Association of Geographers, in New Orleans. It was the product of conversations between what would become the editors and several of the contributors during and around sessions centred on vegetal geographies. The book project further developed through additional conversations at the 2019 edition of the meeting, in Washington, D.C. Many of our great hopes for the book – for it to be the fruit of a truly collaborative writing process, inclusive of a workshop and a mutual peer-reviewing process – had to be re-evaluated in light of the Covid-19 pandemic, which hit us at the start of 2020, and is still with us as we write this in April 2021. The workshop never took place, some of the contributors were forced out of the project by their increased care commitments, and the pace of writing, reviewing and revising chapters was affected. We thank wholeheartedly all of our contributors – those whose chapters figure in the book, and those whose potential contribution remains a ghostly presence – for the time they have made for this project, for their generosity, and for the care they have put into reading and engaging with each other's work. At transcript, we wish to thank Jakob Horstmann for his enthusiasm, guidance and perhaps above anything his patience throughout the life of this book, and Annika Linnemann for making the production such a smooth, seamless process. Finally, we also thank all those with whom we've enjoyed nonhuman labour conversations and debates over the years at events from Islamabad to Washington, Aarhus, and many places in-between.

Author biographies

Jennifer Atchison lives and works in Dharawal Country. She is Senior Lecturer in the School of Geography and Sustainable Communities, University of Wollongong, and an Australian Research Council Future Fellow, awarded 2020. She has a passion for plants and a multidisciplinary background in environmental science and archaeobotany. Her current research seeks to understand the place of plants in past, present and future lives and how life is responding and adjusting to rapid environmental change. She has had the privilege of learning about people, plants and environmental change in Gadjerong Country.

Jeremy Brice is a Postdoctoral Researcher at the University of Oxford and Visiting Fellow in Economic Sociology at LSE. In Oxford, his research examines the role of sustainability, biosecurity and animal welfare metrics in reconfiguring both public debates over and the governance of intensive meat production. Jeremy's doctoral work investigated the economic and environmental transformations engendered by the Australian wine industry's reorientation towards the production of 'wines from somewhere', examining how changing logics of evaluation and accumulation intersect with attachments to place to generate contrasting political economies and ecologies of quality. More recent research projects have focused on the anticipation of crisis and the governance of risk within transnational food supply networks and on the role of digital marketplace platforms in reconfiguring urban economies and cultures of food consumption in the UK.

Can Dalyan is an Assistant Professor of Anthropology at the College of Charleston. His first book project, *Life, Arrested: Genebanking and the Biopolitics of Climate Change in Turkey*, draws on multi-year ethnographic fieldwork in Turkey and analyzes the management of latent plant life inside the country's first national seed bank in juxtaposition with biopolitical projects that seek to arrest social life such as extended emergency rule, refugee camps, and shelter-in-place regulations. His second long-term project, based in Charleston, SC, explores climate adaptation within the context of sea level rise, flooding preparedness, and real estate speculation.

Marion Ernwein is a Lecturer in Environmental Geography at the Open University. Her work examines the politics of urban ecological labour – at once waged, volunteer, and more-than-human. Her current research investigates the changing place of plants in urban environmental management, in areas as diverse as urban design, ecological management, and air pollution mitigation. Her recent publications include the book *Les natures de la ville néolibérale: Une écologie politique du végétal urbain* (2019) as well as journal articles in the *Annals of the American Association of Geographers* and *Social & Cultural Geography*, among others.

Franklin Ginn is a Senior Lecturer in Cultural Geography at the University of Bristol. His research interests are in cultures of nature, environment-society relations and philosophical questions concerning the nonhuman. His previous research projects include green gentrification in Lisbon, religious temporalities and ethics of climate change in Scotland, and plant politics in urban Pakistan. He is currently researching soil cultures in the Himalaya, and the role of nonhumans in space exploration. He is author of *Domestic wild: Memory, nature and gardening in suburbia* (Routledge, 2016), and co-editor of *Environmental Humanities*.

Emilie Letouzey, currently a Fyssen Foundation Postdoctoral Researcher at Ōsaka University's Anthropology Department, investigates relations to plants, conceptions of life and living things in contemporary Japan. Based on in-depth ethnographic fieldwork conducted in Ōsaka's metropolitan area, her PhD in Cultural Anthropology (University of Toulouse Jean Jaurès, 2019) is about traditional horticulture. Focusing on cultivation techniques and human relations around plants, the thesis draws on an anthropology of life engaged with the concrete manipulations of living beings that are at once organisms and artefacts. An attempt to characterize vegetal life in Japan as a "grey zone of life", Emilie Letouzey's ongoing research explores the technical aspect of plants handling in temples and shrines on the one hand, and in ornamental plant industry on the other hand.

Jared Margulies is an Assistant Professor in Political Ecology in the Department of Geography at the University of Alabama. His research explores political ecology, a diverse field of practice interested in the production of environmental inequalities, human-nature relationships, and how matters of social justice intersect with pressing environmental questions. He is currently writing a book, *The succulent subject: A political ecology of plants, desire, and illicit trade*, based on research he conducted as a postdoctoral research fellow with the BIOSEC project, which ran until August 2020 at the University of Sheffield.

Daanish Mustafa is Professor of Critical Geography at King's College London. His research has been funded by the Belmont Forum, International Development Research Centre, Department for International Development, Natural Environment Research Council, National Geographic Society, Royal Geographical Society, and the British Academy. Daanish was the co-author of the first climate change response strategies for Pakistan, in addition to being the lead author for the UNDP in Pakistan's five-year flood response strategy. In addition, he has also undertaken policy-related work with the International Organization for Migration, Stimson Centre, and United States Institute for Peace (USIP). He is author of *Water resources management in a vulnerable world: Hydro-hazardscapes of climate change* (IB Tauris, 2012).

James Palmer is a Lecturer in Environmental Governance in the School of Geographical Sciences at the University of Bristol. His research interests sit at the interface of environmental politics, critical political ecology and science and technology studies. Previously he has researched knowledge controversies relating to transport biofuels policy and road vehicle emissions, as well as governance challenges associated with emerging carbon dioxide removal technologies. More recently he has sought to examine emergent resource-making practices associated with new bioenergy economies and infrastructures in the UK and US, as well as policy controversies relating to wider 'nature-based' solutions to climate change.

Harold Perkins is an Associate Professor in the Department of Geography at Ohio University. He earned a PhD in Geography from the University of Wisconsin-Milwaukee in 2006. His research broadly focuses on the political ecology and economy of environments, including topics of the state, governance, neoliberalization, and environmental justice. He is interested in the political status of nonhuman organisms within capitalist spaces including cities and parklands. In particular his work reflects an openness to the power of nonhumans to coproduce (dis)empowering environmental configurations for humans and other organisms.

List of Figures

Introduction: The work that plants do

Marion Ernwein, James Palmer, Franklin Ginn

A vegetal world

From tree-based climate solutions, green infrastructure, and plant-based diets, to ecosystem services and biotechnological innovations, more hope than ever is being invested in plants to help mitigate multi-dimensional environmental, social and economic crises. Such schemes are the latest refrain in the long history of modernity's instrumentalisation of ecology. Their promissory rhetoric works to distract us from a deeper truth: that economy and culture have always relied on plants. Plants subtend planetary capitalism not just as 'resources' or commodities, but also more fundamentally by providing the basis of planetary life. Despite this, the development of a new array of concepts and tools that serve the common purpose of squeezing yet more out of plant life begs our attention. In response, the contributions in this book ask: What work do plants do, within capitalist ecologies? How does the current crisis of capitalist accumulation transform what we expect from them? And what kind of work might plants do, at the edge of and beyond capitalist relations?

At the end of the 20th century, Wandersee and Schussler (1999) diagnosed an ailment troubling the human sensorium, that of plant blindness: the persistent overlooking and undervaluing of our fellow photosynthesising earthlings. The roots of so-called plant blindness lie in the way a certain conception of life was fundamental to the modernist western project: life as expressed in desire, movement, power and the ability wilfully to channel inorganic and organic energies – in other words, a thoroughly animal and very un-vegetal life. However, plant blindness was always a highly selective affliction, not some universal cognitive condition. There have always been pluriversal worlds comprised by Indigenous cosmology that never trucked in hierarchy and disenchantment (Escobar 2020). And even from within the bowels of Modernity, any gardener, poet, naturalist, biologist, forester, peasant, poacher, shipbuilder, surveyor, or indeed any number of other kinds of labourer, have long worked in intimate relation with plants (Meeker/Szabari, 2020).

Might plant blindness be a thing of the past? In the last several decades, heterodox plant science has advanced our knowledge of plants' remarkably diverse and complex powers of reproduction, dispersal, and communication (Chamowitz 2012). Previously marginal scholarly commitments to the ideas of plant memory, sense, cognition and even intelligence have become the foundational basis of a burgeoning new wave of popular writing, both fictional and non-fictional, on the intricate modes of existence of vegetal life (Mancuso 2018; Powers 2018; Vandermeer 2014). The popularity of new plant science speaks to the waning credibility of individual organisms as the favoured site of ethics or life itself (Haraway 2016). Plants' distributed, cross-kingdom collaborative worldings perhaps offer some imaginative succour alternative to the individualising, deadening world of late capitalism.

This emerging reappraisal of the nature and capacities of plants raises many questions: What are humanity's ethical responsibilities towards vegetal life, once plants have been acknowledged as sensate, communicative, world-making beings? How can 'plant-based' solutions to environmental problems acknowledge and accompany vegetal capacities, without further afflicting plants with the very objectifying forms of knowledge and disciplinary regimes of regulation that gave rise to the environmental crisis in the first place? And what role should there be for scientific concepts and knowledge in reshaping everyday relations with plants?

Although the history of humanity is a history of plant selection and breeding, of variety creation, of tree pruning and grafting, the molecular turn in the life sciences has recently shifted the scale at which plant life can be known and intervened in: through genetic engineering and biocomputation, for example, relations between capital-intensive technologies and plant life are not merely intensifying, but multiplying, often with an explicit focus on accelerating plants' metabolic activities and imprinting proprietorship directly within their basic functions (Kloppenburg 2004). There is clearly therefore no single, coherent direction in which new understandings of plant life are leading, inviting the question: If the future is to be vegetal, then what futures can be built with plants at the edge of, and beyond, a broken capitalist world? This book aims to begin to parse the multiple avenues available for shaping human-plant relations yet to come; it does so by examining a range of particular formations of vegetal power, analysing the modes of work that plants do in planetary capitalism.

Plant turns

Human-plant relations are a longstanding topic within the social sciences. Anthropology, archeobotany and ethnobotany have all played central roles in examining the modes of categorisation used by different societies to know and order the plant world, as well as the sociotechnical knowledges developed to select, breed, and grow plants in practice (Haudricourt 1962). Human relations to plants have also been recognised as pivotal in shaping relations among people for some time, whether through symbolism – as captured, for example, in Laura Rival's (1998) edited collection *The Social Life of Trees* – or in a more material sense, as in Jones and Cloke's (2002) *Tree Cultures*. Countless other contributions to this rich background might just as easily be mentioned here. Yet the more recent 'plant turn' within the humanities and social sciences nonetheless captures something of an onto-logical and epistemological shift. Increasingly, plants are apprehended not merely as socio-cultural artefacts and symbols, but as living organisms "at the fulcrum of [their] world" (Marder 2013: 8), putting their own imprint firmly onto the re-lations within which they are enrolled. To fully understand the emergence of the plant turn, one must – at least initially – acknowledge the important influence of work in multispecies, and more specifically animal, studies. Guided by the motto that "We have never been human" (Haraway/Gane 2006), this wide body of thought highlights the active role that nonhuman processes and organisms play in shaping social life, from slugs complicating gardening (Ginn 2016), through to charismatic birds sustaining conservationists' interest and passion in their work (van Dooren 2016), and even pigeons helping to monitor air pollution (Haraway 2016). More-than-human geographers, for instance, have raised the important point that not only are there animal spaces, ordered by and through human social relations, but also beastly places, made and experienced by animals themselves (see Philo/Wilbert 2000). Paying closer attention to animals' perspectives, lived worlds, and etholo-gies, moreover, is frequently argued to be key to enacting more ethical modes of co-existence (van Dooren/Kirksey/Münster 2016).

The decentring of the "metaphysical image of the human" (Marder 2013: 1), some argue, has been predominantly predicated on a recentring of other animals, their lives, and their entanglement with us. Whilst this move has in many ways redressed the marginalisation suffered by animals, it nonetheless leaves important gaps in the list of organisms deemed to have a legitimate place in our understanding of ourselves, our world, and our responsibilities. Indeed, if animals have long been marginalised, "then non-human, non-animal living beings, such as plants, have populated the margin of the margin, the zone of absolute obscurity undetectable on the radars of our conceptualities" (Marder 2013, 2). By extension then, plant turn advocates can arguably be seen to attempt to achieve – in shifting attention from 'plant spaces' to 'vegetal places' – a recentring of plants predicated on the idea that they not only "are" but "exist" (Vattimo/Zabala, foreword to Marder 2013: xiv). Far from being "decorations on the tree of life" (Coccia 2019: 4, citing Niklas 2016: viii), from this perspective plants are in fact the most fundamental *makers* of the world; they "transform everything they touch into life, they make out of matter, air, and sunlight what, for the rest of the living, will be a space of habitation, a world" (Coccia 2019: 8). As sensory, communicative, and perhaps even intelligent beings, plants clearly do make lifeworlds in ways not like us animals. This has pushed hu-manities scholars to invent new repertoires for cultivating affective connections

with plants, suggesting that speculative fabulation with plants can offer a libera-
tory ethic. Natasha Myers (2018), for example, calls for seeding Planthropos, plant
and human figures joined in involutionary momentum moving towards a less toxic,
less violent world. Key here is the realisation that accounting for plants cannot be
a matter of simple extension, of bringing a new set of beings into the ethical tent;
rather, it mandates a fuller reevaluation of the philosophical and conceptual resources bequeathed to us.

Understanding plant alterity has long been a concern of Western philosophy,
dating back to Aristotle's suggestion that as well as political animals, humans are
'walking plants' (Nealon 2016: 36). Michael Marder's (2013: 3) agenda-setting *Plant-
Thinking*, for instance, reappraises centuries of Western philosophy through "scruti-
niz[ing] the uncritical assumptions on the basis of which [plant] life has been hith-
erto explained", foregrounding instead the "surprisingly heterodox approaches to
the vegetal world" that have germinated on its fringes (ibid: 3, 6). In a similar vein,
Jeffrey Nealon's (2016: xi) *Plant Theory: Biopower and Vegetable Life* seeks to redress the
"elision of plant life in recent biopolitical theory" and to use the unearthing of plant
life to redefine the boundaries of the "wider biopolitical focus on 'life' in humanities theory today" (ibid: xiv). Nealon's compelling argument is that contemporary
theories of *bio*power are thoroughly animalistic, and that different philosophical
moorings rooted in plant *physis*, or growth without telos, are necessary. Nealon
also cautions – a caution we share in this volume – that plant studies should not
move so quickly between vitalist celebration of plants to *any* vegetal ethics or politics.

Critical plant studies – the umbrella term for research within the 'plant turn' –
we suggest, need to retain emphasis on particular constellations of power that align
vegetal, human, material and economic flows – not least because plants cannot be
treated as a uniform green mass (there is a world of difference between phyto-
plankton and loblolly pine). Emanuele Coccia (2019: 124), in this vein, criticises the
writings of Marder, Nealon and others for their insistence "on finding the truth
about plants in purely philosophical or anthropological research, without having
any truck with contemporary botanical thought – which, on the contrary, has produced remarkable masterpieces in the philosophy of nature." Coccia's own work, in
contrast, seeks to revisit philosophy from the starting point of plants themselves,
engaging directly with research into plant life, behaviour, and communication. Yet
he also perceives a need to take some distance from the analogising tendencies evident in some quarters of the plant sciences – or what he describes as the "stubborn
attempt to 'rediscover' organs 'analogous' to those that make perception possible in
animals without trying at all to imagine [...] another possible form of the existence
of perception, another way of thinking the relation between sensation and body"
(ibid: 126). Not dissimilarly, for Karen Houle (2011), everything plants disrupt – the
binary between individual and collective, the idea that communication takes place

between two participants in a dyadic unit – should help to build a case against analogies, and instead provoke more radical and creative thinking that goes far beyond re-readings, however sophisticated, of existing concepts.

There is a fine line, in these accounts, between driving towards an understanding of plants on their own terms and building a new philosophy squarely upon the foundations of natural scientific enquiry, as if decades of work in the history and sociology of science had not given sufficient heed to humanities scholars or indeed social scientists tempted to take expert knowledge claims at face value. Clearly, social scientists should not rely on new plant science as a short-cut to re-enchantment and the revalorisation of plants. This is a point perhaps most forcefully and effectively made by decolonial and indigenous thinkers, who rightly question the reliance, in posthumanist thought more broadly, upon predominantly western philosophy and science (Todd 2016). Indeed, through anchoring their writings within a specific heritage (a line of descent running something like Aristotle-Enlightenment-thought-Heidegger-Foucault-posthumanism-whatever-comes-next) plant thinkers have a tendency to background the very rich veins of plant-thinking that have long existed within non-western philosophies and knowledge traditions (Kimmerer 2020). That these knowledges about plants suddenly appear as new and valid from the vantage point of Western epistemic communities is, in other words, symptomatic in itself of a deeper structural politics (Jackson 2020).

Work on plants in the social sciences has not been left untouched by these ontological, epistemological, and political discussions. While certainly sharing with plant philosophy and humanities an interest in advances in plant science, the specificity of these studies typically lies in the empirically-grounded character of their observations, and in the connections that they establish between broad ontological and epistemological questions and situated practices of plant growing, management and use. The social science 'plant turn' in other terms, has some distinctive features that warrant a specific discussion. Work in this guise proceeds in two principal ways. The first seeks to renew registers of analysis through recentring plant life in interpreting and conceptualising human practices. This approach, exemplified by scholars such as Lesley Head and Jennifer Atchison, develops a methodological sensibility that takes into account the difference that vegetal lifeforms make within specific socionatural settings. Head, Atchison and Phillips (2015: 399), for example, draw on biological research to discuss "the differences" that the "shared capacities of one grouping of beings called plants [...] bring to relations with humans and others." They discuss how accounting for plants' distinctive materialities, the singularities of their movements, their capacities to sense and communicate, and indeed the flexibility of their bodies, can help to renew understandings of and ultimately better inform invasive species management. Plant bodies, Atchison and Head argue, "challenge our understanding of individual and collective bodies"

(2013: 952), with broader implications for thinking about the embodied nature of environmental management. A second approach seeks to reappraise and recentre situated knowledges about what plants are and what they do. This approach does not presume that academic concepts of plant agency, behaviour and capacity need to be centred; instead, it is interested in following the categories that practitioners themselves mobilise to talk about, think about, and interact with lively vegetal processes. Illustrative of this second approach, Jeremy Brice (2014a; this volume) centres social practices of attention and registering in analysing vine growers' relations to the sometimes tumultuous processes of plant growth and ripening. He highlights how specific characters of vine life are registered and monitored, and how this in turn shapes relations between vine agencies and wine production. These two broad approaches are, of course, overlapping and often interconnect; nonetheless, they suggest that plant agency and capacity in fact play two kinds of roles – as categories of practice and of analysis – and that these roles themselves inspire the development of distinct epistemological registers and frameworks.

To date at least, this relatively new strand of research into vegetal politics has been firmly positioned within the more cultural branches of the social sciences (and especially within cultural anthropology and cultural geography). The premise of this book, intended both to contrast and complement such work, is that the conceptual resources of the plant turn(s) in fact also have much to offer to our understanding of contemporary economic processes of value creation, accumulation and reproduction. Indeed, notwithstanding occasional forays into the terrain between plant studies and critical political economy, scholars of vegetal politics have typically tended to appraise plants' roles in shaping the terms of situated, "embodied interrelating", rather than in co-constituting processes "of greater interest to political ecologists, including resource distribution and state-local relations" (Fleming 2017: 33). Accordingly, this book sets out to offer readers a collection of inquiries advancing diverse conceptual, empirical and methodological entry-points for beginning to understand the complex relations between vegetal agencies, resource making, commodity production, and ultimately value creation.

The work that plants do

Inquiry into the roles played by vegetal lifeforms within evolving relations between capitalism, nature, and the state is longstanding. Jack Kloppenburg (2004), for example, drew from earlier work in agricultural political economy in pinpointing the nature of seeds – at once the basis for producing crops and for deriving additional seeds – as a historical impediment to the ability of capitalism to establish full control over the means of agricultural production. From this perspective, the development of hybrid crop cultivars appears as essential not only to markedly increased global agricultural productivity in the second half of the 20th century, but also – given the sterility of those cultivars' seeds – to the establishment of properly capitalist social relations in industrial agriculture, wherein farmers must enter the market for an expanding range of basic agricultural input commodities. In another classic study, Scott Prudham (2005: 13) examined capital's "confrontation with and reliance on ecological processes" not in the sphere of industrial agriculture, but rather the vast Douglas-fir forests of North America's Pacific Northwest. For him as for Kloppenburg, the innate obstacles presented by nature – whether in the form of inherently non-uniform patterns and temporalities of tree growth, or the sheer extent of forests themselves – can only be overcome through an ongoing "struggle over the social (re)production of new natures" (ibid: 13).

While these and other landmark studies are at pains to avoid depicting "the matter of nature" (Fitzsimmons 1989) as a purely recalcitrant realm offering up "rigid limits to growth" (Prudham 2005: 17), an allegiance to theoretical frameworks regarding nature as socially constructed or produced (Smith 1984; Harvey 1996) nonetheless militates against a fuller accounting of "the productive capacities" of the nonhuman world itself (Bakker/Bridge 2006: 11). Such a fuller accounting is perhaps most easily seen in studies that engage with biotechnology. Within so-called 'bio-economies', capital accumulation and value production are driven not just by the (human) labour invested into manipulating biotic material or genetic information, but by the lively potentials of tissues, cells, and other biological materials themselves (Rajan 2006; Cooper 2011). These economies are often highly speculative and promissory: they harness the mutability of life as a field for the production of new commodities or services (or more often, potential new commodities or services). If studies of what has frequently been termed biocapital acknowledge the lively agencies of the nonhuman as a distinct "locus for accumulation" (Barua 2019: 650), they have also sometimes been decried for playing into the fetishization of the basic category of 'capital' itself (Helmreich 2008).

Still more recent work in more-than-human political economy – led especially by animal geographers and environmental anthropologists – has sought to appraise nonhuman agencies not just as a form of "lively capital" (Haraway 2008) that can be tapped into and drawn on, but as co-constitutive of the broader economic realm "from the outset" (Barua 2019: 651). Work attending to regimes of value production centred around animal life, for example, has increasingly advocated a view of the lively capacities of diverse species – in contexts ranging from food production to conservation and even cinema – as forms of "nonhuman labour" in their own right, whether metabolic (Beldo 2017), affective (Barua 2019), or intersubjective (Porcher 2015). That nonhuman nature might be explicitly understood as capable of working might come across as provocative. It would, however, come as little surprise to communities already seeking to capitalise on its supposedly enterprising instincts (Dempsey 2016), for example by extracting ecosystem services in the realm of biodiversity conservation. Yet it is not just an ability to work or per-form labour per se, but a fundamental capacity to shape basic economic processes centred around life – including its commodification, circulation, exchange, stor-age, and even consumption (Collard/Dempsey 2013; Banoub/Martin 2020) – that scholars at the forefront of this new wave of more-than-human political economic research attribute to the nonhuman. In other terms, that tissues, animals, or or-gans need to be and remain alive throughout these processes sets them apart for a range of reasons including the practices and technologies required, the risks that living materials pose, and the potentials that 'surplus' biotic activities bring into processes of value creation. Questions about how nature not only is produced but also *works* in diverse contexts, and indeed about the terms on which 'the work of nature' might be better recognised and responded to (Battistoni 2017), have thus emerged of late not just as pressing theoretical concerns, but as an urgent political problem as well. The studies reviewed above – from nonhuman life as recalcitrant-but-malleable commodities, to the mutability of life as a spur to biocapital, to the work of specific nonhuman actors in shaping economic processes – have increased the conceptual sophistication at our disposal to analyse specific constellations of life, labour and value.

This book's ambition is to explore the heterogeneity of the plant agencies at work in capitalist economies today. In meeting this ambition, the book makes two overall arguments. First, that plants are obligate participants in planetary capital-ism and conduct various forms of work crucial to its maintenance and growth. The book does not however focus exclusively on formal production and consumption – on ecologies already firmly enmeshed in capitalist production. We take a wider view. As well as featuring studies of plants that are already working, the book inves-tigates processes through which plants are made into workers and commodities, as well as processes antecedent even to that moment. If capitalism relies on specific throughputs of nature for extracting surplus value, it also always relies on nature in other ways: to absorb ill-effects (pollution sinks, carbon sinks, and so on), or by supporting social reproduction (water and sanitation, for instance). Plants are, per-haps more than any other lifeform, crucial to these processes. Planetary capitalism also relies on a constitutive frontier, a realm of potential capitalisation: this realm does not simply 'exist' but must be brought into being through various techniques of rationalisation, quantification and instrumentalization – often supported by new institutional or extractive regimes which provide a source for accumulation by more-than-human dispossession (through the extension of agriculture into the Amazon, say). Accordingly, this book investigates moments in which plants move between the realm of potential work, the realm of subtending capitalist ecology, and the realm of providing formalised work.

The book's second argument is that plants' alterity – their difference – makes a difference. Plants require new concepts. They force concepts to change. We know what a worker can do: he or she can drudge and gripe and take their pay, work harder and faster or work less and more slowly; he or she may be able to organise and demand, collectivise, strike, picket. A worker can commit to heterodox identity practices, or draw up a more equitable rota for domestic duties. He or she might compose a ballad, or a tweet, to communicate a wound or voice a demand. But can a worker photosynthesise? What are the implications of saying that plants work, especially in a world economy characterised by the systematic exploitation and abjection of labour? Does it lessen the iniquity of human suffering to say that capital comes not just "dripping from head to foot, from every pore, with blood and dirt" (Marx 1976 [1867]: 834), but also steeped in chlorophyll? Beginning to answer such questions demands experimentation with a wide array of tools, an embrace of diverse empirical sites, types and stages of vegetal life, and perhaps even a refusal – in line with a view of fundamental economic processes as co-constituted by human and nonhuman agencies alike – to reify the category plant itself. As the last section of the book in particular aims to make clear, current environmental issues – ranging from food insecurity to urban vulnerability and climate change – are not just symptoms of the breakdown of existing vegetal economies, but opportunities to experiment with entirely new ways of both living and working with vegetal life-forms. In developing more sensitive understandings of plant work in this volume, the stakes are nothing less than both human and vegetal futures. But we would hesitate to place any bets on what vegetal futures might look like: for we do not yet know what work a plant does.

Overview of the book

The work that plants do explores the role of plants in diverse settings across nine chapters. These chapters are loosely grouped under three thematic headings: planty commodities, vegetal labour and future-making with plants.

Planty commodities

The opening section explores how plants become commodities outside, before and in parallel to formal production and consumption economies. One focus is on how humans channel plants' becoming within aesthetic, scientific and state-making regimes. The chapters each explore specific cases of how human and plant work is co-constitutive, a multispecies reciprocal endeavour. Drawing on studies of multispecies care-work, these chapters emphasise how the micro-relations between humans and specific plants shape wider flows of life, from horticulture to conservation. A prevalent theme is the skill required to achieve plant growth in desired ways – plant death and failure is never far away in these chapters. Another theme is that care-work is never innocent, and can often generate lucrative new markets. This first section, then, focuses on the production of planty commodities – the 'y' suffix here signalling something of the ambivalence attached to ideas of plant vitality and agency shared by these chapters.

Emilie Letouzey's chapter asks the simple question of plant care-work: Who has whom doing what? Her chapter concerns the production and shaping of ornamental plants by Japanese horticulturists in the Ōsaka area, based on long-term ethnographic fieldwork. Her chapter highlights the importance of attending to diverse plant cultures outside western modernity, highlighting the linguistic expression of delegation of action – the 'having do', or 'having something done by another agent', expressed by Japanese language in the so-called factitive mode. This is seen in the work done by wisteria growers who deploy and refine techniques for knowing precisely when and how to intervene in the plants' life rhythms to achieve blooming. There is no clear cut to be made here in deciding who performs in essential vital processes such as reproduction or growth.

Letouzey's study opens up the question of making in capitalist ecologies beyond a simple binary of subject/object, towards a field of genuine multispecies intra-action. Crucially, in her chapter it is clear that the kind of work needed to produce high-quality, sellable plants is not possible on an industrial level. The Ibas, a family of commercial wisteria-growers, cannot simply grow commodities in their nursery. Rather, they are required seasonally to gather new scions from wisteria growing spontaneously in nearby mountains. These are painstakingly grafted with horticultural cultivars. This form of craft horticulture is in decline across Japan, Letouzey notes. Here, as elsewhere, such intensive, delicate commodity-production is being supplanted by large-scale, industrial plant production – the form of commodity production aligned to what Anna Tsing (2015) calls the logic of scalability – projects that can be disassembled and transplanted without regard to historical or geographic specificity. The question posed by Letouzey's chapter, then, is whether the wisteria's ability to flourish can outpace the growth of instrumental horticultural logics.

Jared Margulies' chapter outlines a novel conservation strategy: commodifying rare plants in order to save them. While the work of commodifying plant species for aesthetic consumption and the work of plant conservation are usually seen in opposition, Margulies' chapter explores how these goals dovetail in the Botanical Gardens of The Huntington in Los Angeles County, California, and specifically through its long-running project, International Succulent Introductions. Through fieldwork at the Huntington's Botanical Research division, Margulies notes that the process of reproducing endangered succulents differentiates between species as an epistemological container and plants as living organisms in the world. One point, here, is that the biopolitical calculation involved in saving animal species through forms of 'violent-care' (van Dooren 2016) does not apply. Through tissue culture, one plant can theoretically be cloned an infinite number of times. The individual organism is definitely not the model form of life being worked with in this chapter. The options for multiplying plant life far exceed even the intense metabolic manipulation of broiler chickens – plant cuttings, pupping, selfing, tissue culture, and grafting, in addition to sexual reproduction between individual plants.

The multiplicity of techniques through which succulents can be rendered into more succulents offers multiple routes to commodification. In the case of the International Succulent Introductions project, tissue culture enables the Huntington to access a highly regulated market. The Convention on International Trade in Endangered Species of Wild Fauna and Flora places significant complications and costs on to the trade of endangered succulents, but a plant produced through tissue culture techniques effectively bypasses these complex regulations and can enter the market much more easily (because it cannot possibly be a plant of wild origin). Margulies' chapter also highlights the degree of coordination and technical skill required to maintain a stable plant commodity. Even in tissue culture, genetic variegation is relatively common, showing again how plant's propensity for growth exceeds its instrumentalization. Overall, his chapter is exemplary in showing the pathways from plants-as-subjects made to work in the lab to plants-as-objects working as streamlined commodities for global circulation and consumption.

In chapter three, *Planting Soft Pakistan*, Franklin Ginn and Daanish Mustafa ask how and why plants are put to work by state and private actors in producing urban socio-nature. They unravel the story of how plants mediate a national narrative about Pakistan. They detail how, post 9/11, the Pakistani elite tried to create the image of a 'soft' state, featuring a globalized, corporatized, visual spectacle through exotic plants and horticultural 'projects', and how this image has fatal consequences. With over 1,300 people dying in one week during Karachi's 2015 heatwave, it is evident that the right to the city for the poor and the weak is mediated by plants: shade is essential. Yet aesthetic norms now trump ecological function in urban horticulture, to the detriment of tree's 'shady work' (Atchison, this volume).

The chapter shows plants as workers in more-than-social reproduction. More than this, however, it augurs against any easy connection between the increased presence of vegetal life in urban space and more socio-ecologically just outcomes. In Pakistan, urban plants are put to work (and often deliberately left to die, so that another round of crony investment can be sunk into the soil) for ends that are ultimately about military and elite power. One implication is that, if the scale of analysis widens, the capacities of plants for recalcitrance and resistance fade from view. While highly visible on smaller scales, as outlined by the first two chapters in this section, the shifty agencies of plant-human entanglement seem to offer much less hope when set within a story of elite nature production. A caution emerges, then, that plant's growth-without-telos, their openness to the world and to others is easily channelled in directions critics find unpalatable.

Vegetal labour

The second section tackles the book's core conceptual question: what is the nature of the 'work' that plants do within capitalist ecologies? The section's three chapters highlight how plant agencies are involved in multiple processes of value creation and social reproduction. These chapters argue that recognising plants' productive and reproductive role as a form of labour can help to renew the registers of Marxist critique at a time when the articulation between environmental change and a crisis of labour requires urgent creative thinking (Barca 2017). Although the three pieces share an interest in Marxist analysis, they expand its boundaries by bringing to bear conceptual resources from actor-network theory, feminist theory and the anthropology of time. They closely engage with one or more specificities of plant life – whether plants' metabolism, the peculiar form of their intent, or their capacity to partake in intersubjective relations and to imprint their non-sidereal temporalities upon capitalist processes. Together, they therefore not only bring a different twist to the Marxist labour theory of value, but importantly also highlight the importance of developing a specific conceptual vocabulary to take plants' lives in a capitalist world seriously.

Harold Perkins' chapter, reproduced from a 2007 *Geoforum* article, marked at its publication a key milestone in efforts to bring together materialisms old and new. The chapter offers a sophisticated discussion of how the concept of distributed agency within actor-network theory can help to renew Marxist understandings of exploitation, and to highlight the momentum that different actants gain through their capacity to enrol others' labours. In the chapter, Perkins deploys an extensive understanding of labour, which he draws from Marx's mention, in Capital Volume 1, of 'instinctive' forms of labour. In those lines it appears clear that Marx holds labour to constitute the common ground of all living beings, who transform their environments by the simple act of extracting matter to sustain their basic metabolic needs. To be clear, conventional Marxist analysis usually adopts a much more restrictive definition of 'proper' (i.e. distinctively human) labour, as guided by some degree of intentionality. Perkins, however, argues that it is necessary to take seriously Marx's suggestion and examine its implications for understanding the power relations that unfold through the articulation of different types of labours – whether deliberate or instinctive.

Perkins advances the term 'non-social labour' to highlight the active role that nonhuman organisms play in shaping capitalist processes of production and, in his chapter specifically, social reproduction. This is done by reference to the mass planting of elm trees across American cities in the late 19th and 20th centuries. As lively commodities, grown, sold, purchased, planted, and maintained, trees embody the social labours of arboricultural workers, who direct their growth. Yet, as living organisms their growth remains a biophysical metabolic process, predicated upon trees transforming their local environments through extracting nutrients and transforming the composition of the surrounding air, for instance. The exploitation of this fundamental, metabolic activity marks for Perkins the appropriation of trees' labour, put at the service of a specific capitalist and governmental project of social reproduction through the development of a 'consumption fund'. This chapter offers a daring twist on conventional Marxist discussions of labour, and opens the door to further considerations of the politics of appropriating and enrolling diverse forms of non-intentional, metabolic labour. In that sense, Perkins' ideas lay vital conceptual groundwork for both of the next two chapters.

Marion Ernwein's chapter bears empirical similarities with Perkins', with its focus on urban horticulture and the exploitation of plants' metabolic processes in the production – and maintenance – of urban landscapes. Key to her argument is the idea that plants' labour, rather than being 'non-social' (Perkins, this volume), in fact partakes in wider, always-also social, relations of work. Drawing on research in Geneva, Switzerland, the starting point for Ernwein's chapter is a shift in park management paradigms, from horticultural to ecological approaches. Ernwein argues that this shift is accompanied by the development of ecological labour, a form of maintenance labour "whose raison d'être is keeping nonhuman life alive and setting the right conditions for it to contribute its agencies to urban life" (p. 106). Efforts to make labour ecological "rely on new understandings of the nature of work and of workers themselves", with plants increasingly finding themselves in the latter category (p. 119).

Ernwein's discussion focuses specifically on two contentious points and their implications for the relevance of the term 'labour' in the plant world: plants' presupposed lack of intentionality, and their inability to engage in intersubjective interactions. Drawing on work on domestic and clinical labour, Ernwein develops a conceptualisation in which intent is not a requirement of work at all. In this view, just because plants do not consciously or intentionally labour does not preclude them from having their labour-power exploited. While some argue on the contrary that work is by essence an intersubjective experience, Ernwein takes this as an opportunity to discuss the role that plant labour is made to play in reconfiguring human workers' own engagement in their labour, and their ways of relating to each other. Finally, Ernwein argues that intersubjectivity need not be the primary means through which the relational character of plant labour is understood: ecological labour is also shaped by wider social structures and bureaucratic logics. Ultimately, the chapter positions the question of plant labour within wider debates about contemporary social relations and structural logics of work.

Jeremy Brice's chapter provides an intricate analysis of the modalities through which human and plant temporalities are made commensurable in efforts to organise Australia's lucrative wine industry. Brice's starting point is that discussing whether plants' metabolic activity can qualify as 'labour' through the lens of intent and design partly misses the point. Instead, what makes plants qualify as workers has more to do with their imprint on the temporalities of production. Brice borrows from the Marxist tradition to argue that, as an activity that fundamentally produces conditions "which differ from those which preceded its occurrence" (p. 125), labour "produces time" (p. 124). Time, of course, is central in Marx's conception of exchange value. The history of capitalist development, Brice reminds us, was quintessentially a story of indexing human labour upon an "abstract and context-invariant (or sidereal) time" (p. 124) that allows for labour time to become a fungible quantity. Brice demonstrates, however, that in some industries including winemaking, plants' metabolic activity can "constitute the passage of time" – for example by calling forth or holding back different tasks. Through shaping the time of production, Brice argues, vines "redistribute the capacity to generate worth across species boundaries" (p. 128) and acquire a structuring role within the process of value creation.

Through their different foci – on plants' differential capacities to command power within networks of labour, to organise the broader social relations of work, or indeed to shape the very temporalities of value creation – the three pieces demonstrate that plants are not only enrolled in particular projects of social reproduction and commodity production, but also reshape the locus, modalities, and relations of work within the political economies of urban greening and vine growing. In the chapters by Ernwein and Brice this is explicitly linked to a discussion of the social vulnerabilities that can emerge when the streamlining of work is predicated not on human but rather on vegetal temporalities. Common also between Brice's and Perkins' chapters is an understanding that labour is not merely more-than-human, but also more-than-vegetal, and that plants' performances emerge from specific, and often unstable, arrangements between not only human and vegetal, but also fungal and microbial agencies.

Future-making with plants

In the book's final section, three further chapters turn to examine the involvement of plants in emergent practices of future-making. Anxieties about the growing pace and severity of environmental change – and climate change in particular – are spurring diverse new modes of working with plants across far-flung geographical contexts, and not just in the predominantly rural milieux of agriculture and biodiversity conservation. Efforts to detoxify the metabolic flows and physical infrastructures underpinning large-scale industrial production and contemporary urban life are also increasingly tethered to vegetal capacities, whether as a basis for producing renewable alternatives to fossil fuel, for cleaning urban air, or more simply for protecting urban inhabitants and property from rising temperatures, waters, and extremes in weather. Across these domains, the scope of the vegetal futures being pursued can often appear self-evident: plants and trees are to act as the basis of 'natural' solutions for averting potentially irreversible environmental change and preserving the stability of the so-called 'earth system'. As the three chapters in the book's final section explore however, even while reconfigurations of human-plant relationships are typically advanced under innocuous banners – sustainability, green recovery, even human survival itself – the ideas and understandings of vegetal life which undergird these visions are frequently highly prescriptive and contestable. Moreover, and as the chapters also seek to expose, the actual work entailed in contesting these visions, and indeed in reinscribing alternative futures, may be just as much a capacity of plants themselves as it is of the human communities who variously cultivate, live-with, consume and exploit them.

In her chapter Jennifer Atchison outlines how reductive, essentializing imaginaries of trees – most notably of the African mahogany (*Khaya senegalensis*) – are confounding efforts to counteract future risks posed both by rising temperatures and by increasingly frequent and intense cyclones in Darwin, Australia. Valued for decades as providers of shade, African mahoganies have more recently been demonised in Darwin, particularly following Cyclone Marcus in 2018, as out-of-place, 'towering monsters', with unusually long and large limbs prone to give way at any time. Efforts to improve natural tree canopy shade in the city – before climate change effectively renders some quarters uninhabitable – have thus become intertwined with an increasingly firm commitment to what the city's own council describes as an "arboreal cleansing process" (p. 161). Running just as deep as the nativist tropes that depict African mahoganies as innately ill-suited to the Australian climate, moreover, is an equally problematic tendency to see urban trees of all kinds as lifeforms that can simply be put in their place, as ready-made – and readily substitutable – elements of benign green infrastructure. The appeal of this green infrastructure lens, along with its associated promise of a perfect "botanical recipe for the salvation of urban problems" (p. 160), is felt far beyond Darwin of course. But for Atchison it represents nothing less than an "attempt to seize and structure the future" of urban human-plant interactions (p. 160), one guilty of overlooking much of what trees are and what they can do. Against this agenda, Atchison therefore advocates a closer attunement to what she terms the 'shady work' of urban trees – that is, their propensity to engage in diverse forms of more-than-human labour whose acknowledgement is typically impeded either by its hidden nature, as in the case of subterranean root ball development for example, or else because of its slow-moving, precarious, or predominantly affective dimensions. Far from endorsing the pursuit of definitive or clear-cut 'solutions' to prevailing urban problems then, this lens of shady work incites a more tentative and humble approach to future urban regeneration, one importantly open and responsive to the complicating and disruptive influence of trees themselves.

Concerns about climate change are also at the core of efforts to reshape the future of the so-called working forests of the US South, as discussed in James Palmer's chapter. Rather than offering shade though, it is the ability of the trees growing in these forests to serve as ostensibly renewable bioenergy resources – and moreover to substitute coal as a basis for electricity generation – that drives their enrolment into efforts to cultivate a more clement global climatic future. The expanding production of biomass wood pellets from these forests, and especially from stands of trees comprising fast-growing loblolly pine, has attracted significant controversy, not least because the vast majority are exported to produce electricity abroad, especially in the UK. In seeking to counteract these criticisms, industry groups have placed particular emphasis, Palmer argues, on the benefits that wood pellet manufacturing purportedly brings to working forests' *overall* productivity, with concomitant increases not just in the amount of coal replaced in the global energy sector, but also in the amount of carbon dioxide locked up in diverse wood-based commodities produced by other industries as well. From this vantage point, working forests are imagined as contributing to climate change mitigation not by functioning as carbon sinks, but rather as carbon conveyors – and, crucially, as carbon conveyors that bioenergy production serves to put to work more efficiently than ever before. That trees growing in the US South *should* be put to work for the specific end goal of generating renewable electricity abroad is deeply contestable, of course, not least in view of the region's long history of colonial exploitation and forced labour. But Palmer contends that the starting point for contesting these moves should be an embrace, and not a rejection, of the idea of trees as workers – indeed, as vegetal labourers proper. Recognising and naming the metabolic activity of trees as vegetal labour could offer a potent basis for envisioning alternative forms of collaboration between trees and humans, outside the constraints posed by logics of ecosystem services and natural capital, and oriented instead towards more creative, self-determined ends than those presently offered up by foreign energy firms.

Rounding out the book's final section, Can Dalyan examines the forms of labour which animate the day-to-day work of the Turkish Seed Gene Bank (TSGB), an institution founded only a few months prior to the international adoption, in 2010, of the Nagoya Protocol on Access to Genetic Resources and the Fair and Equitable Sharing of Benefits Arising from their Utilization. While Turkey may be party to the broader UN Convention on Biological Diversity under which the Nagoya Protocol was adopted, Dalyan's analysis reveals significant fault lines between the TSGB's outlook and the explicitly universalist perspectives associated with other prominent seed banking projects, such as the Svalbard Global Seed Vault and the Millennium Seed Bank at London's Kew Gardens. Indeed, Turkey's history of imperial losses and decline, not to mention its status as one of the world's key crop biodiversity hotspots, offer flimsy foundations upon which to build an image of seed banking as an endeavour concerned principally with 'collaborative survival'. Instead, Dalyan argues, TSGB employees enact a distinctly protectionist brand of conservation, routinely denying access to foreign researchers, and internalising a view of the latent genetic potentialities embodied by seeds stored in the Bank's vaults as a precious stock of national biowealth. That the institution presently lacks the ability to sequence and license most of the crop species which make up that biowealth, moreover, does little – given the likely impacts of climate change upon future crop yields and food security – to prevent its potential value, as a source of new crop breeds and forms of crop resistance, from steadily increasing. As Dalyan puts it then, it is not strictly the future survival of humanity that the TSGB seeks to secure, so much as "the sorts of reparations that Turkey will be able to accrue" in that future, from what amounts to the systematic accumulation today of biological contingency and possibility itself. In the meantime, moreover, the already-existing potentials of seeds to facilitate alternative social relations around crops and food production – especially those predicated upon sharing and experimentation – are rooted out and extinguished as threats to the Turkish state's future power and legitimacy, both domestically and on the international stage.

While the three final chapters traverse radically different empirical cases, each of them examines how plants are currently being enrolled into future-making projects that take for granted the goal of enhancing the collective capacities of earthly life, whether to endure, to metabolise, or even to create new kinds of vegetal lifeforms – and vegetal capacities – altogether. In their efforts to stretch windows of urban habitability, to intensify metabolic exchanges between the biosphere and the atmosphere, and to diversify the genetic profiles and living potentials of food crops, the initiatives discussed in this final section arguably all affirm a view of life itself as something to be intensified and expanded, both spatially and temporally, in the quest to overcome pressing global social and environmental challenges. While the visions of future human-plant relations at the core of these projects are highly developed, all of the chapters also discern apertures for plants and humans to begin to work together in alternative ways, and potentially even to push back against deeper logics of enhancement, expansion and improvement themselves. Rather than viewing plants as the basis for what Stefania Barca (2020: 60) calls "an even higher level of mastering earth-systems", these apertures instead raise the prospect of working with plants to instil slower, more faltering, and perhaps even diminished future life-worlds than those typically envisaged under economic logics of efficiency, productivity, growth and profit. Indeed, as both these final chapters and the collection as a whole hope to make clear, the provocation of new ideas about what an economy should ultimately be for may just be the most crucial form of work that plants could yet undertake in the turbulent times ahead.

SECTION I
Planty commodities

Chapter 1 – Whose performance?
Agencies in Japanese ornamental horticulture

Emilie Letouzey

Questions from the field

April 2015, Ikeda (north of Ōsaka). In their horticultural nursery, Mr and Mrs Iba are occupied from dawn to dusk by the grafting of the 300 to 400 wisterias they produce annually. At the top of a two-and-a-half-meter long trunk, they graft scions of cultivars belonging to the species *Wisteria floribunda*. Their technique is known as "grafting in height" (*takatsugi*), adapted to the flat trellises used to train ground-planted wisteria. A couple of months before, the Ibas spent weeks roaming the forests of Kansai region, seeking dozens of wisteria trunks to use as rootstocks. The trunks must be straight. Given the baroque shapes spontaneously generated by this liana, this step is in itself a feat. When the time of grafting comes, the trunks are lined up on the ground. Mr Iba refreshes the cutting wound with a circular saw; opens three or four notches in the – remarkably solid – wood with his knife; inserts the scions and sinks them with a quick and precise movement; firmly ties the sticks to their new base (Figure 1.1). Mrs Iba then covers the crown-like result with a generous amount of humid sphagnum moss and wraps it all in a plastic sheet. Once the grafting is done, the wisterias are bathed for several days, then planted in tight rows along bamboo structures, evoking giant licorice root sticks. Now, they will grow branches, and produce new roots, since the original ones were almost totally pruned during the collection in the mountains.

Two weeks later and a few kilometers away, Ōsaka's Fukushima ward. The Noda Wisteria Festival (*Nodafuji matsuri*) has just started. *Nodafuji* is the vernacular name of the species *W. floribunda*, which stems from the toponym "Noda", a village once renowned for its wisterias before being absorbed by expanding Ōsaka.[1] The Noda Wisteria Association's volunteers put on their purple jackets to welcome the visitors

---

1   There are two endemic species of wisteria in Japan: *W. floribunda* and *W. brachybotrys* (*yama-fuji*, "mountain wisteria"), whose clusters are shorter. As both species grow in Kansai's mountains, the Ibas collect either one or the other; in Fukushima ward, although the focus is on *W. floribunda*, part of the wisterias are in fact *W. brachybotrys*, especially in public parks.

who come to admire the blooming of the ward's numerous wisterias. Since 2006, when the Association was created, they have been planting and cultivating more than 250 wisterias, spread all over this densely constructed area of central Ōsaka. The first edition of the Noda Wisteria Festival, which celebrates the flowerings, was held in 2007.[2] Each year, throughout the festival, the wisterias and their clusters of flowers are skillfully arranged and displayed, surrounded by various decorations such as flags or lights when the night falls. The volunteers are especially proud because many of them – shopkeepers, craftpersons, housewives, employees – knew hardly anything about plants when they joined the group. However, one can feel a certain apprehension floating in the air: despite the collective all-year-round effort, some of the wisterias won't bloom. Indeed, flowering is not a given. This is why volunteers devote so much energy to research and experiments, in order to answer the following questions: why won't some wisterias flower, and how can they "make [them] bloom" (sakasu)? All kinds of measures have been taken to program the blooming, so to speak.

Let us dwell on the main operations mentioned in these two vignettes: graft and make bloom. What is grafting? For plants, the technique consists of uniting two (or more) plant fragments, by having the vascular tissues of the incised parts enter into contact. It is not a mere 'cut and paste': a connection – a living connection – must be established in order for the recomposed plant to keep going. Katchaku 活着, the Japanese term for successful graft formation, means something like "hold on alive". The Ibas say they reach a 100 per cent graft success rate, while their neighbors mention a rate of 40 to 70 per cent for the pines or fruit trees they obtain by grafting (depending on varieties, conditions and type of graft). "When we graft, [it] comes out 'buaaaaaaa'!", says Mr Iba, mimicking the growth of the branches with an onomatopoeia to express the gushing, as if the process was both sudden and irrepressible. However, while Mr Iba undeniably puts the vascularized sections into contact ("grafting", tsugiki 接木, literally means "trees in relation"), it is the plant-organism itself that achieves the vessel connection, which the circulation of nutrient fluids – and ultimately the "holding on alive" – depend on. It is also the plant-organism itself that grows roots and branches. For Mr Iba, both the grafting operation and the assembling of several plants seem to go without saying. For my part, I am impressed as much by the technique as I am by the plant.

The second main operation is to make bloom. In Noda Wisteria Association, the corresponding verbal form, sakasu (shortened form of sakaseru, "make bloom"), is more than a key word: the volunteers literally speak sakasu, as the word can be deployed in multiple ways. Sakasu is a so-called factitive form, which expresses the

---

2   Others local events celebrating wisterias had been occasionally held since the 1970s, organized by individuals or local groups, but they had stopped for several years prior to the relaunch in 2007.

idea of a delegation of the action, like a "have do" ("[an agent] has [another agent] do [something]"). In this case, humans cultivate wisterias, but it is the wisterias themselves that generate the flower clusters. Since this flowering process is not systematic, the actions that the members of the Association carry out on the plants can maybe favor it in anticipation (as bud initiation occurs the year before flowering), but this is not guaranteed. Whether the volunteers predispose the plant to flowering or coax it to do so is unclear – with some of them, I had many opportunities to experience how a horticultural or biological bibliographic investigation only makes the flowering process more complex and mysterious.[3] As for the apprehension floating in the air at the festival, it reminded me of a similar hesitation that I often encountered on my fieldwork about horticulture. These 30-130cm long clusters of flowers showering on visitors' heads beg the question: whose achievement are they, after all?

This chapter is based on ethnographic fieldwork research on horticulture I conducted from 2013 to 2017 in Kansai area, Japan.[4] It deals with the question of plant agency, in the case of relationships between cultivators – amateurs or professionals – and the plants they grow. Garden-scale horticulture often leads to speculation about the development of the plants in terms of agency and performance. Anthropological descriptions of garden practices or horticulturist societies suggest that even when powers are attributed to an invisible entity whose favors humans have to win, negotiations between humans, plants and other agents are constantly at work (Malinowski 1978[1935]; Descola 1986; Coupaye 2013). It is on these negotiations that we will be focusing. In the production and in the appreciation of wisterias, the technical actions that come one after another all correspond to vital vegetal processes, which have been appropriated by plant growers in order to control the plants as closely as possible. In grafting, for example, processes such as divisibility, replicability, connectivity of sap vessels, healing or growth are all involved at different steps of the operation. Sometimes, this appropriation seems complete, as with the Ibas; more often, it seems to be subjected to a persistent proportion of uncertainty or randomness, as it goes in the Noda Wisteria Association. Focusing on the articulations between vital and technical processes (Coupaye/Pitrou 2018), we will move away from the positivist 'making' that characterizes production, and consider actions on plants as being much more like a 'having do'. Here I describe

---

3   In Japanese or English-speaking biology manuals for example, while some authors point the yet unknown aspects of the flowering process, many describe it as a succession of distinct steps (floral transition, bud initiation, flower induction, etc.) occurring at cellular scale, thus unlikely to be apprehended by the cultivators or controlled by common horticultural actions.
4   I studied horticulture as a wide set of technical practices, that can be connected to traditional gardens but is independent, and has its own history. From a technical point of view, and also in people's daily lives and practices, horticulture has much more to do with agriculture.

ordinary horticultural actions that are, if we consider them, more complex than they seem. They put into question the narrative of a unilateral human control over plants. This brings us to the question: ultimately, who/what operates? And who has whom doing? Of course, modes of doing are integrated to horticulture as a craft and as a market: the cases of the Ibas' nursery and the Noda Wisteria Association enable us to sketch a picture of traditional ornamental horticulture as a paradoxical sector, an artisanal domain with its own technical and economic paradigms, whose history is marked with fads and speculative bubbles, appearing today like a precarious niche assemblage.

Figure 1.1: Mr Iba grafting, 2015.

Image: Emilie Letouzey.

Domesticating plants

To introduce the notion of agency, let us start from two fundamental notions: domestication as a particular tendency of humans and other living beings' common evolution, and plantness (Darley 1990) as the set of features that characterize the vegetal as a form of life.

First, domestication. A still widespread view of domestication assumes that humans initiated the project, appropriating and dominating a set of passive species – here we recognize one of the 'branches' of the classic story of the mastery-of-nature-by-humans. This view has been challenged by Stephen Budiansky (1992) whose striking "covenant" thesis, based on archaeological research, emphasized animals' initiative in domestication history. Many complex scenarios, in which the agency of nonhumans is considered, were explored since then (for example,

Zeder 2015), so that recently, domestication narratives have been retheorized as hybrid communities (Stépanoff/Vigne 2018) or multispecies worlds (van Dooren et al. 2016). By investigating "what humans do with non-humans (and their world-making projects), but also what non-humans do to humans (and our worldmaking projects)" (Tsing 2018: 236), multispecies ethnography fully assumes such narrations. Together with approaches such as extinction studies or more-than-human geographies (van Dooren et al. 2016: 5), they form the flourishing field of multispecies studies, which keeps defying the human-mastery tale by calling agencies into question.

Questioning agency in our relationships with other species through a switch in narratives, however, is not a new idea. A decade after Budiansky's essay, Michael Pollan (2001) convincingly depicted cultivating humans as manipulated by the evolutionary strategies of plants. To expand their ecological niche, tulips, potatoes, apple trees or cannabis (the examples developed in the book) have taken advantage of human desires from the very beginning. Far from being a product of human will and technical performances, the cultivation of species – including diversification, reproduction, care – can thus be seen as an evolutionary performance by the species themselves. An important support to this perspective is the fact that plants have always used a multiplicity of external agents to assist their locomotion or reproduction (animals, wind, water, etc.). Following archaeologist Marijke van der Veen (2014), we can even consider this reliance upon others' agency as one of the essential features of plants' mode of existence on the planet. In this view, humans have carried this agent role out with tremendous fervor.

Plants as a form of life have long been maintained in a relative indifference in Western science and thinking (Hallé 2002), for cultural reasons (Hall 2011) and with political consequences (Brancher 2015). Although a "pervasive plant blindness", as anthropologist John Hartigan Jr. (2019) puts it,[5] somehow persists today, there has recently been a profound engagement in plants as a form of life. Both natural sciences and humanities are – in part at least – plant-turning. Striving to move plants away from their status of "borderline beings" (Findly 2002), scholars are rehabilitating the vegetal as fundamental planetary agents, supporting life on Earth (Myers 2016), creating worlds and cosmos (Coccia 2018). To this end, they look at what plants are: sentient? intelligent? persons? a network? This is not what we will do in this chapter: rather than an ontological approach, I will here be taking an agency-based relational perspective, and insist on the interest of looking at what plants and humans have each other do. The description of plant-cultivator relationships makes it possible to assess the action of vegetal power on people, and to think about how

---

5   The expression "plant blindness" was proposed by Wandersee and Schussler in 1999 in their article "Toward a Theory of Plant Blindness", and discussed since (see for example Knapp 2019).

plants affect the humans who craft, manipulate and admire them. Plants are thus brought back to the forefront, in their essential role, without having to speculate on their nature.

The case of Japan is particularly interesting in this respect. Far beyond a simple enthusiasm for seasonal spectacles of nature that would occur to experience, Japan, as a "civilization of the vegetal", has based its calendar, its aesthetics and its material culture on plants (Gourou 1948). Love of plants is generally considered to be one of the fundamental traits of a supposed national character – geographer Augustin Berque (1986) explained for example that some Japanese scientists have gone so far as to seek vegetal features in the 'Japanese mind', as if to naturalize this affinity. Yet there is nothing more cultural than plants in Japan: aside from a vivid attraction for spontaneous mountain plants, almost all common plant species are domesticated. Far from being 'natural', the national plant cover has been artificialized for centuries, as if portions of territory had been gradually grafted onto others. The ardor in celebrating the landscapes echoes the energy spent in carrying out these extensive plant transfers over time. Of course, we can consider exploitation, instrumentalization and control of environments and plants by humans. But if we switch the perspective, then the extraordinary 'successes' of rice, black pine or cryptomeria appear. The case of the cherry tree speaks for itself: although it was an endemic species with many varieties, millions of clones of a single horticultural cultivar – *Cerasus x yedoyensis*, known as Somei.yoshino – have been planted throughout the country since the 19th century.

Somei.yoshino was obtained during the horticultural boom that took place during the Edo period (1603-1868). Although ornamental horticulture is very ancient – especially among the nobility – from the 17th century it became more and more popular in pacified Japanese society. Countless *ukiyo-e* (woodblock print) and horticultural treatises published at this time show an extraordinary enthusiasm for plant cultivation. While nurseries were competitive in their creativity for inventing new plants (with double flowers, new colors, variegated leaves), amateurs were collecting cultivars with monstrous traits, which they displayed during competitions. Pots, stakes or shelved greenhouses became common accessories in homes and streets. Famous sites (*meisho*) from across the country were represented in guides and series of prints, strengthening associations between (human planted) species, landscapes and toponyms. All these aesthetic and technical models are well-known today, and many have been maintained. Elsewhere in the world, other famous historical examples of horticultural booms can be found that periodically aroused collective passions: the case of the Dutch tulipomania in 17th century Holland is famous (Pavord 1999), but in 13th century China, a peony boom had already provoked sudden value increases for certain varieties (Needham 1986). As for 19th century England, Keith Thomas (1983) describes a horticultural enthusiasm similar to that of Edo in many regards; 19th century France can also be mentioned here

(Cueille 2003; Bergues 2011). For each of these examples, scholars' analyses call on the lexical field of passion, recalling the "desires" of Pollan's book. Imagining all these people caring for their plants or spending money to acquire rare cultivars, are we not tempted to see plant agency at work? With ornamental plants being the category that counts the largest number of domesticated species (Gessert 1993) – while failing to satisfy any vital need for humans – aesthetic agency is surely one of the more efficient components of animal-oriented vegetal strategy. As such, it calls for both esteem and scrutiny.

Let us return to Ōsaka. I couldn't actually say to what extent wisterias have the Ibas and the Noda Wisteria Association's volunteers act. Yet, as Jeremy Brice (this volume) puts it, plants enact the passage of time, and it is a fact that the cultivators' daily schedules are partly harmonized with the plant's annual cycle. As the next section will show, the wisterias' vital characteristics do have the Ibas collect and graft at a certain time; they do have the volunteers organize their activities in accordance with flowering and its programming.

Figure 1.2: The Noda Wisteria Association's volunteers showing a print of "Nodafuji" (Satonoya Yoshitaki, around 1860), one of the "Hundred views of Naniwa" (Naniwa hyakkei). The print depicts Noda's village wisteria climbing on pines and represents the landscape inside Kasuga shrine. Behind the volunteers stands current Kasuga shrine and its non-blooming wisteria.

Image: Watanabe H., 2012.

"Having do" and "benefiting from"

Noda's wisteria and its numerous cultivars happen to be one of the iconic 'Edo style' plants. The ways it was – and still is – appreciated appear on several famous prints: on flat trellises, the long clusters of flowers showering at head height, or in pots, trained as a self-maintaining dwarfed tree (an appropriate pruning permitting to shape the climbing vine this way).[6] From this point of view, the Edo period's Noda wisterias were an exception: they climbed around pine trees in sparse groves, as they spontaneously do in the mountains of Japan (see the print in Figure 1.2). This landscape did not survive the Meiji period's industrialization but some wisterias were eventually maintained on Kasuga shrine's grounds until World War II's destructions. Today's wisterias grow on horizontal trellises, in parks, flowerbeds or pots. Yet, due to the plant's vigorous woody agency,[7] in Fukushima ward one can see wisterias escape their pots to plunge into a fortuitous crack in the cement, climb up on a nearby tree or creep along a metal gate (which the plant slowly distorts). The wisterias are cultivated with so much enthusiasm by the Noda Wisteria Association's volunteers – and by neighbors, school children, shopkeepers – that I am tempted to say that people are *themselves* the actual substrate of plants, in which they most surely flourish and multiply. Around thirty volunteers share the maintenance of all the wisterias cared for by the Association, according to a rigorous distribution. Most of them are in charge of several wisterias in their district of residence, and also grow wisterias in their homes.

To "make bloom" (*sakasu*) is the main goal of the Association, which brings the volunteers together several times a month and occupies some of them almost every day. Even when they look disconnected from the flowering process, all collective activities are conceived as flower-oriented in some way (Figure 1.3). The annual cultivation cycle of wisteria, with its necessary operations and its diverse hazards (urban climate uncertainty, pigeons swooping on flower buds), is the matter of never-ending discussions within the volunteers' group. The branches of each plant are carefully scrutinized throughout the year. They are all trained and tied, in parallel lines according to the so-called barcode method, or in curves according to the so-called natural method. As for pruning, depending on whether one follows the Tamura manner (*Tamura-ryū*), the Hirooka manner (*Hirooka-ryū*) – both named after members of the Association – or "one's own manner" (*jibun-ryū*), one will prune twice, three times or more, counting the buds while working. For non-blooming

---

6   For example, "Wisteria and Half Moon Bridge at Kameido", one of the most famous Utagawa Hiroshige's *ukiyo-e* (1957) depicts a wisteria landscape; potted *fuji* (wisterias) can be seen in many Edo period New-year auspicious images, a type that gathered miscellaneous things containing the sound "fu" (evoking "happiness").

7   I am adapting here the "weedy agency" discussed by Kawa (2016).

wisterias, various measures have been tested, like soil aeration using pneumatic drills or luminosity adjustments with spots or tarpaulins. In order to adapt their techniques and to clear up the causes of non-flowering, the volunteers constantly seek to learn more about the functioning of the plant, by themselves or by calling for external knowledge, like professional gardeners or wisteria producers. They even invited a mycologist from the Museum of Natural History of Ōsaka to a monthly meeting to talk about root symbiosis.

One day, during a special monthly meeting entitled "How to make non-blooming wisterias bloom?", the volunteers discussed the relevance of trying a "root cut" (*nekiri*) on a wisteria that has never flowered. The shock caused to the plant by this radical action, some argued, would make it react. Feeling threatened, the wisteria would endeavor to produce fruits in order to leave offspring – and produce flowers in the process. This measure is advocated elsewhere in the world,[8] but it gives an accurate example of the 'factitive' mode: the "have do" expressing the delegation of the action, which is both immediate (a cut in the plant) and indirect (the plant itself will – hopefully – provoke flowering). From a technical point of view, and aside a possible fundamental parting between actions performed on living matter and on inert matter, operations carried out on living beings often imply the participation of the organism itself to accomplish them (Ferret 2014). It is also the case when the action is delegated to an environmental parameter (soil, light, temperature, etc.) assumed to affect the plant. The subject reacts immediately or later in time, but can also be recalcitrant, or react in a way that is unexpected or imperceptible to humans. Although this is not specific to plants (we experience it every day in our own bodies), this "have do" is rarely discussed. Such operations belong to a different sort though: they are more a programming than a production. Far from the vegetal evolutionary agency mentioned earlier, we are here at the level of 'small agencies': as Darwin advocated (1881), small as they may seem, they are nevertheless fundamental modes of action of beings or things one onto others. Domestication makes it so that from the evolutionary to the small, plant agencies and human agencies are enmeshed.

8   See, for example, "Don't worry about wisteria. You can beat it up a bit and it'll still bloom", August 7, 2016 (www.theglobeandmail.com/life/home-and-garden/gardening/dont-worry-about-wisteria-you-can-beat-it-up-a-bit-and-itll-still-bloom/article13645046).

Figure 1.3: Volunteers at work in 2015: spreading an anti-pigeon net on a trellis (left); organizing a budding workshop in a school (right).

Image: Emilie Letouzey.

In the Ōsaka area, the wisteria's flowering period occurs at the end of April. Accordingly, so does the Noda Wisteria Festival, which is ten days long. Every day during the festival, several volunteers visit the wisterias' main sites, to check and communicate the blooming degree, in the same way the famous cherry bulletin (*kaika jōhō*, literally "flowering information") is established.[9] The wisterias are displayed both as horticultural productions and as local community emblems: the species has been the "ward flower" (*ku no hana*) since 1995. Visitors enjoy the flowers by contemplating, photographing and commenting. The volunteers appreciate them in a more assessing manner, counting the clusters and measuring their size, taking notes and comparing with previous years. Aesthetic and technical appreciation allow, everyone agrees, for a better enjoyment and understanding of the blooming phenomenon. However, as in a garden where one does not know whether to admire the capacities of the plant or those of the gardener, none seems to be of any help in answering the question: whose performance is it? For most of the volunteers of the Association, the wisterias are more or less reluctant partners with whom we negotiate all year long. They are just as reluctant to appropriate the flowers.

Still, every year, visitors congratulate and thank the volunteers for their work. Hirooka H., for example, proudly shows the postcards he received from neighbors or visitors: "Thank you for having the flowers bloom"; "Thank you for the flowers this year again", and so on. The volunteers themselves often repeat how much they are personally grateful and even indebted to wisterias: the plants stupefy and inspire them, they diffuse their energy (*chikara*), they are a reason for living (*ikigai*). A tree doctor (*jumokui*) and former member of the Association, even claims he had his "life

---

9   Although the cherry tree bulletin is the result of a year-long high-tech meteorological measurement system. In comparison, Noda's bulletin is totally empiric.

saved by the soul of a wisteria", the day he collapsed near a wisterias' trellis after a pruning session.

Even if affects involved in personal relations to plants rely on conceptions of non-humans' status in general, and as such can vary considerably according to individuals, the volunteers are delighted by the idea of cultivating relationships of mutual care and gratitude with the plants. Although wisterias are never seen as persons, many value a "giving relationship", rather than a mere production by humans for their own benefit. The expression of acknowledgment and gratitude towards others (humans, but also non-humans, tools, the elements) is one of the remarkable aspects of the Japanese language. The so-called 'beneficial' mode can be found in grammar textbooks, often presented only as a mark of deference. Yet, terms of benefaction are omnipresent in everyday conversations (especially in the Kansai area) and produce an impression of perpetual acknowledgment of others' agency, which not only is expressed, but towards which one feels gratitude. The use of such a mode by people can be sometimes playful, which reinforce the listener's impression – as vague as it is persistent – of a certain inclination to extend the distribution of achievement.

Engineering plants

Let us return to the Ibas, who produce wisterias. "In February-March, we go for rootstocks; in April we graft; during the Summer we spray pesticides; in the Fall, [the wisterias are] ready: we can sell!" So goes the annual production cycle according to the Ibas, like a sequence of simple operations without any suspense, from the quest for wild wisterias in the mountains to the alignment of disciplined artifacts in palisades (Figure 1.4). Yet we have seen that collecting and grafting mature wisterias as they do is quite a logistical and technical performance, to the extent that another producer whom I tell about the Ibas claims that such a method is implausible. While their neighbors praise their dexterity – "They are able people (*udekiki*), aren't they!" – the Ibas are all but boastful about their skills. The same goes for the double aggregate they carry out: first the aggregate of hundreds of trunks from various mountains they gather in their property; then the aggregate of (cloned) horticultural cultivars and spontaneous individuals (from a seed) by grafting. A clone on a seedling is the most common association in grafting. The former, 'fixed' by vegetative propagation, constitutes the upper part of the plant and carries the desired production; the latter provides a robust rootstock that safeguards the underground part of the plant's life. In the Ibas' property, the scions are taken from no more than three or four wisteria cultivars considered to be abundantly flowering, growing freely on loose supports. Regarding the rootstocks, although their cultivation on site at the Ibas' property could allow to shape them from the start instead of searching for straight trunks in the mountains, it would require both space and time – at least ten years. Above all, the Ibas object that it would require them to pay too much attention to the growing conditions, while the plant is considered to grow best spontaneously in its own milieu, taking care of itself perfectly.

Although among the most intensely rooted and entangled in its immediate surrounding,[10] wisteria is an extremely dynamic and powerful vine that luxuriates in shifting environments – as were the ancient Noda's woods that grew from the Yodogawa river's alluvium deposits centuries ago. Creeping and climbing, it can suffocate its support tree and get the upper branches tangled (needless to say, Japanese woodcutters hate wisteria). Also, when the dried pods burst, they can throw seeds quite a distance away. Considering these traits, the Ibas' technical sequence, although characterized by mastery and control, can also be seen as a process that enhances the wisteria's endeavor to disperse and travel. Furthermore, the Ibas have completed the optimal process to achieve what we can call, following Fleming (2016), the graftability of wisterias. Graftability involves concrete materials that are both fluid and solid (and even particularly dense in the case of wood), but also processes, the most obvious of which are connectivity and growth. Plant connectivity is due to the vegetal ability to divide, merge and heal (to "hold on alive", as the term goes). As for growth, in the case of wisteria it is so vigorous that Mr Iba describes it with an evocative onomatopoeia (*buaaaaaaa*). In this way, grafting can be considered as an enhancing manipulation.

Figure 1.4: The Ibas, taking a short break during a grafting day. On the right, the grafted wisterias have been planted the day before, after being bathed (2015).

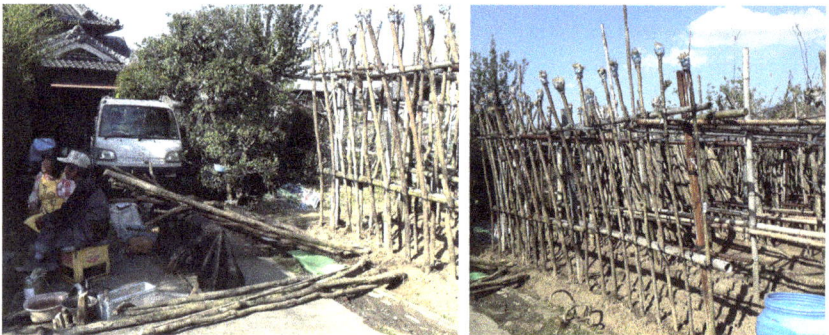

Image: Emilie Letouzey.

---

10   Due in particular to the complexity of the root symbiosis that the plant develops thanks to their root nodules, like most plants of the Fabaceae family (or legumes; see Ibáñez et al. 2017).

The kind of work the Ibas accomplish on – or rather with – wisterias corresponds to a technical paradigm of patient and skillful individual shaping. This paradigm is declining. From the era of craftsmanship that characterized traditional Edo style horticulture, Japanese horticulture is gradually shifting to an industrial production and genetic engineering era, which obviously involves a very different kind of intimacy with plants.

In the Ministry of Agriculture, Forestry and Fisheries' (MAFF) national data, floriculture (*kaki*) belongs to the horticulture branch – that officially consists in fruit trees, vegetables and floriculture – and usually refers to cut flowers industry only.[11] Although most of Japan's emblematic flowers are tree flowers, flowering trees (*kaboku*) constitute a smaller category, that appears in specialized documents and is invisible in agricultural pie charts – both at the production type level and at the economic weight level. The floriculture and flowering trees categories consist of various subcategories whose proportions vary considerably depending on the production area and whether they are cultivated in pots or sold in cut branches; the same plants can be included in different categories.[12] The ornamental domain is today led by *shisetsu engei*, which literally means "facility horticulture", and refers to intensive greenhouse cultivation. A well-known product of industrial capitalism, this model is based on financial investments and characterized by high-tech and fossil fuel voracious facilities, and by the growing role of biotechnologies, patents and branding. By contrast, the vegetal economy described in this paper comes under a tiny-scale handcrafting model, characterized by high skill and low tech. Of course, a wide range of cultivation models unfold between these two extremes – the crafting model and the industrial model – but it is the latter that constitutes the economically significant part displayed in the pie charts. Businesses like the Ibas' are very representative of the traditional tendency in Japanese ornamental horticulture: they manufacture thousands of plant units and they are part of a rich mosaic of similar businesses. Still, one has to search in town council data to find such trades, in the same way that one has to zoom in on satellite images to find out the location of north Ōsaka's nurseries.

In facility horticulture, cultivation labour tends to be entrusted to sophisticated measurement devices and automated machines. The nature of "have do" thus

---

11   According to MAFF's 2020 data, portions of horticultural production in total agricultural production is about 40 per cent, principally constituted of vegetables 25.6 per cent, fruits 9.3 per cent and floriculture 3.7 per cent. By comparison, rice is 19.2 per cent and livestock industry (*chikusan*) 35.5 per cent of that total.

12   Floriculture category encompass four types of plants: cut flowers (*kiribanarui*, that include cut leaves (*kiriha* and cut branches *kirieda*), bulbs (*kyūkonrui*), potted plants (*hachimonorui*) and young plants for flower bed use (*kadanyōnaerui*). Flowering trees and the likes (*kaboku nado*) category encompass three types: flowering trees (*kaboku*), grass (*shiba*) and ground cover plants (*chihi shokubutsu rui*).

changes, as cultivating actions – whether on the plants or on their environment – are enacted by sophisticated machines, whose programmed agencies seem to lead the process. However, for many common plants, grafting – described by philosopher François Dagognet as an archaic biotechnology (1988) – remains necessary.[13] Setting aside the topic of intimacy with plants induced by this horticultural model, another example suggests the limits of high tech's superiority over hand skills. The recent creation of a genetically modified blue rose by Suntory Flower's teams has received much media attention,[14] making the technical possibilities of ornamental plants lab engineering look endless – especially since they enable genetic manipulations that are restricted or prohibited for edible plants. It is however remarkable that no biotechnology has yet made it possible to re-create the yellow ipomoea cultivar that was obtained during the Edo period (as evidenced by 19th century horticultural treatises), which went extinct later on.

Vegetal economies, bubbles and value-creation

A crafting practice based on plant breeding and cultivation, Japanese traditional horticulture's vegetal economy is also made of booms, bubbles, and speculation processes that often end up creating asset-like goods out of ordinary commodities. From the Edo period the cultivation of ornamental plants flourished continually until the 20th century, especially during the 1970s and 1980s: depending on fads, entire categories of plants were then prestigious possessions, collected with care and displayed with pride. All the producers I met are nostalgic about the plant booms (azalea boom, bonsai boom, *omoto* [Rohdea japonica] boom) that succeeded one another. Some even mention suitcases of money spent in plant nurseries. Although I suspect these are legends, I did meet housewives whose husbands had indebted their family to satisfy their vegetal passion. The burst of the Japanese economic bubble marked the end of this epoch. As many cultivators explain, the high price period could not resist Japan's economic crisis of the 1990s. Even if business somehow lasted until the 1990s in various horticultural areas, it has globally been decreasing since the 2000s. Cultivation and crafting labour is no longer valued: the producers frequently blame a deep change in Japanese "sense of values" (*kachikan*), now unfavorable to the production of traditional plants, whose value is produced by time-consuming techniques, especially when it comes to the shaping

---

13   Grafting can be mechanized for vegetables seedlings, but not for woody plants, especially fruits trees, conifer, and many ornamental species.

14   For example, Tyell, Eric (2004): "A thorny tweak for the rose." In: Los Angeles Times, August 13; "My love is like a blue, blue rose", October 21, 2012 (http://news.bbc.co.uk/2/hi/asia-pacific /8318511.stm).

process. The complaint that current prices do not even compensate the effective working time is frequently heard in Kansai's nurseries and "planted trees" (*ueki*) whole markets.

It is just as true that today few producers are willing to put so much "effort and time" (*tema hima*) into crafting ornamental plants, especially as this dedication is no longer appreciated by the clients, who cannot 'read' it in the plants from a lack of aesthetic and technical knowledge or interest. Many of the best breeders, grafters and plant-shapers are more than 70 years old. Many of their sons and daughters are not taking over the family business, or choose to develop them in new directions, for example in the import and finishing of Mediterranean plants, supplying the garden shops and hardware stores ordinary people go to. Most importantly, more than ever producers have to be versatile. They take advantage of their skillfulness to face a precarious professional condition. That is why, although traditional horticulture remains a popular hobby for the elders, professional production is declining.

The Ibas come to the same conclusion. They are indeed versatile, as they also cultivate different types of woody plants such as bamboo or crape myrtle (*Lagerstroemia Indica*) and occasionally work in other nurseries. However, they are an exception in at least two ways. First, being located in Ikeda, a city whose horticultural production mainly consists of seedlings and young trees,[15] they receive orders from the cities and private institutions in relation to urban greenery or big scale events (many producers mentioned the yet to come 2020 Olympics when I did my fieldwork). Second, in their case, the common use of wisterias in urban public parks to procure shade in the summer ensures an annual outlet, as the heat island phenomenon occurring in Japanese cities have lately pushed Park services to promote such measures. That is why most of urban parks have a wisteria, whose dense foliage is part of the street furniture as is the bench lying under it – flowers, in this case – appear like a bonus.[16] Thus, the Ibas are holding on. Who will make such an effort in ten years though? In any case, not their children.

Finally, let us pay a last visit to Noda Wisteria Association in Fukushima ward. At first glance, the volunteers' activity within the Association, based on the unpaid labour of enthusiastic citizens, stands away from production and market paradigms. Does this mean that Noda's wisteria has no economic value? On a regional scale, Noda wisteria is – economically speaking – invisible: in the twelve million people agglomeration Ōsaka is the heart of, the Association blends into

---

15   In 2005, about 75 per cent of the municipal horticultural production consisted of seedlings, young trees and so forth (*shubyō, naegi, sono hoka*). The proportion has not changed much since then.

16   On the contrary, many Japanese gardens, temples, shrines and other *meisho* (famous places) that include a flowering wisteria prohibit to tread under the trellis to prevent soil compression.

hundreds of similar local projects. Yet on a local scale, the economic dimension of the wisteria clearly appears. I do not refer here to the festival, which is a minor event in this regard, as it is – at best – an occasion for shops to attract clients and for associations to promote themselves through small craft merchandizing. A mere budget-related concern for Noda Wisteria Association, money recently became a major subject matter. As for many associations, much monthly meeting time is devoted to accountings: annual membership fees and various donations – as the Lion's Club's regular contribution (*kifu*) – finance the group activities and the maintenance of the plants (that includes treillises, tools, material, etc.). This routine got troubled in 2017 when a mysterious benefactor made an astronomic donation to the Ward office (and not to the Association) for "the flourishing of Noda Wisteria". "With money like that, you could buy a flat!", a volunteer said as I frowned when he told me the news:[17] suddenly, Noda wisteria and its flowers went priceless.

The volunteer's remark echoed another aspect of the wisterias' local economic dimension, less obvious and even ambiguous. As historic and emblematic local heritage, the plant and its flowers are also seen as a means of valorizing the reputation of the ward – its symbolic value, its "image" (*iméji*) – and therefore very concrete monetary value in terms of real estate. Significantly, the first wisteria cultivation project in Fukushima ward in the 1970s was initiated by local notables, some of whom owned real estate businesses. Many local historic figures, landscapes, objects, products and so on, can be used for such purposes in Japan. Economic value-creation is not a role limited to plants, although they are privileged objects. Maybe because of the historic role of Ōsaka as the "merchants' capital" (Wakita 1999), this value-creation aspect is not concealed or considered inappropriate: quite the opposite, it is viewed as a good thing for the neighborhoods, including among local volunteers' associations. First an intuition, this value-production reading gradually became one of the lenses I see Noda Wisteria's Association's activity through. It would confer a non-assessable value-creating role to the wisteria's emblematic flowers, different from the vine's foliage "shady work" – as Jennifer Atchison puts it (this volume) – humble but much more tangible.

Epilogue

Although apparently motionless, plants are tirelessly making, producing themselves and the environment around them. Their photosynthesis process, as well as their pluripotent cells able to produce any organ, are both the tools and the symbols

---

17   In Japanese, big amounts of money are expressed in "thousands of ten-thousands [of yens]", implying in my case a double calculation and conversion operation I am not good at.

of this perpetual making. Striking work about plant life – Darwin's plant studies, early time lapse cinema (Castro 2019), the forest's 'wood wide web' to mention just a few – emphasize this making by describing its fascinating mechanisms. Human appropriations use this potential. However, from crop domestication to plant engineering, such appropriations appear as a feeble inversion of the work – and the worlds – that plants do. Besides, understanding of vegetal agency hardly challenges our concept of production, even in Japan. Of course, plant-based material life and aesthetics have been at work for centuries to increase plant presence in society, name them, connect them to history. Today emblematic plants have a biography, or appear like significant others for many caring people. However, Japanese culture has acknowledged vegetal agency mainly to appropriate it for human purposes. This has enabled some to use plants as ideological instruments: Berque (1986) and Shirane (2013) analyzed the role of plant praise in the process of mistaking culture for nature, thereby enlightening the paradox – which up to that point remained baffling – of nature being celebrated while serious environmental damage was being caused; Rambelli (2001) and Rots (2017) showed how Buddhism and Shintō have used the vegetal as power-establishing instruments. In Japan, critical plant studies would have much to do to untangle such deep misunderstandings.

In the global context of a plant turn and while anthropologists endeavor to "interview" plants (Hartigan 2017), I often wondered what place I should give to the vegetal in my research. The focus on what people in my fieldwork were focused on offered a large part of the answer: through their stories and activities, the ethnographic inquiry naturally became an inquiry into the vegetal form of life and into the intricated human-plant agencies. The Ibas and the volunteers, who chose wisteria as a livelihood or as an emblem, have it partly occupy their hands and their heads. Taking a close look, cultivation techniques help us to see human and plant agencies meet (or confront?) at an individual level – even on the scale of a flower bud. These techniques are based on canalizing vegetal processes that are pushed or impeded. They result in straight and parallel wisterias, rooting in concrete pots and expanding on square trellises. Yet the vines still gush, escape, show reluctance. While most domesticates have, so to speak, picked a side – humans or the wild – wisteria's real performance may be their remarkable ability to flourish both with or without humans, constrained or unconstrained.

Acknowledgements

I am deeply grateful to the cultivators in Ōsaka who have been enduring my enthusiastic-yet-intrusive participant-observation for years, and to the editors of this book for setting up a stimulating, meticulous and warm elaboration process, and for providing generous and insightful comments on early versions of this chapter.

Chapter 2 - Care for the commodity?
The work of saving succulents in the laboratory

Jared Margulies

The work of saving species threatened with extinction is of critical importance. But what that work entails, who performs such work, and for whom this work is done has transformed and evolved alongside conservation as an academic discipline and scientific endeavor, a governmental and non-governmental industry, and more recently as a major financial enterprise (Braverman 2015; Dempsey 2018). The conservation of plants, however, with the very notable exception of agricultural crops, has not elicited the intense kind of global interest, financing, opportunity for capitalist accumulation, or at-times violent character (thankfully) such as that seen in the world of animal conservation (Duffy 2016; Margulies et al. 2019). As a small sliver of the plant kingdom, the cacti and succulents I focus on this chapter are experiencing a moment of phenomenal popularity with global consumers, both as household plants as well as in visual and iconographic forms, their images plastered across social media platforms, wallpaper, coffee mugs, and t-shirts, among other consumer goods. The work of commodifying plant species for aesthetic consumption, and the work of plant conservation, however, are traditionally understood as distinct activities with divergent interests. In this chapter I focus on a space of vital overlap between them through species care work, to consider the work of caring for endangered plant species and the more-than-human laboratory labors this involves.

My attention turns to the shared work of plants and persons in a botanical garden laboratory setting, and a decades-old project at the Botanical Gardens of The Huntington in Los Angeles County, California. The project, International Succulent Introductions (ISI), aims to reduce threats to endangered succulent plant species through their commodification – the mass reproduction of plants as lively commodities. In cloning laboratory plants, ISI represents a market-oriented intervention into curbing the illicit collection of wild plants by making cultivated specimens available for purchase. Drawing on notions of lively capital (Haraway 2008: 46), lively commodities are defined by Collard and Dempsey as "live commodities whose capitalist value is derived from their *status as living beings*" (2013: 2684, original emphasis). Through the setting of the laboratory and the work of laboratory laborers, the work of species care is extended to plants with the intent of offsetting pressure on these plants' wild relatives that are oftentimes restricted in habitat or naturally rare in number. In focusing on this laboratory setting and the mainte-nance and reproduction of endangered species, I became interested in these acts of commodification as a means to better understand the economy of saving plants and what it means to consider care of the species as "an alignment of interests and practices, applied across species boundaries [...] developed and promulgated through advances in genetic procedures and techniques" (Hartigan 2017: xiii). How might this laboratory work of species conservation be understood both as a matter of care and an effort of co-laboring between plants and persons?

In considering how plants are both made to work, but also fostered as species through the work of conservation care, thinking with Besky and Blanchette's (2019: 7) notion of "troubled ecologies" is useful, which "make the boundaries between subjects and objects blurry, while forcing those who subsist in them to grapple with the inadequacy of ingrained capitalist concepts and binaries such as work or na-ture". In a similar register, attending to the frictions at the heart of this species care work aligns with the project of posthuman political ecologies, an effort of destabi-lizing taken-for-granted ontological 'givens' in analyses of environmental inequal-ities and power relations (Sundberg 2014; Margulies/Bersaglio 2018). As plant con-servation work, the notion of more-than-human care extended through capitalist logics both complicates what it means to perform care work for nonhuman organ-isms and also who or what performs such work (Puig de la Bellacasa 2017). This chapter is a speculative effort to think with plants through the troubled ecological webs capitalism weaves through nature and vice versa (Moore 2015). Practices of succulent commodification interlace with 'caring for the collective' as biopolitical strategy aimed at the maintenance of populations (or species) deemed worthy of sustaining where the targets for care are not individuals but broader categories of interest (Srinivasan 2014). Rather than strictly complementary practices, there is an emergent tension between the fostering of life and its commodification that mate-rializes in the laboratory around the practice of 'saving species'. This tension finds resonance with other examples of appropriating nature in which new techniques devised to monetize natural resources while also reducing natural resource degra-dation instead simultaneously maximize economies of both "growth and repair" (Fairhead et al. 2012: 242). Before tackling the subject of succulent propagation, in the next section I clarify the terms of more-than-human care work.

The work of species care

In the broadest sense, care encompasses activities and forms of attention directed towards the maintenance and sustenance of others, other things and others' interests. To clarify my use of this terminology, I start with one of the most common definitions from Joan Tronto and Bernice Fisher:

> On the most general level, we suggest that caring be viewed as a *species activity that includes everything that we do to maintain, continue, and repair our 'world' so that we can live in it as well as possible.* That world includes our bodies, our selves, and our environment, all of which we seek to interweave in a complex, life-sustaining web. (Fisher/Tronto 1991: 40, cited in Tronto 1993: 103, original emphasis)

While care is conventionally understood in everyday usage as inflected with empathy, concern, love, or affection, care is also detached, ambivalent, even violent; to care does not exist outside the cultural and political milieu of those engaged in the work of care, inclusive of the uneven power dynamics produced through and across histories of race, class, gender, and other forms of social difference (Puig de la Bellacasa 2011; Murphy 2015). As care has emerged as an important analytic, particularly within feminist geographies and (feminist) science and technology studies, Murphy (2015) urges deeper engagement with unsettling care, questioning care and caring that presumes only positive affects. I take this work of unsettling to mean both granting attention to and working against inequalities present in the work of care and the uneven social contexts within which care is pursued (Martin/Myers/Viseu 2015).

In turning to matters of the more-than-human in the context of care work, it signals a flourishing interdisciplinary area of scholarship concerned with developing language and theory to explore, analyze, and learn to be affected by the entangled and complex relations between bodies, individuals, collectives and earth system processes that co-fabricate the world (Whatmore 2002; Greenhough 2014; Giraud 2019). Thinking with care in more-than-human registers, I became interested in a question posed by Puig de la Bellacasa (2017: 65), who asks: "for what worlds is care being done for?" Her question speaks to my interest in practices in which scientists within the conservation division of a botanical garden conduct care work for endangered species through the propagation and cloning of individual plants to sell over the internet. In whose interest do these practices of interspecies care occur? Does a rare species of aloe plant only known from two locations near a small village in the Mudug region of Somalia care if laboratory technicians in California produce hundreds of clones from a single individual of the species? What does it mean to extend care across species lines when those receiving care are collectively indifferent – as far as anyone knows – to such actions, but where individual lives are also arguably sacrificed or brought into existence for the care of the much more abstract concept of a species or population? I will fail to answer all these questions, as echoing Hartigan (2017: 217), "these dynamics of care become a good deal more complicated when they are enacted or exerted across species lines". Hartigan's choice of words is important as they tilt at agency, and beget yet another speculative question—how does one make determinations between *enactments* and *exertions* of care work, expressions with differing connotations of agency, force, and detachment in how work is pursued? Puig de la Bellacasa (2017: 7) again offers insight, suggesting the question to pursue – "how to care?" – transforms care from "a predetermined set of affective practices" into "an analytic or provocation". As a provocation then, the reproduction of rare plants in the laboratory is an avenue for considering both possibilities and limits to the work of conservation as care, attentive to the political economy of the more-than-human relations emergent through conservation work.

The laboratory is a particular site through which I consider the work of plants, but my interest in the lab extends beyond either the techniques or the economy of maintaining and reproducing plants. At the same time that the plants at the heart of this chapter were – through their entanglements with laboratory technicians, petri dishes, agar medium (the product of another plant), botanical gardens, and rare plant collectors – transformed into living commodities, the human labor of reproducing them is also unambiguously intended as an act of what John Hartigan Jr. (2017) calls "care of the species". Care of the species names the relationships forged as "forms of care as cross-species engagements", but specifically it turns on the work of caring for species rather than individual organisms (ibid: 98). Hartigan (ibid: 97) centers the plants – in this case, forms of maize – as the central focus of his ethnographic investigations, but with particular attention, drawing on the work of Foucault, to the meaning of the self in relation to the species, or namely "one species acting on and sculpting the self of another". But where Hartigan's work focuses on one of the worlds' most important food crops, here I am interested in the cultivation of species which do not serve the immediate sustenance of human life. Hartigan (ibid: xiii-xv) notes this is an important expansion in the work of care from concern for agriculturally useful crops to species with innate 'biodiversity value' through the distinction between artificial and natural selection, writing that: "Escalating efforts at conserving and cultivating biodiversity are extending such forms of care to species with little or no direct value for humans, blurring an important contrast with the domesticates we have transformed over millennia". In the case of the succulents I focus on in this chapter, these contrasts become blurrier still: because collector desire is incited by the possibility and availability of new species (or new phenotypic expressions), species care work and the sustaining of succulent biodiversity very much hold immediate value for the human subjects the ISI project engages with. Simply put, the more kinds of plants that exist, the more plants there are to plausibly collect.

The blurring of the natural and domestic Hartigan speaks to mirrors the troubled and blurred distinctions between the more-than-human care work of conserving species, and the work of cultivating lively commodities in the laboratory. As Hartigan (ibid: 247) later adds on these distinctions between the work of caring for the "domesticated" versus "the untamed", he questions the ability to maintain such clear distinctions. I agree, arguing the work of cloning individual plants is not a purely innocent endeavor of perfect and indefinite genetic replication of species life. In particular, in the laboratory setting which I focus on, decisions are made about which individual plants should botanically represent the species as an epistemic category, but these decisions also determine how representations of species are economically appraised and valued by succulent collectors as living commodities for consumption. At the same time, as I discuss later in the chapter, plants too, through their physiological responses to the stresses of repeated clonal propagation, can resist the smooth and endless processes which render them into identical vegetal commodities (Shukin 2009). In coming to focus on the labors of plants and laboratory technicians working to propagate rare wild species, important connections also emerge between this work as species care and the growing emergence of seed banks, cryogenic freezing operations, and botanical gardens as sites where extinction operates as a speculative biocapital accumulation strategy (Helmreich 2008; Churlew 2017; Harrison 2017; Breithoff/Harrison 2020). While the activities I focus on in this chapter are not being pursued as a new form of bioaccumulation strategy, the plants situated at the heart of these endeavors nevertheless are shaped by capitalism and its logics.

Beyond articulating another rich example of the entangled lives within socionatures that make various accumulation strategies possible (Braun 2006), it is worth considering what is advanced more precisely by recognizing such entanglements of species life through acts of care work. Writing on the tensions of such articulations of entangled relationality, I am motivated by Giraud's recent (2019) assessment of the need to question whether recognition of relations begets more ethical responses. Much of the literature on relational ethics presumes that revealing or articulating modes of relating generates affinities and greater capacity for interspecies intimacies (ibid: 2). This work therefore extends problematizing more-than-human relational ethics, questioning "the assumption that an ontology of relation and vitality can provide a route to a full more-than-human ethic" (Ginn 2014: 534). Attention to such indeterminacies and ambivalences in ethico-political registers is especially pertinent for thinking about more-than-human care work as an evolving set of laboring relations between persons and plants emergent through species care.

Botanical gardens as sites of species care work

The Huntington is one of the largest private research libraries in the world, an art museum, and collection of numerous botanical gardens located in Los Angeles County in San Marino, California.[1] The cactus and succulent 'living collection' of the Desert Garden is nearly 100 years old and is considered one of the most important succulent collections in the world, boasting over 2000 different species of desert plants. As part of a larger research effort studying global succulent plant trade and conservation, in 2019 I spent a little over a week visiting the Botanical Research division of the Huntington to interview and spend time with cactus and succulent researchers, conservation practitioners, and garden staff, hoping to better understand the role of botanical gardens in succulent conservation work. Botanical gardens perform a vital function linking together the epistemological activities of knowing, describing, and archiving plants with the work of plant cultivation, care, and public education (Hartigan 2017: 217). Whom or what that care work serves has evolved over time; in previous centuries, botanical gardens were crucial (and problematic) sites of empire building and nation-making (McCracken 1997; Schiebinger 2004; Endersby 2008; Herbert 2012; Baber 2016). Over the past half century, and especially in the past few decades, botanical gardens have become more active sites of ex-situ conservation work. This ex-situ work is done in the name of preserving living biodiversity and involves working to maintain living collections, seeds, and plant genetic material for, among other things, their potential future value to repopulate degraded or destroyed ecosystems with rare or threatened species (Prance 2000; Heyd 2006; Hawkes et al. 2012).

Within this vein of thinking about the botanical garden as a site of ex-situ conservation, but also a space concerned with engaging the public, I wanted to learn more about a program run out of the Botanical Research division at The Huntington called International Succulent Introductions (ISI). ISI was formed in 1958, and after operating out of various private commercial operations, it formally moved to the Huntington in 1989. ISI's mission is to "propagate and distribute new or rare succulents to collectors, nurseries and institutions. In keeping with sound conservation practices, field-collected plants are not sold" (The Huntington, no date). Clones of field collected plants or their progeny are sold, however, as a goal of ISI is to meet the demand of specialist collectors who might otherwise – so it is believed – take plants "from habitat" (an expression used throughout the collecting and conservation community). ISI is unique for bringing together matters of plant conservation

---

1   The Huntington and its supporting endowment were formed through the amassed wealth of real estate and railroad tycoon Henry Edwards Huntington, who created the Huntington with his wife, Arabella Duval Huntington, the former wife of his deceased uncle and railroad business partner Collis P. Huntington.

care with their commodification, as well as for the connections it makes between private collectors passionate about succulent plants and the threats plants may face from the activities of the very same community. I therefore conceive of the ISI as an intervention of species care work, and an attempt to mediate particular ways in which succulent collectors encounter and collect plants understood as either ethically 'good' or 'bad.' I must clarify my usage of, and slightly modify, Hartigan's (2017: 133) conceptualization of care of the species here, which he says "*aims toward knowledge production of species themselves*, in order to guide or direct their plasticity and cultivate their modes of diversity" (original emphasis). Here, the ISI is not an effort of knowledge production, but a set of tools and practices very much concerned with how to "maintain, continue, and repair" species by shaping human-plant encounters (Tronto 1993: 103). Embedded in this practice of caring for the species then is not only a moral claim to proper ways of caring, but also ethico-political determinations of what kinds of plants within a species are included in specific acts and attention of species care (and the work of care), and which are not.

It is for this reason – how the species as a matter of care for conservation both includes and excludes plants from acts of care based on their status as a 'wild' organism or not – that I situate this work as species care rather than care for plants, though the former does not preclude the latter. I understand 'species' as performed and enacted scientific classificatory constructs (Kirksey 2015). Presented in the form of a written binomial – a species is the joining of a Latin genus and species name as the indicator that a grouping of plants exists as a specific, immutable type.[2] The species binomial works well within the logics of capitalism, as it orders and standardizes vegetal life in a structured and hierarchical form that belies the far more promiscuous and porous nature of plant life. Acknowledging this disjuncture between epistemological ideals of plant types and their ontological realities would complicate efforts of commodification and the production of species demand for consumers. This demand production is important because it taps into collector desire to possess representatives of species as well as type specimens, a botanical category described in greater detail in the next section. In the process of caring for the species, this care work differentiates between the species as an epistemological container for living organisms that very much exist in the world (even if they are represented quite poorly by the formal taxonomy that 'species' represents), and the organisms being grown in the laboratory through this care work as living representatives of the species. The species of conservation interest then is increasingly distanced from the actual work with plants in the laboratory

---

2   The Linnaean taxonomic system using Latin binomials for species names has been widely critiqued for decades as an inadequate means of categorizing and classifying life, especially life beyond the animal. See e.g. Ereshefsky (2000).

and the process of objectifying individual plants as lively commodities. Reiterating a position taken by Martin, Myers, and Viseu (2015: 627), care "circumscribes and cherishes some things, lives, or phenomena as its objects. In the process, it excludes others". One way to understand this differential species relationship between the plants of concern (wild plants – out there) and the plants being worked on (clonal propagules – in the lab) is to frame the endangered succulent plants living beyond the laboratory as the subjects of care, while those plants under replication in the laboratory are worked into commodified objects through whose reproduction care of the conservation subject is pursued. But in being worked on, these plants also work (metabolically) themselves, and it is ultimately this co-laboring of species that comprises species care work. Species care work is further complicated and temporally extended into the lives of plants through incorporating cryobiotechnologies as a technique capable of suspending life itself.

Tissue culture, cryopreservation, and the cycling of vegetal life in the lab

During an hour-long conversation in 2019 with the Huntington's Plant Conservation Specialist, we spoke over a cup of coffee on the conservation work of gardens. We touched on all matters of work and activity that takes place in the Botany division, and how the work of the garden is connected to concerns about the maintenance of wild life. Weaving across various thematic threads relating to trade, conservation, plant preservation and cryogenics, eventually we arrived at discussing the ISI as an activity bridging these topics. He explained the program's value:

> Every year we offer plants that are either rare in cultivation or rare in the wild with the intent that people won't poach them from the wild if we give [the plants] to them first. We're targeting plants that we think are either new to the trade, or are uncommon. We mass propagate them artificially and then we try to satisfy the market. (Interview with Plant Conservation Specialist, January 28, 2019)

Prior to 2008, propagating plants for ISI focused on traditional methods of vegetal reproduction, such as taking plant cuttings, rooting them, growing them up, and cutting them again, a process he described as:

> [...] a ten-year process. Whereas we were able to fast track that to 18 months or less through tissue culture. It was a time issue [...] As long as you keep a plant in what we call the multiplication phase, you can, theoretically, get as many plants as you want, you can stop it whenever you want. (Interview with Plant Conservation Specialist, January 28, 2019)

Tissue culture in plants involves taking small cuttings of meristematic plant tissue (called explants after excision) and then rearing them in a sterile growth medium (Figure 2.1). Meristematic plant cells have the ability to regenerate into any other plant cell and organize a complete organism, a cellular ability known as totipotency, a capacity much more restricted in animals. This means minuscule plant tissue cuttings can produce fully fledged plant clones in a matter of weeks, a process that, as noted above, can theoretically continue indefinitely. But more than providing time management advantages (reduction in necessary labor time to reproduce individual plants), reproduction of plants via tissue culture enables an additional avenue for plant reproduction when other methods of reproduction are not possible:

> Our tissue culture program was originally created as a propagation tool for plants that were difficult to propagate by other means, either it was a plant that was slow to produce flowers or didn't produce flowers, a plant where we only had a male or female, we didn't have both, and/or a plant that we knew was really hard to keep alive. These are candidates we looked at for using tissue culture to try to propagate them clonally. (Interview with Plant Conservation Specialist, January 28, 2019)

Figure 2.1: Agave morani tissue culture explants in sterile growth medium on laboratory bench prepared by the author.

Image: Jared Margulies.

At the Huntington the scientists and technicians I interviewed explained the tissue culture program was an important phase of vegetal life in the lab linking the gardens' 'living collections' with mid- and long-term ex-situ preservation of species through plant cryopreservation – the process of storing desiccated plant tissue and seed at very low temperatures in liquid nitrogen cooled vessels. Cryopreservation is an evolving technology that extends biopolitical governing of life into blurrier thresholds of lively and not-so lively existence, and thus has also become a recent area of research interest for more critical scholars concerned about the biopolitics such practices produce or enable (Friedrich 2017; Radin/Kowal 2017). But while cryopreservation can serve as a practically indefinite form of storing value, coupled with other biotechnologies, it can also be applied to botanical and conservation problems that move plant life in and out of the varied biological temporalities and rhythms extreme cooling enables. As Friedrich (2017: 61) explains: "Prevented from aging and spoiling, cryogenic life is the result of the sociotechnical effort to detach organic matter from its natural life cycle".

The Huntington's Cryopreservation Research Botanist offered me a primer on cryogenics and botany one afternoon at her desk attached to the Huntington's tissue culture lab. We pored over powerpoint slides of the cryopreservation process on her computer screen, and she narrated the various figures and diagrams for me:

> So you collect a plant that might be wild collected, then you can keep it in a botanical garden, in an ex-situ collection, in a field collection. As I said before, that plant might die for different reasons. If you have the chance to have a backup collection – that is what actually the cryopreservation collections are – *they are living collections, but they are [also] backup collections*. They are not the only collection in the group for the plants. (Interview with Cryopreservation Research Botanist, January 30, 2019, her emphasis)

She showed me a figure illustrating how this process begins with either garden plants or wild specimens as sources of "donor material". This living material is then used to cycle explant material in and out of cryogenic preservation and tissue culture propagation, sending some of those newly produced clones back into the cryogenic storage vessel, while sending the rest out to where they are needed. The destination might be the garden's outdoor collections to replace old or dying plants, other gardens or research centers, commercial entities or private collectors (such as through the ISI), and perhaps one day, she speculated, even into habitats where wild plants are no longer found. During our discussion, she made sure to clarify we were not discussing "freezing" seeds or plant tissue through cryogenics, but "cooling" them. Freezing would imply ice crystal formation – a process that would be deadly to plant material as water expands when frozen and thus would cause plant cells to lyse. In cryopreservation, the water content of the plant material is first largely removed, and the plant tissue or seeds are treated with cryoprotectant chemicals to further shield them from freezing. She explained to me that in contrast to freezing plant material, cryopreservation is about the maintenance of life in suspended form for future use, unrestrained by the normal temporalities of plant time.

The role of cryopreservation at the garden mirrors similar efforts in zoos to cryopreserve endangered animal reproductive materials (Chrulew 2017); in fact, cryopreservation is much more well-established in humans and animals, and remains more experimental in plants. But unlike sperm and unfertilized eggs, cryopreserved plant matter is already existing life in suspension rather than only its future possibility. There is a distinction therefore between the way the botanist talks about the living status of plants in cryopreservation compared to its parallels for animal life. While this distinction is subtle, it speaks to the drastically different reproductive possibilities of plants and animals and how they might be put to work, and what these modes of reproducing life enable or disable in efforts to conserve them. Cryogenics enables a vital form of stable storage for plant life, suspending value in ultra-cooled plant tissue until its circulation is later desired (Banoub/Martin 2020). But which plants of a species enter cryopreservation, and which do not? Here the formulation of plant species as fixed botanical taxonomies, both by botanic gardens as well as avid collectors, is an epistemological concern determining how species care work in the botanic garden is pursued in relation to the value of certain plants. The botanist explained:

> The reason why do we do it [plant reproduction] clonal is just because we want to keep the *true-to-type plant*. So we want to keep the same plant. [For instance] if we want to plant it later in the garden [...] In the case of the agaves, and the species we are working with, many of them are type plants, as you might know, they're the plants that are used for the description of the species. So they have a botanical value. *It might not be a value for conservation itself, but it's a botanical value.* (Interview with Cryopreservation Research Botanist, January 30, 2019, my emphasis)

Her reference to "type plants" here is important. "Types" refer to a specific botanical specimen, an actual living or preserved plant, that serves as the reference plant for describing an entire species. Somewhere, every formally described plant species in the world has a type specimen comprised of preserved plant material affixed to an herbarium sheet with its description, location of origin, who collected and described the plant (often different people), among other essential data. In cloning types, cloning and cryogenic technologies are put to work to reproduce and store the individual organism that ties the species concept to a specific biological being. While the cryopreservation botanist points to the botanical value of these plants, as type specimen clones, these plants are also valued more highly by many collectors as 'the best' or 'true' representations of the species. Cryopreservation therefore also further enables a form of standardization and replication – at least in theory – of plants seen as more valuable than others of the species and prioritized by the botanical garden and collectors alike as such. While this concern for species types and reproduction of 'true' or 'pure' species might seem to contradict previous statements made by others I interviewed about the conservation value of the ISI, the focus on type specimens is a space of concern for intervention because the private collectors they are producing plants for, and whose behavior they are seeking to modify, are specifically desirous of collecting the species. While there are many kinds of collectors motivated by various aspects of plant collections, many succulent collectors are equally concerned with the provenance and acquisition of plants that are representative of the type or closely affiliated with it through plants sharing the same provenance as the type's locality. Thus, although the cycling of clonal plant material in and out of cryopreservation and tissue culture may seem entirely removed from the lifeworlds of existing plants out in the world (the plants the program seeks to foster through their intervention), the production of these clones is very much linked to how the succulent collecting community constructs stable notions of species kinds, which in turn mediates their desires to possess and obtain wild-collected plants. Thus conceived, the work of conservation in the laboratory links together epistemologies of the species with forms of care work increasingly distanced from the plant lives for whom care work is pursued.

The multispecies work of cloning commodities

My time spent physically working with plants at the Huntington enabled a greater appreciation for species care work as a form of co-laboring. At the Huntington I was introduced to the basics of tissue culture propagation as well as more traditional propagation techniques such as grafting and taking succulent cuttings. I found cutting plants to be a generative task for theorizing about how different plant lives are valued through care work. In revisiting these practices, I wish to pay attention to what changes in the course of analysis if it is permitted that these plants in the lab are "working subjects, not just worked objects" (Haraway 2008: 57). It is in this speculative grey area between working subject and worked object that the labor of more-than-human care work clearly expresses both a relational endeavor of co-laboring between plants and persons, as well as an extension of species care by humans interested in the maintenance of species constructs, or classifications of a kind whose representations as species come to express forms of value.

One afternoon in one of the Huntington's succulent greenhouses I turned a pile of rat tail's cactus (*Discocactus flagelliformis*) stems about one meter long into a much larger pile of shorter cuttings. In the course of an hour I quintupled the number of cacti laid out before me. The only difficult part of the task was remembering to keep the new cuttings all facing the correct direction – new roots would only sprout from one end and growth would only occur in the other, so if I accidentally reversed them, they would die. The curator overseeing my small operation corrected me when I made this error. Unlike him, I was unable to easily discern up from down just by looking at the plants, and for several days after I worried whether I had accidentally switched any others around, subjecting them to a slow, upside down death by desiccation. As I became more confident in my cactus cutting, I became aware that the care I extended to the plant(s) seemed to decline as the pile of new cactus cuttings grew; what started out as careful surgery soon felt like repetitive and mechanistic chopping. Another day I was tasked with propagating a particular aloe hybrid named 'Wiley Coyote' (Figure 2.2). To my untrained eye, the process of splicing the plants under sterilized conditions was not only awkward and tedious, but ambiguous. I thought it would be clear when one aloe should become two or three. My lack of skill spelt uncertainty – should this explant become two or three clones? I was clumsy with the scalpel and other tools, preoccupied with maintaining a sanitized laboratory space. Eventually I developed a rhythm in splicing the plants. In a matter of weeks the process would begin again. One to three, and so on, until there were hundreds of new aloes, all the clonal progeny of a single plant.

Figure 2.2: Frame from film of aloe 'Wiley Coyote' micropropagation by the author.

Image: Jared Margulies.

There are other clever techniques cactus collectors and conservators use for speeding up the propagation of cacti. One brutish method is to simply cut a large hole into the top of a cactus – in response to this injury, many types of cacti will respond by offsetting, or creating a slew of tiny new propagules, or pups, at the site of injury. I once watched an expert grower demonstrate this technique during a meeting of the Sheffield branch of the British Cactus and Succulent Society, an association I had joined in the course of my fieldwork. He took a pen knife, jabbed it into the center of a round cactus, gouged out the top, and said that's all it took, in a matter of months there would be half a dozen new cacti growing out from the top of the mother plant. These, like the progeny of tissue culture, would be clones. Deciding when a plant is no longer one but multiple starts to feel more slippery or uncertain at this juncture. What counts as an individual in the world of plants? To most growers, the only distinction between having one and many is the moment of excision of the pups from the mother plant into its own pot, its own kind of artifice of boundary-making in the vegetal worlds curated by collectors. It isn't a terribly profound question to consider whether to count a plant cut in half as one or two, but it does gesture towards the unsettling of clear distinctions between efforts to save species and vegetal commodification, and whom or what is engaged in species care work.

Despite the uneven dynamics of choice, agency, and power embedded in these acts of multispecies work, at the ISI the clonal cultivation of plants is a relational endeavor of sustaining plant life through variously inducing or encouraging plant reproduction and growth into desired forms. The use of tissue culture, alongside a variety of other reproductive tools and techniques the staff at the botanical garden utilize in the pursuit of species care, highlights an important and under-theorized facet of the work of plants in the commodification of life: the indeterminacy of plant cellular life and its diverse reproductive capabilities, especially when coaxed and activated by human-technical activity. In comparison to plants, animal reproduction appears remarkably limited: taking cuttings, pupping, selfing, tissue culture, and grafting, in addition to sexual reproduction between individual plants, all are means by which plant life (sometimes under human care, sometimes not) is sustained and expands (on the political ecologies of grafting see Fleming 2017). While the technologies themselves may remain more or less consistent in these pursuits, the cloning and propagation activities conducted in the laboratory value plants in remarkably different ways. At times the succulents being worked on in the lab are recipients of conservation care, a practice aimed at fostering and sustaining genetically diverse life through the suspended ex-situ preservation of individual plants. At other times, however, these activities of preservation and growth seem actually to diminish the vitality and valuing of plants as individual beings through processes rendering them as lively commodities. Vegetal standardization, mass replication, and the reduction of species diversity places emphasis on the valuing of plants as species types, or as representatives of endangered species rather than as individual plants. In the ISI lab, species care work thus conceived retains both a biopolitical shape fostering certain plant lives, while at the same time it reshapes others – often of the same species – into lively commodities through activities of purification and standardization. Within the same laboratory space this tension in how plant life is both valued and replicated is not only maintained, but linked together through the shared and distinct desires of conservationists and collectors and the technological capabilities to make plants work. This tension between practices of conservation and commodification speaks to the 'troubled ecology' of species care work. Practices of cutting, propagating, grafting, and cloning, all practices intended to sustain and foster endangered or rare plant life, also lessen how conservationists value these same plants as individual subjects by literally working them into living objects in the name of species care.

Tissue culture and affiliated technologies not only accelerate the embodied capacities of succulent plants to reproduce, but also further their commodification through streamlining them as (seemingly) homogenous entities for mass market consumption. Tissue culture opens up additional means towards international commodification and trade that can be hindered by more traditional methods of vegetal reproduction. Where once the ISI was a truly international program, today only tissue culture plant materials are shipped internationally (to one commercial lab in Europe); full size plants are restricted to sales within the United States due to the complications and costs associated with complying with international species trade regulations under CITES, the Convention on International Trade in Endangered Species of Wild Fauna and Flora (Interview, January 28, 2019). Because tissue culture successfully serves as 'proof' that a plant was artificially propagated (and thus, cannot be confused with a plant of possible wild origin or wild origin seed), tissue culture side-steps many of the complex regulations and certification requirements for selling and shipping plants internationally demanded by CITES. As laboratory grown plants, they are recognized as unambiguously artificial in origin and not of concern to the conservation of the species.

Not all succulents are suitable for tissue culture, however, which affects the speed with which mature plants can enter the marketplace. At the Huntington they focus more on agaves, aloes and other succulents compared to members of the cactus family, which reproduce less well under tissue culture. While certain types of plants are amenable to tissue culture due to their own evolutionary adaptations, others, such as cacti – with their spines, areoles, wool, and rough microtopographies where bacteria or fungi live on plant bodies – are not. As the curator spoke, I scribbled in my notebook, "cactus resistance to commodification?", self-conscious of my overt adoption of agential language to describe how the biological and material existence of particular organisms shapes the possibilities for their transformation into commodified form. This perspective finds resonance with Youatt (2008) who writes:

> Because nonhumans constitutionally (rather than intentionally) refuse to internalise the meanings of human language, they are able to resist becoming self-regulating subjects to a significant extent, relying instead on their own semiotic interpretations of the environment and acting accordingly: for example, through migrating, reproducing, consuming resources and filling ecological niches in un-

expected ways biotic nonhumans are constantly challenging the normalising will of biopower. (Youatt 2008: 394-395)

As a constitutional refusal then, many cactus species resist vegetal commodification via tissue culture, while remaining amenable to other accelerated reproductive techniques such as grafting.

The practice of tissue culture both distances plants as matters of concern in relation to the species as a still evolving, genetically diverse grouping of plants, while simultaneously facilitating their transformation into carefully manipulated commodity-forms. Just as in other industries, here we see how practices of standardization and mass-replication through tissue culture accelerate plant commodification by smoothing out the frictions erupting from biological heterogeneity within global supply chains. But let us consider this possibility of vegetal 'resistance to commodification' more seriously, as there are ways in which plants in the ISI lab do unsettle and trouble these clonal practices through specific responses to their environment and condition. Following Youatt's (2008) notion of constitutional refusal, I interpret ruptures in the smooth operating of tissue culture as plant resistance to efforts of total objectification. One site of resisting the reproductive work that enables their commodification is through phenotypic plasticity. Despite the promises of tissue culture as a means of indefinite and standardized vegetal reproduction, through the interplay of genetics and clonal techniques, errors invariably emerge in the tissue culture laboratory, as small, random gene mutations occur in the proliferation of species, creating new phenotypic expressions:

> So, it happens, in tissue culture occasionally, actually with surprising frequency, that what you get out ends up looking a little bit different than what you put in. Maintaining genetic stability is the goal, of course, but things happen […] Variegation tends to be a frequent result, but the tissues are being abused and manipulated so much that may be a factor in stimulating mutation. (Interview with Desert Gardens and Collections Curator, January 02, 2019)

As a metaphor, these phenotypic expressions rupture the theoretical possibility for indefinite replication of individual plants as expressions of a 'true' species form – more than organic machines, plants are not infinitely reproducible entirely, and treating plants as living machines would represent a form of "bio-mechanical reductionism" of their vegetal vitality (Beldo 2017: 115). But these ruptures also hold possibility for further commodification: sometimes the resulting somatic mutations produce desirable aesthetic effects, similar to the work of crossbreeding hybrids, and they can lead to exceptionally lucrative new (and patentable) plant varietals. Thus even when plants' metabolic labors might be seen to go awry or 'resist' their indefinite duplication, their induced self-reproduction can become yet another new site for speculative biocapitalist accumulation (cf. Marx 1976 [1867]:

283-284).[3] This exemplifies the tension between plants as both subjects made to work in the ISI lab, and their position as worked objects as plants are transformed into streamlined commodities for global circulation and consumption.

As demonstrated through the case of the ISI program at The Huntington, the act of replicating plants through modern clonal techniques entwines matters of more-than-human care, species epistemologies, plant conservation, and vegetal commodification through species care work. In the laboratory, the particular reproductive capacities of plants are put to work in order to satisfy human desire as a means of pursuing their protection. But they do not always 'work' as well as human technicians would like, and they are not, in practice, always the infinitely replicable 'organic machines' that theory suggests. In many ways, the ISI, as an intervention, is a stopgap measure within a very troubled ecology, one in which human pleasure, emotional experience, and affective relations are gained and sought through caring for plants, but as a kind of care work that can reverberate with negative repercussions for plants. The botanists and technicians at the Huntington are therefore responding to a very immediate and real threat to species survival in increasingly fragmented and damaged landscapes, destruction which, perversely, can at times aid in making certain plants all the more desirable to passionate collectors by increasing their rarity. But while these intentions of species care work are benevolent, and may help reduce pressure on wild plant populations, the practice also reproduces notions of purified and static species categories in the valuing and fostering of certain forms of vegetal life at the exclusion of others. In the laboratory, species as epistemological sites of care move ethical concern away from plants as vital beings worthy of consideration as subjects, and work to transform them into objectified commodities through exertions of species care work. Attention to the reproductive workings of plants through tissue culture is therefore an effort of careful political ecology (Hinchliffe 2008), bringing the empirical specificity of vegetal vitalities in the laboratory as corporeal sites of care work to the fore. The plants at the center of this care work unsettle notions of mechanistic practices rendering them into objects, revealing plant capacities for exceeding the binaries of 'working subject' and 'worked object' that foreclose possibilities for interspecies caring beyond the commodity-form.

---

3   For a valuable discussion of metabolic labor of nonhuman life, see Beldo (2017: 119): "There is no reason to suppose, however, that labor needs to be deliberate or consciously directed to count as labor. Metabolism is a process yoked by capital that creates surplus value. It should not matter if it is microbes or cellular structures that labor instead of subjects."

Acknowledgements

This research would not have been possible without the support and generosity of Professor Rosaleen Duffy and the broader community of the BIOSEC project at the University of Sheffield in the Department of Politics and International Relations. This work was supported with funding from the European Research Council (ERC) under the European Union's Horizon 2020 research and innovation program grant agreement No 694995 (BIOSEC: Biodiversity and Security, Understanding Environmental Crime, Illegal Wildlife Trade and Threat Finance). I am indebted to the generous staff of The Huntington for permitting me to spend time at the Gardens in order to better understand their work with plants; particular thanks go to Sean Lahmeyer and John Trager who facilitated my visit in a number of key ways. Finally, I would like to sincerely thank Franklin Ginn, James Palmer, and Marion Ernwein for their insightful and important feedback and editorial guidance on earlier versions of this chapter. Any errors are, of course, my own.

Chapter 3 - Planting Soft Pakistan

Franklin Ginn & Daanish Mustafa

> It is unfortunate that Pakistan's image abroad has been tarnished so badly that the world associates it only with terrorism and extremism [...] I have therefore tried to project a truer image of Pakistan which I call a soft image, through the promotion of tourism, sports and culture. (President Pervez Musharraf, 2006: 320)

As the 21st century dawned, Pakistan found itself in a familiar place when, for the third time in the country's history, the military took command of its government. Just as Generals Ayub and Yahya Khan sought to pull Pakistan into the American century of development in the 1960s, just as the dictatorship of Zia-ul-Haq aligned the country to the socially reactionary free market ethos of the 1980s, so too General Pervez Musharraf aligned the country with the prevailing international mood of the day: neoliberal globalization (Daechsel 1997; Musharraf 2006).[1] Aware that his military dictatorship might ring geopolitical alarm-bells, Musharraf eschewed the preferred title of his predecessors, 'Chief Martial Law Administrator'. Instead he anointed himself the 'Chief Executive' of Pakistan, clearly signaling his embrace of corporate capitalism. On Musharraf's watch Pakistan also joined the war on terror and was duly rewarded by the USA with the status of 'strategic ally' and 'frontline state' (Talbot 2012). Musharraf's domestic policies ran with the fox and hunted with the hounds: they supported the religious right while simultaneously continuing apace in the war against religious-inspired terrorism. The Pakistani state also repressed progressive labour, ethnic and women's movements, even as it privatised and liberalised the media. The Chief Executive's one consistent principle was to court domestic and international capital, foreign direct investment peaked in 2008 as state assets were privatised.[2]

---

1   Musharraf was president of Pakistan from June 20, 2001 to August 18, 2008. The trend is not limited to Pakistan's military presidents: tactically aligned with an anti-globalisation position, Pakistan's current president, Imran Khan, rides the ebbing global wave of reactionary populism.

2   The main sources of FDI were USA, UK and UAE.

Musharraf's substantive shifts in national politics were refracted through a new national narrative. Pakistanis began to tell a new story about Pakistan to themselves and to the rest of the world, a story wrapped up in postmodern tactics of miscegenation and the cultural logic of late capitalism (Jameson 1991). The classic developmental state made its territory legible and manageable through dams, highways and other mega-infrastructure. 'Seeing like a state', as James Scott (1998) put it, meant engineering territory and society through rational order. By contrast under late capitalism, Musharraf's realignment of Pakistan's bureaucratic, military and political troika duly required a different kind of a project. Instead of seeing like a state, the more pressing question for soft Pakistan became 'being seen like a state', both by its own citizens and by its international allies and enemies. The story's central actor was, as the epigraph from Musharraf shows, a *soft Pakistan* – a modern, religious state ready to do business with the world.

Hilary Clinton visited Pakistan as US Secretary of State in 2011. She landed amid a fog of mistrust between Washington and Islamabad, a fog created by the recent execution of Osama Bin Laden by US special forces. American hawks expressed incredulity that Pakistani officials had no idea that Bin Laden had been holed up in Abbottabad; Pakistani hawks derided Musharraf's pro-US stance and protested the blatant breach of sovereignty. Clinton's visit was highly orchestrated to present an image of soft Pakistan. Before she landed at Benazir Bhutto airport in Islamabad, huge effort had gone into to tidying up urban poverty and greening the city. Twenty million rupees (about two percent of the city's parks budget) were spent on planting trees and Korean turfgrass around the airport and along the route taken by Clinton's motorcade. While a negligible proportion of the city's 22 billion rupee budget, this money (equivalent to £100,000) was wasted as most of the trees have since died, due to a combination of poor maintenance and water stress.

There is of course nothing new in leveraging plants for political theatre. The point, however, is that the story of soft Pakistan exemplifies a wider 21st century shift in the work that plants do in consolidating political and cultural power. As we explore in this chapter, plants are increasingly made to work in urban and national metabolisms in ways that refract Pakistan's security state and create pervasive urban precarity.[3] The work that plants do often leads to new socio-ecological patterns of inclusion and exclusion, wrapped up in economies of gentrification and property-based accumulation, mediating the 'right to the city' for different groups. How and why does the security state, with its corporate allies, put plants to work in producing soft Pakistan?

---

3   This chapter draws on interviews conducted as part of a wider project. The authors conducted 54 interviews between 2016 and 2018 with city planners, nursery owners, seed importers, maali (gardeners) and homeowners in Islamabad, Karachi and Lahore.

Elite nature

Ayub Khan's military regime (1958-1969) selected Islamabad as the site for the country's new capital to isolate the Pakistani state apparatus from the 'corrupting influence' of wider urban society. In the original capital, Karachi, commercial and proletarian elements encroached too closely for the comfort of the state. Islamabad's Greek architect, Constantinos Doxiadis, modelled the city on the colonial hill station. The city was laid on to the physical landscape in a square grid pattern, overwriting its rich human heritage with a modernist state-centric landscape, drawing upon 19th century German spatial formulas.[4] Government servants were to have few connections with each other and hierarchies of bureaucratic rank were to be etched into the spatial organization of the city. The square grid pattern of residential sectors was to run along the spine of the central district of the city, now called the Blue Area. In the wilder dreams of its modernist planners, this East-West city axis would sprawl inexorably into a pan-Eurasian urban belt spanning half the globe. Architecturally, the military regime was obsessed by ornamentation and monumentalism (Daechsel 2013), an impulse carried into the extensive horticulture undertaken to transform the well-trodden agricultural landscape of fields and rangelands into a cosmopolitan, modernist urban centre.

A military vision of Pakistan's future dominated the early urban form of Islamabad. The Capital Development Authority (CDA) became the main civic body for municipal services in Islamabad, and its first chairman was Brigadier – later General and President of Pakistan – Yahya Khan. A mass plantation of Islamabad and the nearby Margalla hills with Australian exotics like lantana and eucalyptus, chosen for being fast-growing, easy-maintenance urban trees; planted along highways and avenues they sped to growth of a clean, modern-looking, functional city (with a nod to cosmopolitan international outlook). The mass planting was conducted like an invasion on two fronts: helicopters dropped seed bombs from above, while an army of poorly-paid amenity workers planted saplings from below – a project exemplary of modernist state-making practices (Scott 1998). Embodying the pervasive contradiction of Pakistani urbanism, city planning left no room for the underclasses – sanitary workers, domestic help, deliverymen, maids – who actually keep a city functioning: Islamabad was based upon mass expulsion of the local population with nominal compensation relative to the value of land, in a tortuous process that is still ongoing. Horticulture, too, ignored local and working-class concerns with nutrition by eschewing fruiting trees. Even today these workers find themselves living in informal settlements, many in the flood plains of local streams (Mustafa 2005).

---

4   Constantinos Doxiades was trained at the Technical University of Berlin and many of his design elements for Islamabad had a German heritage.

Subsequently, the CDA formed one of the first plant nurseries in the country. Across the affluent zones of the city (which is to say, most of it), avenues were planted with a mix of South Asian and exotic species chosen for their appearance but also reasons of shade and dust filtering: chir pine, jacoranda, fiddlewood, kanak, silver oaks, ficus pelican. Employing landscape architects and foresters from Japan, Australia, UK and Germany, Islamabad's horticultural planning became a metonymic motor of the country's modernist future. The CDA was pathbreaking in the way it integrated horticulture into urban design, creating a legacy of extensive numbers of trees doing 'shady work' across the city (Atchison, this volume). Before independence, urban forestry and gardening were limited to the elites and royalty, and the British in their cantonments: "rich people would form their own landscapes", as a former CDA horticultural director put it. The CDA ensured a more widely dispersed green landscape, as plants became a medium through which elite nature moved across the cityscape, articulating a vision for what the Pakistani polity should be about, all the while excluding the urban poor.

Echoes of the story of Islamabad can be found across the country. A walk around the rookery of the politico-military and bureaucratic elite, Aitchison College, in Lahore, reveals remnants of modernist military visions rubbing shoulders with novel emblems of cosmopolitan Pakistan.[5] The late 19th and early 20th century parts of the campus feature shady *Ficus religiose*, also known as Peepal, and local Banyan trees. A substantial portion of Aitchison's sprawling 200-acre estate used to be dedicated to crops like wheat, fruits and vegetables. Today, much of the grounds have been converted to grassy lawns and kaleidoscopic borders of Mediterranean Ericeira, South East Asian Alstonia, tropical banana and palm trees. The vast battalion of working men and women on the Aitchison grounds who used to benefit from the nutrition produced on the college grounds, mostly from their own labour, now must turn to the market for their nutritional needs. These most recent horticultural interventions on the campus employ the 'Dubai aesthetic' of exotic foliage. Widely noted by growers, gardeners, importers, landscapers and planners, this aesthetic began emerging after General Musharraf's coup in 1999. The aesthetic privileges high-input lawns, date palms and other exotics with an emphasis on the visual spectacle – its uptake represents a move away from both precolonial and colonial landscape legacies and the modernist impulses of mid-20th planning (exemplified in Islamabad's CDA original emphasis on trees' ecological functions), towards an

---

5   The closest English equivalent of Aitchison College would be Eton, where twenty of the UK's prime ministers were educated.

alignment with the newly potent form of Islamic cultural capitalism emanating from the United Arab Emirates.[6]

Figure 3.1: Plants outside the Principal's office at Aitchison College, Lahore.

Image: Franklin Ginn.

Functionaries in Pakistan's extensive system of military-run elite residential areas now enact the visual grammar of soft Pakistan through plants. As one director, now retired, lamented, "Before 2003, we maintained the natural contours and plant areas for greenery and shade [...] after 2003 we have changed it to levelling the grassy areas and making it look neat". The standard operating procedure, set by the whims and preferences of elites (many trained in Aitchison), has shifted from an ecology designed to deliver shade as well as greenery to "maximum colour and maximum visual attractiveness". The trend has changed state-run landscaping in Islamabad, as well. As an ex-Director of Islamabad's Capital Development Authority put it, "since 2000 the visual aesthetic has taken over environmental amenity

---

6   The UAE has longstanding bilateral ties with Pakistan and accounts for a rapidly growing proportion of the country's FDI; the Gulf states offer a huge range of employment opportunities for Pakistanis, from property development and finance to construction and domestic work.

considerations," such that the imperative is for cities that "look like an urban man-
icured garden". A much younger greenspace manager, working in the military-run
Clifton cantonment board in Karachi, contrasted modern landscaping and the as-
cendant Dubai aesthetic to memories of an older Pakistan now seen only in old
movies, in which "song and dance numbers would take place which would have
roses, jasmine and Saru (*Cupressus* sempervirens) trees". The multiple functions of
urban horticulture – shade, soil conservation, habitat provision, dust and pollu-
tant absorption – have been superseded by the visual in private, state and military
landscaping.

Like living abroad

An old joke of the car-driving classes holds that Islamabad is 'five minutes from
Pakistan'. In the joke, the unplanned 'twin city' of Rawalpindi, a short motorway
trip away, stands in for the muddling chaos of the rest of the country's urban spaces
(Hull 2012: 14). If Islamabad is insulated from the country by five minutes' fast travel
down a wide highway, then a new quip might be that Bahria Town is a hundred
million rupees from Pakistan. Since the 2000s, when early property buyers were
largely expatriate Pakistanis rushing back to invest in Pakistan in the aftermath
of 9/11, Bahria Town has grown into *the* landmark, Dubai-style gated development
in Pakistan.[7] This was also the first development where horticulture was deliberately deployed to increase property values. If Bahria Town's horticultural currency
is exotic plants, then the largest denomination bill is the date palm. Date palms
not only evoke the luxury lifestyle of Dubai, but also have religious undercurrents.
Muslims break their Ramzan fast with dates, following the tradition of the Prophet.
In the amplified pan-Islamist identity politics post-9/11, religious idioms and imagery have been readily deployed for financial gain. As Humeira Iqtidar (2017) argues, there is a convergence between the numerically based notion of counting sins
and good deeds in mass Muslim piety and being a neo-liberal subject. From Islamic
banking to stamping religious symbols and calligraphy on roadsides to date palms,
religion is a way of branding products, including real estate, in Pakistan.

The cultural and economic value of foreign plants is not supported by everyone. The greenspace manager of Bahria Town, one of six brothers and educated at
an Agricultural University, plays a horticultural game. He would prefer to use less
water- and labour-intensive local species such as Jaman, Neem, and Dharek, but
his employer remains so "deeply impressed by Dubai" that he has to plant these
local plants in less obvious locations, out of his owner's roving, but ecologically

---

7   When the current round of expansion is complete, the various Bahria developments now
     located across urban Pakistan will house more than one million residents.

uneducated, eye. Yet, "when it is dates season [like in Ramzan], he needs to give a rapid impact and he has to sell properties. So he orders me to plant dates". The horticulturist keeps a sharp eye on the commercial value added by exotic plants, but balances this with his affection for local plants (Figure 3.2). There is a mischievous refusal to submit to the visual rhetoric of soft Pakistan. Another manager elsewhere recounted a tale where a homeowner in the elite F8 district of Islamabad demanded a permit to remove an acacia tree (*Acacianilotica*) he found offensive. The manager's staff reported that the tree posed no threat to property or electric wiring. The homeowner, however, "just hated it because it was just a wild tree and he wanted a beautiful tree, like an Australian bottlebrush":

> To me to remove that tree was a perversity. I said to him that to cut that tree for bottlebrush, would be like divorcing your own wife and bringing in a white woman for a wife. He said, 'Are you that sentimental about it?' I said, 'Absolutely! I am sentimental about it, but I also have scientific reasons.'

The former Islamabad manager and the horticulturist in Bahria Town had sentimental as well as sound environmental reasons for using local plants, which were not consonant with the internationalist sensibilities of their clients and bosses. Local plants do not have the same cultural and commercial cachet because they are often deemed to be *jungli* (wild), a code for uncouth. Even horticulturists trained in Pakistani institutions never learn about local plants, only about exotic plants, mostly those circulating in the global gardening industry. There is simply no local research or curriculum that covers indigenous plants. This coupled with the fact that the exotic plant trade and seeds is dominated by multi-nationals like Sakata of Japan, Benary of Germany, and many others from the Netherlands, Thailand, Italy and the United States, means that there is major international and domestic capital involved in the projection of exotics and that Pakistan – as the breathy market researchers put it – is "one of horticulture's fastest-growing emerging markets" (Euromonitor 2016).[8] The buying power of Bahria Town and the aesthetic of soft Pakistan has changed urban ecologies across Pakistan. Plants are deployed, as a typical real estate advertisement declares, to make these developments feel *'Like Living Abroad!'*

---

8   The global gardening industry was worth US\$ 83,258 million in 2016. Euromonitor, *Gardening Global Overview: Social, Sustainable and Smart*, 2017.

Figure 3.2: A nursery owner explains to one of the authors how he grows and imports certain plants for profit (such as this large date palm), but prefers dealing with more established species and indulging his love for roses.

Image: Franklin Ginn.

Real estate development in Pakistan at the scale of Bahria town is simply not possible without the patronage of the security state, however. Bahria Town's billionaire founder, Malik Riaz, began his career as a smalltime clerk, and then became a contractor for the Military Engineering Services in Rawalpindi. Working his way into the good graces of the military high command, he landed the contract to build a gated community for Pakistan Navy personnel in the mid-1990s. Subsequently the Navy pulled out of the project under a pall of financial irregularities, which cost the then Naval Chief his job. In a remarkable act of largess however, the Navy sold its shares to Malik Riaz. 'Bahria' in Urdu means Navy, and Riaz quite sensibly retained that brand, even though Pakistan Navy retains no formal links with the development. Today Malik Riaz is perhaps one of the most influential and visible tycoons in Pakistan, with strong links to the security state. Bahria Town does not represent a triumph of entrepreneurial, private housebuilding: behind it lies the military, and the military remains the biggest real estate player in the Pakistani market (see Siddiqa 2017).

The Pakistani military has always used its political power to secure land for its upper echelons, with benefits carefully trickled down through the ranks to enforce discipline through patronage. Defence Housing Societies (DHA) – areas of housing originally earmarked for military families and comprising some five per cent of Pakistan's urban land – are headed by corps commanders and managed by retired brigadiers or colonels. While land is sold only to officers, these officers are then free to resell the land at a substantial mark-up to civilians. Those with the savvy to manipulate information about land development can turn a high profit. The trend to sell outside the military spiked post 9/11, and after a decade of speculative investment civilians now outnumber the military in most cantonments. Karachi DHA, for example, expanded by 4000 units after 1999 to an estimated value of Rs 400 billion ($3.22 billion). Stable price escalation is ensured in such real estate developments by more visible, if not necessarily more effective, security and a higher level of infrastructure and amenity provision (Siddiqa 2017). There is little evidence that this illusion of security is at all overtly concerned with climate change (cf. Anguelovski et al. 2019). Historically, it was more directly associated with safety during the very violent period of the 1990s and 2000s in Karachi, with kidnapping (or the fear of kidnapping) a concern, as well as more everyday desires for a reasonably steady water and electricity supply. Certainly, military cantonments evidence a water resource grab by the elite: Pakistani cities are reeling from the demands of providing safe drinking water to their booming populations – yet up to 70 per cent of domestic water supply in semi-arid regions is used for landscaping (Mini et al. 2014, Balling/Gober 2007, Mayer/DeOreo 1999). Plants, then, are not simply token markers of exotic consumption or quasi-religious piety contributing to the illusion of invulnerability to the risks of urban living in Pakistan: they substantially reorient urban metabolic flows to their own sustenance. The work and care that sustains plants in the elite urban spaces of Pakistan is work that also sustains privilege, exclusion and wealth.

Gardening work

Akbar was born in the agricultural area of Charsadda, in Punjab, and moved to Islamabad after finishing school. He has since been employed as a *maali*, a jobbing gardener, for over a decade. His client base consists of seven to eight private households, sufficient for a full day's work. While not his first choice of career, Akbar has some autonomy, some fondness for the job, and – most importantly – opportunity to make money from rich sahibs' embrace of soft Pakistan's new visual aesthetic. Akbar is typical of a new, entrepreneurial generation of *maali*. Clients who know nothing about plants are best. For these householders, he doesn't "have to change anything for the entire year – they just don't seem to care". Strategically performing the lazy country boy is a solid tactic in dealing with such clients:

> Four-to-five days ago, a madam said, 'Plant flowers'. I said, the season is over and you must wait ten-to-fifteen days. I delayed her for three-to-four days and then told her that the new flowers are here, and I am going to go get them. She would yell at me every day for not replacing the flowers, and said that I am lazy, but I kept quiet. But finally, I told her that with the new flowers I would get them in five days, but then I took eight days and thereby saved her sorry ass from a major loss. But she yelled at me all the way through.

Elite householders like to complain that the city's growth has created a glut of labour, an oversupply so pronounced that anyone can get a job as a *maali*. Hiring the entrepreneurial poor risks the elite homeowner finding that "in two months he has killed everything in the garden", as a Karachi resident complained.

Alongside such youthful game-players as Akbar, older garden hands are making serious cash. As Bahria town and the military-run Defence Housing Associations provided the medium for accumulation of cultural capital through plants, the social transformation did not go unnoticed by petit bourgeois *nurserywallahs* (nursery owners) who made fortunes riding on the back of this new demand for landscaping services and exotic plants. They nevertheless maintained an antipathy towards the consumers that made their social mobility possible. Over a tray of mangoes, one old hand at the nursery game reminisced that his grandfather had moved to Islamabad "wearing no shoes". "It used to be that if you were rich", he recalled, "you would show off by getting drunk and buying whores".[9] Today, smitten by Pakistan's soft visual grammar, the same kind of people have "realized that they can also show off through plants". Hot-housed exotics, force-grown palm trees, aged Italian fig

---

9   While selling alcohol to and consumption of alcohol by Muslims in Pakistan is illegal and carries severe penalties, the elite indulge in expensive branded imported liquor in their homes and private clubs with a large degree of impunity; if the poor indulge in domestic moonshine they risk imprisonment or corporal punishment.

trees – the nursery owner has poached this new grammar to his own benefit – "We're making monkeys out of these folk!" – and gestures to his gleaming Toyota Land Cruiser parked outside. The young entrepreneurial *maali* and the older breed are united by wry bemusement at the follies of the wealthy. They see lawns, tropical plants and flowering annuals as a stupefying waste of resources. As an experienced Islamabad *maali* put it, "These are big rich people. They don't care about things that we poor people worry about". If this man had full run of his employer's land, he would simply "grow more food'" He would "get rid of this lawn" and plant "wheat, sugar cane, food crops like that".

If the maali occupies a liminal position between a new, soft Pakistan and visions of an older imagined community bound to productive soil, then the visual grammar of domestic gardens hovers uncertainly in the same area. On the one hand, a display of colorful exotics and water-hungry lawns is essential for a showy reception. The Pakistani elite may purchase pre-grown date palms that have been tended by nurseries for a decade for upwards of $5000. It is a crude metric: the bigger the palm, the greener the lawn, the more status is displayed. Through a visitor's casual glance at a lawn or plant, influence and power might be cultivated – just a little – as social ties thicken and twist. Yet, at the same time, even the most hard-nosed career politician or businessman might well make room for the sentimental. While the garden is what Goffman called a 'front stage', it also must have its 'back stage' (Goffman 2002) (Figure 3.3). Older garden traditions rub against newer preferences (Ginn 2016). Local plants, fruit trees, vegetables might take their place in a back garden, where scent and memory floats from long-loved plants, transporting the garden-owner to another time and place; a childhood on the railways, or spent moving between sprawling cantonment gardens. Status of a different kind emerges here: biographical continuity, forms of identity that exceed internationalist, soft Pakistan and the creep of the Dubai aesthetic. These preferences are of a piece with the horticultural directors discussed earlier, who still value local species (the looked-down-upon *jungli*, or wild), over imported palms. In some sense, then, the grammar of 'soft Pakistan' is anything but soft: it seems narrowly obsessed with visual aesthetics in a hard-nosed, profit-minded orientation framed against the sentimental, nostalgic preference for other forms of planting.

Figure 3.3: One of the authors in front garden showing a Dubai aesthetic; to the rear of this home, however, lies an extensive vegetable and fruit garden.

Image: Franklin Ginn.

Conclusion

On April 30, 2018 the market town of Nawabshah, in the Sindh province of Pakistan, logged the highest ever temperature recorded on Earth in the month of April – 50.2°C. Between June 17 and 24, 2015, 1300 people died in a Karachi heatwave: most of them were working class poor. It may sound trite, but to live in a city, you have to perform remunerative labour in the city, and this labour has to be offered somewhere. How do you get to that somewhere in the absence of air-conditioned cars or public transport? How to be at that somewhere in temperatures of 40°C plus? What if you are a day labourer, fruit hawker or domestic worker, who has to commute somehow, from one end of town to another to clean someone's toilet, tend to someone's garden or wash their dishes? Outside Bahria town and elite military housing authorities, armies of women and men must endure the interrogations and humiliations of the private security guards simply to get to their jobs. Once into elite areas, they must walk – there is no transport, and no shade. A fruit and vegetable hawker, a traveling salesperson, or a *maali* has nowhere to seek shade in the blaring Pakistani sun, in urban landscapes designed not for them, but for automobiles. Palms and flowers may vicariously transport the automobile riders to Dubai or Los Angeles, but for pedestrians and cyclists date palms make for poor shade.

The state's choice of a different story for Pakistan – one projecting the image of a soft state, featuring a globalized, corporatized, visually obsessed nation, with exotic plants and the security state as key characters – has fatal consequences. The very right to the city for the poor and the weak is mediated by plants. In a burning hot concrete metropolis no shade can mean death. And temperatures will rise, with growing heat islands driven by breakneck urbanization, climate change and the indifference of the elite. Date palms and lawns siphon off the life-giving ground and surface water, which could otherwise hydrate and cool people. Until recently small kitchen gardens, indigenous fruit and shady trees had been a source of nutrition, shade and spiritual solace for South Asian urbanites. Some plants can make city life possible, or at least more bearable, for those forced to walk, work or live on the street. Soft Pakistan has been very hard on its poor.

Acknowledgments

The research for this article was funded by the Royal Geographical Society-Institute of British Geographers (RGS-IBG), Environment & Sustainability Research Grant no. 1/16. We thank everyone who spoke to us about plants, as well as Marion Ernwein and James Palmer for comments which helped improve the chapter, and audiences at the Bristol Environmental Humanities Centre, LEAD Pakistan, and the AAG Conference 2019.

SECTION II
Vegetal Labour

Chapter 4 - Ecologies of actor-networks and (non)social labor within the urban political economies of nature

Harold Perkins

International standards for phytosanitary measures are prepared by the Secretariat of the International Plant Protection Convention as part of the United Nations Food and Agriculture Organization's global programme of policy and technical assistance in plant quarantine. This programme makes available to FAO Members and other interested parties these standards, guidelines and recommendations to achieve international harmonization of phytosanitary measures, with the aim to facilitate trade and avoid the use of unjustifiable measures as barriers to trade. (Jacques Diouf, Director-General Food and Agriculture Organization of the United Nations, International Plant Protection Convention, 2002)

In 2005 the United States and European Union began restricting the entry of commodities shipped from abroad in wood packaging materials (WPM) that do not conform to internationally recognized phytosanitation measures.[1] Endorsed by the UN Food and Agriculture Organization, the regulations are put forth in order to "practically eliminate the risk for most quarantine pests and significantly reduce the risk from a number of other pests that may be associated with that material" (IPPC 2002: 6). Before entering countries bound by the Convention, all relevant forms of WPM must be sterilized[2] in an accepted manner spelled out in the Fifteenth International Standards for Phytosanitary Measures (ISPM#15) agreement and subsequently stamped with an internationally recognized symbol.[3] If com-

---

1   Eighty countries are now party to WPM regulations defined in the International Plant Protection Convention's Fifteenth International Standards for Phytosanitary Measures. Regulatory exceptions apply to wine and liquor barrels, woodchips, sawdust, veneers, or thinly cut pieces of wood present in processed board materials that are not considered likely harbingers of insect pests and fungal pathogens (IPPC 2017).

2   Sterilization includes heating WPM to 56°C for a minimum of thirty minutes, fumigation with Methyl bromide, irradiation, or a combination of said processes (IPPC 2017).

3   The symbol must provide a code for the country in which it was produced, the producer of the WPM, and treatment method employed (IPPC 2017).

modities are shipped to participating countries on WPM lacking a stamp indicating sterilization compliance, the commodities must be refused entry and shipped back to their country of origin or to another country without restrictions on non-sterilized WPM. These actions stem from the high price paid for the impact that introduced pests and pathogens have upon production (Robbins 2001; Gandy 2005).[4] The damage 'rogue' organisms cause compels further theorization of the proliferation of nonhumans within capitalist urban political economies.

In general, Marxists have scrutinized the enlistment of nature within their relational studies of capitalism to elucidate the impact of accumulation on ecologies (see Smith 1984; Swyngedouw 1996; Harvey 1996; Foster 2000 for representative works). Of particular importance, O'Connor (1996) developed the concept of the 'second contradiction of capitalism' as nature in various forms is incorporated into production and considered a free good that tends to be undervalued, resulting in its over-exploitation and decreased ability to contribute to further production (see also Boyd et al. 2001). This emphasis on the social production of nature has bearing on human-induced species relocation as their potential long-term costs are not often calculated into short-term production scenarios within capitalist economies.

While Marxists have paid increased attention to the import of social labor in relation to nature, some scholars are more interested in the agency and political status of nonhumans (see Callon 1986; Latour 1993, 2004; Murdoch 1997, 2001; Whatmore 2002; Wolch et al. 2002; Walker 2005 among others). These theorists suggest that actor-network theory (ANT) can better account for the political status of nonhumans. A self-characteristically non-modern critique of the sociology of science, ANT links humans and nonhumans alike in assemblages or associations in which power is diffused throughout according to the ability of certain actants to convey, strengthen, or resist their bonds with other objects (Latour 1986, 1993, 1994; Law 1994; Murdoch 1995, 1998). Central to this theory is symmetry, whereby diffusion of power throughout networks renders structures the result of human *and* nonhuman activity. In this manner, the power of sociability is attributed to nonhumans, as scallops for example, are credited with agency based on their ability to reject essentialist categorization by scientific investigators.

This emphasis on symmetry causes some Marxists to take a cautious approach to the ANT ontology based on its tendency to attribute as much causal ability in network formation to nonhumans as humans. According to Castree (2002: 135), "advocates of a strong ANT agenda risk ignoring the possibility that some actants 'marshal' the power of many others and, in so doing, limit the latter's agency and

---

4   Pimental (2007) suggest that the costs incurred in association with introduction of exotic species into the United States, alone, are approximately 120 billion US dollars per year. These costs include the lost productivity of ecological systems, as well as efforts implemented for suppression and eradication of pests.

circumscribe their existence." On this basis Kirsch and Mitchell (2004: 698) suggest the importance of considering a crucial ontological difference between ANT and Marxism based on Marx's description of living and dead forms of social labor:

> Only living labor can bring the dead labor of the past – the network associations of the machine – to life. Compared with the mechanical metaphor of the network, Marx's dialectic of agency here is infused with a far more organic vocabulary: life itself, and the difference between living and dead labor, constitutes a crucial ontological divide [...] For Marx, the otherwise 'lifeless mechanism' of the factory is animated by living labor, and by a highly structured set of relations between people and things that is characteristic of the labor process [...] What Marx rejects outright [...] was any notion that the machinery was itself generative of the value frozen in the objects produced.

In other words, the ontological priority resides with social relations of production (including nature) that govern the interaction between humans and objects within a capitalist political economy, not the objects themselves as proponents of ANT would have us believe.

A purpose in unity?

At first glance then, it appears that there are significant discrepancies between the contributions of Marxist approaches and those of ANT to the study of nature/society relations. However, as Castree (2002) suggests, further scrutiny reveals that the critical approaches of Marxism and ANT are in some respects overlapping. This is particularly the case in their mutual materialist basis and their resulting negations of nature/society binaries. As an ANT theorist, Latour (1993) is critical of the categorization of objects as natural and/or social based on what he describes as a false, anthropocentric dichotomy between nature and society that deemphasizes the materialist basis for all relations in nature. As Gareau (2005) indicates in his defense of theoretical reconciliation, Marxist dialectical inquiry also resists such an anthropocentric dichotomy because it considers humans as material extensions of nature who have no choice but to engage it with their labor. Thus Marxists also negate simplistic binaries between nature and society (see also Harvey 1996). Marxism and ANT therefore share a common, if partial, ontological basis and epistemic potential that can be expounded further through an expanded definition of labor.

Why though is this specific articulation of their mutual constitution lacking in the political ecology literature? The reasons are primarily epistemic and twofold. As Castree (2002) and Gareau (2005) suggest, unlike Marxists, ANT practitioners are often reluctant to concede the fact that some actants and their associations or networks command and conserve more power than others. Thus, they deemphasize the prominent role of *social* forms of labor in environmental transformation. This stems from a tendency within ANT circles to discount the legitimacy of macro level analysis in favor of micro level investigation between individual objects (Allen 2004; Fine 2005). Second, as Gareau (2005) reminds us, unlike ANT, Marxist analysis hints at but tends to neglect the sociability of biophysical actants. In other words, Marxists deemphasize the potentially destabilizing role of *nonsocial* forms of labor in environmental transformation. Thus they are frequently guilty of sidestepping the idea that nonhuman organisms can labor within capitalist environments, actively contributing to their form.

The (re)articulation of social *and* nonsocial labor as an internally heterogeneous ontological category aids in formulating new accounts of the relationship of nonhumans to use, exchange, and abstract values within capitalist networks. And this is important because as Castree (2002: 139) states, "the material effects that 'natural' entities have upon capital accumulation are variable and contingent, but rarely passive." Accordingly, Braun (2005: 646) asks: "Must the real actors in urban political ecology be always already social?" This question can here be extended to ask, what then can the full incorporation of nonsocial labor into Marxist political ecology look like?

The argument here presented is that an account of urban hybridity based on a dialectic comprised of the social labor relation and an apolitical nature is at best an incomplete project. Articulating a synthesis of Marxism and ANT via their mutual constitution in labor can tell us more about the political status of humans and nonhuman species which together act to form urban environments. To further such an objective, this piece demonstrates: 1) that Marxism and ANT share a foundation in labor as a metabolic, yet internally differentiated ontological category and 2) epistemologically speaking, the nonsocial portion of the labor dialectic that comprises urban environments is more fully articulated as a political definition of the labor relation is extended to include the actions of nonhumans in network (de)stabilization. 3) Finally, as Castree (2002) indicates, and recent writings on the subject of theoretical reconciliation indicate, the debate lacks empirical specificity (see Rudy/Gareau, 2005). In response, the epistemic benefits of asserting labor as the ontological priority will be articulated by using a dynamic species of nonhuman organisms as a case study that represent a threat to urban elm forests.

Ophiostoma ulmi and *Ophiostoma novo-ulmi* ssp. – a family of fungal pathogens better known as Dutch elm disease (DED) (Brasier 2001) – will be discussed as examples of nonhuman organisms, or actants dependent upon networked production relations (global commodity flows) to come into contact with new host ecologies. Despite its reliance upon international flows of commodities for introduction into new ecologies, DED is a dynamic organism that contributes to networked production conditions and also impairs networked consumption relations by wreaking havoc on extant urban elm forests. As experience with DED suggests,

tree pathogens are inherently dynamic organisms that capitalize on socially networked landscapes, rendering them impossible to eradicate, or even difficult to
suppress (Hubbes 1999). This results in urban ecologies mediated by the tensions
between global production and consumption as shaped in part by the nonsocial
labor of biophysical actants like fungi.

Ecologies of labor within urbanized production networks

Some Marxists argue that urbanization is the penultimate political ecological manifestation of the transformation, or metabolism, of social and material environments vis-à-vis the labor theory of value (see Marx 1976 [1867]; Harvey 1973, 1996;
Smith 1984; Swyngedouw 1996; Foster 2000). Their argument is founded on the
ontological priority of human- or socially necessary- labor as the means whereby
humans are a part of, and engage with, nature. Accordingly, Swyngedouw and Heynen (2003: 907) suggest: "[I]t is on the terrain of the urban that [the] accelerating
metabolic transformation of nature becomes most visible, both in its physical form
and its socio-ecological consequences". In other words, the social labor process –
as it relates to the transformation of nature under capitalism – is most intensely
concentrated in cities throughout the world. And Marxists acknowledge the increasingly complex, yet networked relationships that social forms of labor assume
under contemporary, urban iterations of capitalism.

They suggest that intensifying nodes of metabolic activity occur globally as
greater proportions of our planet's human population live in an interconnected
network of 'global with a small g' cities (Keil 1995, 2003; Luke 2003). These interconnected cities are increasingly impacted by hegemonic forms of neoliberal capitalism (Peck/Tickell 1994, 2002; Brenner/Theodore 2002) that, among other de-
structive tendencies, effectively reduce barriers to international trade and employ
laborers to shape urban ecologies for the sake of exchange value, or profit (Hey-
nen/Perkins 2005; Heynen/Robbins 2005; Swyngedouw 2005). With little regard
for healthy and egalitarian forms of social reproduction, Harvey (1989, 2000) notes
that social labor is redirected by capitalists to continuously reorganize the composition and flows that comprise and sustain these 'global with a small g' cities.

This continuous reorganization of network relations – or the annihilation of
space by time – gives rise to urban ecologies that result from heterogeneous, yet
increasingly interdependent associations of social labor (Keil 1995; Luke 2003; Hey-
nen/Perkins 2005). Thus, transportation and information systems (just two examples) have rapidly accelerated the (re)distribution of information and commodities
across the planet, contributing to the commodification of urban environments in
accord with dictates of increasingly globalized modes of accumulation. As Cronon
(1991), Harvey (1996), and Gandy (2002) each demonstrate in their works on the na-

ture of Chicago and New York, urban form is in part built by, and out of, these dynamic networks of human labor and other objects enrolled to produce profitable and often unhealthy relationships with nature. But how do these associations help to relate social labor to the production of local urban ecologies?

Urbanization processes are ultimately composed of complex, yet interwoven divisions of social labor. Social labor can be further internally differentiated, thus revealing the complexity of the production of urban environments in relation to the biophysical realm. For Marx, productive forms of capital (value in motion) are dependent upon the employment of living labor purchased from individuals so that biophysical materials may be transformed, among other things, into commodities for renewed production and consumption in later labor processes. Once completed, the commodities are objects that embody abstract value in past or 'dead' forms of social labor. He elaborates (1976 [1887]: 287): "Instruments of this kind, which have already been mediated through past labor, include workshops, canals, roads, etc." Kirsch and Mitchell (2004: 696) also contribute to the concept of dead labor:

> One of the main points of Marx's analysis is to show that while the means of pro-
> duction may be a certain faction of capital removed for a time from circulation,
> they are also more than that: they are 'dead labor,' work ossified and made con-
> crete in the shape and form of a machine, a building, a finished commodity, a
> technological artifact, a piece of property, or even nature itself.

This twofold composition of social labor has relevance for changing relationships between urbanism and ecology. Accelerating and intensifying metabolic interactions and associations via living and dead forms of social labor contribute to ever more complex urban environments as biophysical actants are increasingly incorporated in production processes, both past and present. As capitalist commodities, urban forests (just one urban ecological example) represent the activity of dead and living forms of social labor because laborers planted them in the past and they continue to require maintenance to retain use, exchange, and abstract values within urban political economy.

Critical studies in political economy have linked the development of urban forests to social labor under increasingly globalized capitalism. Based on Moll's (1995) description of trees as commodities with exchange-value, Heynen (2003), Perkins et al. (2004), and Heynen and Perkins (2005) employ a Marxist perspective to describe urban forests in relation to the consumption fund for the reproduction of human laborers and social labor relations. Subsumed within Harvey's second circuit of capital,[5] the consumption fund is an association of commodities pro-

---

5   Harvey's second circuit of capital includes the production of commodities with use-values for
     human social reproduction. For greater elaboration of the second circuit of capital and the
     consumption fund, see Harvey (1999).

duced by social labor as directed by capitalists and state governments so that human laborers can consume them in their own process of rejuvenation. Only by consuming the use-value of these objects can laborers return to their toils well rested, ensuring continued human social reproduction and renewed accumulation (Harvey 1999).

Since urban forests and lakes (Perkins 2006) are included in consumption fund formation, the fund can be extended to include urban elm forests intentionally planted for their aesthetic and utilitarian benefits consumed by urban dwellers (Campanella 2003).[6] Their long, arching limbs enveloped neighborhood streets in green cathedrals, giving them a unique identity. But in addition to their symbolic contribution, their hardiness and ability to grow to great heights and stature quickly provided laborers relief from the heavily industrialized settings in which much of the working class toiled. In other words, the contribution of the American elm to the reproduction of social labor led to their planting (itself an act of living and dead forms of social labor) in unprecedented numbers and density throughout growing industrial cities of the Northeast and Midwest during the latter nineteenth and early twentieth centuries (Schreiber/Peacock 1979). In this manner elms were a requisite component of the urban environment which also contributed to the (re)production of class relations within urban industrial capitalism.

But while the incorporation of trees by social labor into a network production ontology tells us a great deal about how people relate to nature, it tells us less about the political effectivity of nonhuman organisms in transforming urban networks. Social theorists here lose an opportunity to more fully expand epistemologies of urban development when they relegate the mechanics of nonhuman proliferation – including urban elms and by extension DED – to the background of relational social theory. Since social labor and material nature comprise the urban environmental dialectic, it makes sense to further theorize the political status of nonhuman organisms as they relate to human or social action (Castree 2002). The problematic relationship between social labor, urban elm forests, and DED is a starting point.

As living components of capital's consumption fund prior to their demise by DED, elms thrived in cities. But their development as urban organisms was not solely due to social labor. Tree growth is decidedly a biophysical and material action; as organisms they had to adapt to and metabolize their changing environment in order to survive and proliferate after they were planted. And to add complexity to the urban elm situation, DED appeared to emerge without the aid of social labor that facilitated the growth of elms. A closer investigation reveals, however, that both elm growth and DED proliferation are dependent on social *and nonsocial* forms of labor.

---

6   The benefits urban forests provide to the public are well documented. For an overview, the reader is encouraged to see Nowak and Dwyer (2007).

Ontologically speaking, both social and nonsocial forms of labor are based on the application of energy and matter to the environment as directed by organisms for various purposes including reproduction, proliferation, and profit. Simply put, organisms (social or otherwise) must struggle with their material environments in order to survive – suggesting strongly the materialist link between both human and nonhuman activities and environmental metabolism. Marxists are at pains to describe the social appropriation of environmental metabolism in its contemporary profit-oriented form as well as its resulting alienations. But Marx himself (1976 [1867]: 283), by hinting at human emancipation from "instinctive forms of labour", suggests that other organisms do toil for their survival. It is then a small epistemic leap to attribute nonhuman organisms with the capacity to transform urban environments via their own forms of instinctual or nonsocial labor.

Nothing in Marx's writings precludes the idea that nonhuman organisms labor. It should be noted, however, that for Marx (1976 [1867]: 284): "what distinguishes the worst of architects from the best of bees is that the architect builds the cell in his mind before he builds it in wax". In other words, Marx strongly privileges the capitalist appropriation of the social labor process as the basis for class struggle and thus by extension contemporary Marxists legitimately use this as the basis to theorize urban environmental transformation. But if the nonhuman capacity to labor is directly acknowledged, the notion of the appropriation/exploitation of labor can also be extended to include the metabolic processes performed by nonsocial organisms. In essence, the exploitation/appropriation of social and nonsocial forms of labor comprises the 'enrollment' process which endows both Marxism and ANT with their relational political import.

This complex, yet under-theorized realm reveals another potentially powerful ontological bridge between Marx and ANT because both social and nonsocial forms of labor are comprised of living laborers that generate products (as embodied in past or dead forms of labor) that can be enrolled in future labor processes. Thus, if we account for the possibility of dead forms of labor embodied in the products of nonhuman organisms, the perceived schism between Marx and ANT based on living and dead forms of labor is destabilized and decentered. These relationships can be examined in more detail to expose potential theoretical coalescence.

While the appropriation/exploitation of social labor and its product within capitalist associations is geared toward transforming relationships or associations into abstract values, nonsocial labor is also appropriated in the process and is demonstrative of the multidirectional process of enrollment. The example of elm forests can again be visited to elaborate the point. Elm forest production was in part dependent on public urban forestry programs. Municipal governments underwrote program actions by appropriating and redirecting monies from capitalists and the laboring class via taxation to enroll forestry laborers, equipment, and trees into associations conducive to social (re)production. Therefore, most of those trees planted and maintained by urban laborers in part owed their existence to the net-worked relations of past, or dead, social forms of labor. And as Kirsch and Mitchell (2004: 700) suggest: "... dead labor demands fresh living labor". Hence arboricul-tural workers as living labor were trained to prune urban elm forests in order to direct their growth and ensure future vitality and value.

But elm trees exploited via social labor for social (re)production are also the products of nonsocial labor; they performed the 'work' of growing in part by en-rolling or appropriating/exploiting the labors of the afore-mentioned social actants thereby producing networks conducive to their own benefit.[7] Elm trees and forests prior to their demise by DED were simultaneously living laborers and the products of their own past or dead forms of nonsocial labor. As embodied in, and embod-iments of living and dead configurations of social and nonsocial labor, the elms themselves contributed to the total labor of consumption fund formation via their own growth. This totality of metabolic activity between people and trees represents "congealed labor" (Latour 1994: 40) which manifests as dynamic urban form. But be-cause it is comprised of myriad social *and* nonsocial actants, the consumption fund – including urban elm ecologies – is inherently a dynamic network of uneven and unstable relations (Castree 2002).[8]

The contribution of nonsocial labor to the production of urban environments does little to negate the import of a relational Marxism, because while elms re-late to urban metabolic relations via their growth, they don't wield as much power within the network relation as the people who chose to plant, maintain, and remove them. In this light, Castree (2002: 135) suggests: "... agents, while social, natural and relational, vary greatly in their powers to influence others; and that power, while dispersed, can be directed by some [...] more than others". Marxists then need only extend their purview of the labor ontology to further theorize the politics of urban environmental transformation.

But this instability of power within networks is anathema to practitioners of a strong version of ANT, because they generally resist the long-term possibility of uneven power configurations, otherwise known as 'asymmetry' in associations. Here a consideration of complex divisions of, and relationships between, social and nonsocial labor as the enrollment mechanism within ANT betrays a difficulty with

---

7   'Network' and 'ecosystem' can here be used synonymously because ecosystems represent complex and dynamic interactions or relationships between heterogeneous actants within space, forming more or less discernable interrelated community structures that call into question the 'balance of nature' thesis (Sprugel 1991; Reice 1994; Zimmerer/Young 1998; Westley et al. 2002).

8   Although important, it is not the aim of this piece to address the unevenness of urban forests. Implicit within this network of capitalist urbanity is the possibility that relations between capitalists, bureaucrats, and laborers dictate that urban trees are unevenly distributed. For more on this, the reader is encouraged to see Heynen et al. (2006).

the application of 'symmetry' and requires strong practitioners to make a critical concession. A compositional analysis of the process of association via enrollment (exploitation/appropriation of social and nonsocial forms of labor) should reveal that in any given space-time, some laboring actants garner heightened abilities to exploit/appropriate the labor of others. Heightened enrollment of some laborers and their products by others can further strengthen and weaken associations within and without networks depending upon the actions of all of the other laborers in proximity of the given space-time. In other words, the enrollment of laboring actants and/or their products by other actants sequesters resources and power which 'curve' network dynamics into and out of symmetries as conceived within a strong version of ANT.

But the concept of symmetry in strong versions of ANT is misconstrued. The motion associated with complex articulations of labor exploitation/appropriation never ceases, giving rise to only momentary and fleeting instances of uniform power distribution (symmetry) within networks. As some actants labor to increasingly enroll the labor and products of other actants, a *uniformity of direction* through space-time can result whereby the momentum of a whole collective of laborers (both social and nonsocial) and their product is reoriented, if only temporarily and within a certain geographical extent. Epistemologically then, replacing 'symmetry' with *uniformity of direction* does nothing to preclude variegated (intra)networked relationships from tending toward a common objective – it in fact liberates them to do just that in an unlimited number of possible articulations. It seems then that Marxist political ecology and ANT are essentially synthesizable, when amended to include the import of nonsocial labor and its role in shaping the directed uniformity and momentum of network relations. But what advantage does this synthesis provide the study of urban environments?

Here the relationship of nonsocial to social labor becomes critical in understanding the politics that can thus be attributed to people, urban elm forests, and their vulnerabilities. This is potentially significant for theorizing the politics of nonhuman organisms such as DED, which unlike elms, labor in ways that are detrimental to urban networks uniformly directed via social labor for social (re)production. While political relationships are generally considered by Marxists to encompass actions between actants in the social realm – particularly class struggle as it relates to the labor relation – struggles between social and nonsocial labor for resource allocation also gives rise to a less visible but powerful politics.

Ultimately, a most basic of political relations is comprised by, and generative of, the exploitation of living labor and its product (embodied dead labor) for the (re)distribution of energy and material resources. And it doesn't matter in which direction the exploitation occurs, for if it is accepted that no part of our environment remains free of social and nonsocial alteration via the labor of animate beings, then every act of labor upon and within it, even by nonsocial organisms, is exploitative/appropriative of the living and dead labor produced by other actants. The political realm can therefore be extended even to relationships of exploitation/appropriation between nonsocial actants like DED and urban elms. The sociomaterial configuration of urban elm trees across the United States prior to the DED epidemic is illustrative of this political relationship.

Prior to the 1940s, the socio-ecological momentum of elm forests in urban areas in the United States grew at a staggering rate (see Sherald 1982; Campanella 2003). As elms were planted and quickly grew large in urban spaces to the detriment of other tree species, the mass of elms within urban ecosystems diminished competition with other trees for space and resources. As Holling and Gunderson (2002: 44) elaborate: "... the actors, whether species or people, develop systems of relationships that control external variability and, by doing so, reinforce their own expansion. That is, connectedness increases". In other words, the amount of social and nonsocial labor embodied in the production of elm forests produced a substantial political and ecological momentum or uniformity of direction.

Troubling for such ecologies however, novel associations of social and nonsocial labor in urban settings create unanticipated opportunities for other nonhuman organisms to labor and command power within networks. In keeping, Wolch (1996), Haraway (1997), Whatmore (1999), Wolch et al. (2002), Castree (2002), Kirsch and Mitchell (2004), and Latour (2004), all suggest that many nonhuman organisms do not comply with the requirements of profit-oriented urban metabolic relations. Unlike elms, they may resist network trajectories, or relate to them in varied and complex ways, often changing their own attributes or effecting further change in urban metabolic form itself – resulting in substantial changes in the uniformity of direction in any given network(s). The unprecedented accumulation and connectedness of mass and energy tied up in elms within the urban ecological network rendered it prone to a catastrophic act of disturbance (Holling et al. 2002: 73) in the form of the fungal pathogen, or actant causing DED. In this respect elm forests – a major facet of the consumption fund employed by social labor to ameliorate the effects of intensifying urbanization – fell victim to the enrollment of another nonsocial actant laboring within the intensifying interconnectedness of urban political economy.

A 'rogue' fungus decomposing the networks of capitalist rationality

Despite its name, DED is caused by a family of fungal pathogens *Ophiostoma ulmi* ssp. whose origin remains an enigma (Brasier 2001).[9] The presence of the fungal mycelia in elm tissue causes vascular disease, whereby the living tissue beneath the bark responsible for carrying water and nutrients throughout the tree become colonized and clogged, essentially starving the canopy as the tree reacts to its invader (Hubbes 1999). Following the death of the tree, fungal mats develop beneath the bark and cause it to rupture, where insects can gain access and inadvertently pick up fungal spores (Sherald 1982). Elm bark beetles, both native (*Hylurgopinus rufipes*) and foreign (*Scolytus multistriatus*), specialize in feeding on the soft tissue of elms, primarily between the joints on young twigs (Webber/Brasier 1984). Bark beetles that have emerged from trees infested with the pathogen introduce its spores into the vascular systems of uninfected trees where they can take hold and cause infection anew.[10]

O. ulmi first caused widespread damage to elm ecologies during the 1910s, causing ten to forty per cent mortality rates in the infected elm forests of Northern and Western Europe. By the 1940s the fungus had run its course through Europe, perhaps due to the resistance of European varieties of elm and the spread of deleterious fungal viruses that inhibited further proliferation of DED (Mitchell/Brasier 1994; Brasier 2000). *O. ulmi* made its first recorded appearance in North America in 1930 when American elms in Cleveland, Ohio were found infected. Its introduction at ports in Cleveland and later New York was attributed to imported infected elmwood materials shipped from European markets (Peace 1960). Despite the mobilization of federal, state, and municipal forestry programs to resist its diffusion, it quickly spread throughout New England and into the Midwest, causing nearly 100 per cent mortality in American elms (Campanella 2003).

During the 1970s, a new outbreak of DED emerged in Northwest Europe, caused by a newly discovered fungal pathogen, *O. novo-ulmi*. The new source of DED was more virulent than its predecessor, causing fatality rates near 100 per cent for European varieties of elm, decimating that continent's remaining elm forests that survived the first outbreak (Brasier 1990). Investigations into the origins of the new pathogen determined that it simultaneously appeared in Eastern Europe and the Southern Great Lakes region in the US during the 1940s. Subsequent research

---

9   The name Dutch elm disease was ironically attributed to the Dutch scientists who first investigated the pathogenic fungus at the beginning of the 20th century. There exists no evidence to suggest that it originated in the Netherlands (Hubbes 1999).

10   Despite the high distribution efficiency of a mobile insect vector, the pathogen also spreads through networks of root grafts that are associated with trees that grow very close to one another.

by Brasier and Kirk (2001) later revealed that *O. novo-ulmi* found in the Great Lakes region varied enough from the European race that they could be renamed as subspecies *O. novo-ulmi* ssp. *novo-ulmi* and *O. novo-ulmi* ssp. *americana*. Ssp. *americana* soon found its way to Europe via contaminated elm-wood shipped from a Canadian port in the 1960s, where it encountered ecologies occupied by *O. novo-ulmi* ssp. *novo ulmi*, resulting in subspecies hybrids (Pipe et al. 2000; Brasier/Buck 2002).[11]

While the fungal organisms are capable of spreading on their own and in conjunction with insect vectors, *O. ulmi* and *O. novo-ulmi* ssp. have been primarily dispersed to new ecologies based on their relationship to global flows of commodities, particularly inferior wood products used to secure shipments between ports. In this manner, scores of other tree pathogens and pests have been introduced into the US from abroad and from the US to other continents as well. Britton and Jiang-Hua (2002: 122) indicate the scope of the problem with 'biopollutants': "In the United States [...] 70% of all imported goods arrive on wooden pallets and spools, or wedged into metal cargo boxes with pieces of wood. Such wood is usually inferior in grade, and may contain many insects and disease organisms". They go on to suggest (ibid: 122): "A system of regulation and inspection has been established in most developed countries to safeguard against pest introduction, but it is so overcome with the volume of trade, that in the United States, we can inspect only 1% of incoming freight".

Unsurprisingly, the increasing interconnectedness of urban metabolic process is potentially detrimental to the momentum of urban ecologies. While the production of urban forests for human social reproduction may have been a localized process in the past, the expansion and integration of global commodity networks now means that urban forests are directly enrolled into new and increasingly extralocal socio-ecological configurations. In other words, the formation of human social reproductive networks within contemporary capitalism involve an increasingly global and urban political economy as consumers purchase commodities produced great distances away from their homes (and their urban trees).

But the relationships that make up an increasingly global association of actants open up the possibility for new and contradictory forms of network associations not planned by human actants who labor to metabolize urban form to their advantage. Boyd et al. (2001: 561) state: "the particular risks, uncertainties, and surprises associated with biological systems can have profound influences on industrial organization". So, for example, when human actants labor to produce WPM in order to safely ship commodities to consumers abroad, they purposefully enroll the labor

---

11   Evidence suggests that both subspecies have replaced *O. ulmi*, from which they are distantly
     related, perhaps even causing its extinction (Brasier 2002). It is suggested that *O. novo-ulmi*
     ssp. are likely better suited to temperate climates than *O. ulmi*, which evidence suggests fa-
     vored warmer temperatures (Brasier 2001).

of trees as production conditions and relations.[12] But the process of WPM production creates opportunities for other nonsocial actants to exploit/appropriate the social and nonsocial labor that gives extra-local tree ecologies their momentum.

As *O. novo-ulmi* ssp. and its bark beetle vector demonstrate, such organisms are far from passive actants riding on the flows of commodities within the profit-oriented networks of urban political economy. Once introduced into new urban spaces following their transoceanic journeys, they give rise to new forms of environmental politics as they labor to curve the associations comprising capitalist ecologies to their own advantage. They do this by exploiting/appropriating through their labor elm ecologies rendered vulnerable to attack by their own sheer ecological density and momentum. And while the DED fungus metabolizes the mass and energy produced by past social *and* nonsocial forms of labor within elm ecologies, it sequesters power to its own advantage within the new network association, rendering a new (a)symmetry of politics and power between humans, trees, and fungi.

During and after network reorganization, the actants that labor toward networked production and consumption relations for capital accumulation thus have to labor to curve the new (a)symmetry of politics and power between humans, trees, and fungus back to its former (ir)rationality. Orchestrated by actants within the spheres of capital and the State, humans responded to the DED crisis by enrolling tax monies, knowledge, other human laborers, equipment and nonhuman organisms to counteract *O. novo-ulmi* ssp. Thus municipal forestry departments expanded their operations by employing manual social labor in the form of sanitation practices meant to curb the rapid spread of DED (Cohen 1999). Genetic research (intellectual social labor) conducted at universities continues to investigate the possibility of developing DED resistant elm cultivars like the recently released "Valley Forge" and "New Harmony" (US National Arboretum 1996; Schlarbaum et al. 1997). Internationally, the FAO has implemented WPM sanitation guidelines to combat further spread of DED and other plant pathogens.

But the political dynamic of network reorganization is continuous; DED pathogens having sequestered much of the energy of urban elm networks continue to integrate with capitalist production/consumption ecologies, further transforming them. Sanitation efforts implemented by municipal forestry departments failed ultimately to stop the disease, and as a result, hundreds of millions of urban elms in the northern hemisphere have died (Hubbes 1999) while the fungus continues to evolve (Pipe et al. 2000; Konrad et al. 2002). Investigations conducted into the possibility of fungal hybrid introgression (Brasier 1995; Pipe et al. 2000) suggest that viable hybrids ssp. *novo-ulmi* x ssp. *americana* are emerging

---

12   For an encompassing overview of the problems associated with incorporating mineral and
      forest ecologies as production conditions within capitalism, see Bridge (2000) and Prudham
      (2005).

throughout Europe as a result of cross fertilization and horizontal gene flow via mycelium contact in infected trees. Brasier (2001: 126) states: "the hybrids could act as 'genetic bridges,' allowing unilateral gene flow from one species to the other". This is problematic as hybridization likely acts to trigger speciation, whereby new genetic variants of an organism emerge, facing extinction or escalation based on their ability to exploit/appropriate their ecosystem. Brasier (2001: 129) sums up the import of this ability in conjunction with episodic selection:[13]

> This glimpse of the migratory history of O. novo-ulmi from the 1940s to the 1990s demonstrates clearly how the "escape" of a fungal pathogen beyond the routine selection constraints of its endemic environment presents it with new evolutionary opportunities. It also shows that the traditional focus of concern about the risk posed by introduced exotic plant pathogens – namely, disease impact – must be extended to include the risk of accelerated pathogen evolution and the emergence of new or altered pathogens.

Despite the ability of human actants to employ their social labors to curb the fungus, it demonstrates a remarkable ability to respond and adapt to new network configurations quickly. This is problematic for newly engineered DED-resistant elm cultivars because it is possible that once planted they will be exposed to genetically variant offspring of O. novo-ulmi ssp. as the fungi proficiently capitalize on changing conditions within the ecologies of capitalist production and consumption. The capability within these organisms to labor adaptively and to spawn new political economic configurations is therefore a formidable political force. In order to protect commodity networks in the interest of continued capital accumulation, social labor must be employed to collectively give rise to global institutional reforms like the phytosanitation measures adopted by the International Plant Protection Convention. The costs associated with phytosanitary measures are significant,[14] but the relations that comprise capitalist urban ecologies must also be protected if human social reproduction is to continue to occur in the face of unpredictable nonhuman actants that are every bit as resourceful at curving network dynamics in their favor. O. ulmi-novo ssp. is but one nonsocial actant among many with this capability.

---

13   Episodic selection refers to sudden environmental disturbances that alter ecosystem dynamics which further impact the ability of an organism to thrive and evolve. Geographic transposition via human activity is an example (Brasier 1995).

14   Britton and Jiang-Hua (2002) suggest that treating WPM can raise the price of pallets from 0.5 to 1.5 US dollars each. They also state that WPM sanitation standards adopted by the European Union curtailed approximately seventy million US dollars worth of exports from the US in the first year of implementation.

In conclusion

By considering social labor as the ontological basis for human engagement with nature, Marxist urban political ecologists presciently articulate the production and consumption of urban environments. But in privileging social forms of labor in relation to apolitical nature, something has indeed been lost within the urban environmental dialectic. The dialectic is more fully balanced, however, if: 1) it is acknowledged that Marxism and ANT share an ontological foundation in the metabolic, yet internally differentiated process of laboring, and 2) that environmental politics is therefore extended to include the possibility of exploitation/appropriation of all forms of labor and its product by nonsocial actants as well as their social counterparts in the formation of networks. Finally, 3) the political process comprised of the dynamic relationship between laboring actants rarely leads to networked symmetries, but rather a uniformity of direction or momentum which implies instability rather than stasis in associations.

What advantage does the recognition of this ontological basis provide to those interested in the study of urban ecologies? In relation to the metabolization of urban environments, the import of social labor is retained while political status is attributed to nonhumans like the fungus *O. novo-ulmi* ssp. As laboring actants, organisms like DED assert their ontological status via their remarkable capacity to articulate their political power within heterogeneous associations. But this assertion does not deemphasize the power that humans wield in relation to other organisms via social forms of labor; consideration must be made for the possibility that social actants garner heightened abilities to shape network relations at the expense of others. It does mean, however, that people who employ their labor to build complex commodity networks out of nature have to deal with the emergent contradictions based in the politics of laboring nature.

Thus, in acknowledging the ontological status of nonhuman organisms like DED, the political struggles surrounding the socio-material development of institutions that seek to preserve global commodity chains and consumption-oriented ecologies is better accounted. The ability of fungus to relate materially to social labor is here requisite for a fuller understanding of the development of said institutional structures. Without the laboring capacity of a rogue fungus, why would social labor be directed toward implementing DED sanitation programs and WPM regulations in the first place? The answer lies in the fact that fungus and other nonhuman organisms can and do have serious political-institutional ramifications via their capacity to enroll the energy and products of social labor. And this political reality necessitates that social labor be (re)employed to curve the dynamic of power between humans and organisms like DED back toward urban metabolic relations less detrimental to social reproduction and accumulation.

Viewed in this manner, certain actants can curve urban ecological conditions and relations disproportionately, if only for a short duration. But the balance of power is always contested during political struggles, resulting in dynamic associations without static or predictable outcomes. Not surprisingly then, a global war against a variety of 'biopollutants' continues unabated on the ever-shifting landscapes of capitalist production, trade, and consumption. With this in mind, Castree (2003a: 209) suggests that we consider the "political effectivity" of nonhuman organisms like DED. In doing so, we acknowledge the contributions of humans *and* nonhumans to a universe of urban ecological possibilities. And so we can consider the politics surrounding capitalist commodity flows, WPM guidelines, research into disease resistant elms, and municipal forestry programs as being mediated in part by fungi.

Acknowledgements

A previous version of this chapter was published in *Geoforum* in 2007 (38/6, pp. 1152-1162). Many thanks to its editorial team for permission to reproduce it here. I would like to acknowledge, without implication, Nik Heynen, Anna McGuire, Jamey Essex, Brad Jokisch, Ethan Yorgason, and the anonymous reviewers for their comments on previous iterations of this piece. I would also like to thank my father, Harold E. Perkins, for his assistance in compiling research materials, without which this project would not have been possible.

Chapter 5 - Plant labour in the ecological regime of urban maintenance: Reproduction, collaboration, uneven relations

Marion Ernwein

In 2017, after just short of a decade of austerity, the park service of the north-eastern city of Newcastle-upon-Tyne (UK) had lost over 90 per cent of its budget and made every single one of its 20 park-keepers and most of its 20 rangers redundant, leaving the service's remaining six rangers responsible for maintaining the city's 500 hectares of parks and green spaces. Dozens of volunteers stepped in to work by their side and sweep paths, cut brambles, and keep the parks open. Any observer would note that the parks were increasingly going wild. The grass was cut less often, the trees pruned less frequently; flowerbeds gradually disappeared, and benches were taken over by spontaneous plants. This might sound like the starting point of an exciting new experiment in urban rewilding. And indeed, the appeal of wild nature resonated well with the volunteers who stepped up, many of whom shared with me their interest for "wildlife-y type of stuff".[1] A somewhat comparable story had unfolded a few years earlier in Geneva (Switzerland). Following the tightening of municipal budgets, between 2011 and 2015 the park service had been depleted of over ten percent of its more than 200-strong workforce, a decrease which coincided with the adoption of a new approach to park management, which introduced less intensive, more 'ecological' forms of management, and led to 'wilder' park aesthetics.

These stories of urban rewilding differ in more than one way. The scale of the cuts, the percentage of staff laid off, and indeed the degree of financial autonomy of local authorities vis-à-vis their national state, are all very different. In Newcastle, parks were included in a larger multi-service restructuring effort led by a team

---

1   This chapter draws on insights from two research projects. One research project was conducted in Geneva (Switzerland) between 2011 and 2016 on the role of neoliberal imaginaries and instruments in reshaping the politics of urban nature, the other one between 2016 and 2017 in Newcastle (UK) on the transformations of environmental volunteering in a context of austerity. In both research projects, interviews were conducted with service managers, workers, and volunteers within the municipal park service.

of senior managers from outside the park sector. In Geneva, on the other hand, even as it was laying off some of its staff, the green space service simultaneously increased its capacity to deploy state-of-the-art ecological design and maintenance principles through the targeted recruitment of highly skilled individuals at a planning and design level. Despite these differences, common to the two cases is a profound rethinking of where labour can come from when it is not only from core paid staff, of how to enrol it, and of how to manage it. While Newcastle's park service recruited a vast volunteer workforce, Geneva's followed another, somewhat more surprising, path: it drew on knowledge about plants' capacities to mobilise 'vegetal intelligence' and redistribute some previously distinctively human tasks to plants themselves. Geneva's rewilding experiment in fact embodies a logic of enrolment of plants' dynamics within a novel management framework oriented towards resource optimisation, whilst Newcastle's remains a largely unplanned consequence of the ongoing deprofessionalisation of the park service.

This chapter argues that naming plants' enrolment in park maintenance 'labour' opens up new, fruitful ways of understanding the politics of urban maintenance work. The argument proceeds in three stages. The first section positions the chapter within current discussions of urban maintenance work. It argues that recent shifts in urban design towards enhancing and harnessing the contributions of nonhuman life to urban resilience – for instance in the form of green infrastructures – call for a new conceptualisation of maintenance labour. Indeed, as urban infrastructures are increasingly understood in ecological terms, so are the skills and types of work needed to maintain them. The term 'ecological labour' is advanced to designate those forms of labour whose raison d'être is keeping nonhuman life alive and setting the right conditions for it to contribute its agencies to urban life. The second section then focuses on plants within said ecological labour and advances a view of them as workers. The section highlights both the imports and limits of writings on nonhuman labour – which are often based on accounts of animal work – for capturing what plants do under an ecological urban maintenance regime. It deploys Marxist-feminist writings on reproductive and regenerative labour to tackle the problem of intentionality in thinking about plants' contributions as labour. The final section highlights the need to understand how structural power relations shape plant-human work relations. The section cautions that the mobilisation of plant labour offers no guarantee that values of mutual flourishing and collaboration will take over the workplace, highlighting instead how plants can also work for, rather than against, alienation.

In sum, through highlighting plants' reproductive-regenerative labour, their partaking in collaborative work, and their contribution to uneven work relations, the chapter offers three avenues for both theorising maintenance labour in more ecological terms and conceptualising the specificities of plant life within the ecological labour force. The chapter finally insists that there remain aspects of plant life excessive of work relations and questions the political work that plant labour and its excesses can perform.

Maintaining the stuff cities are made from: the birth of ecological labour

The notions of infrastructural and maintenance labour foreground the concrete, embodied, and yet oft-invisible labours required to maintain, repair, and adapt the built environment. Those working with the notion of infrastructural labour seek to do away with the idea of urban infrastructures as hard, inert things, which once built, acquire permanence. Instead, they foreground the role of labour in joining fragmented segments of infrastructure together and linking pipes, waste collection lorries, and so on to the social fabric of the city (Simone 2004; Lawhon et al. 2014; Fredericks 2018). In cognate fields, the notion of maintenance labour helps to foreground the many invisible labours required to keep streets clean, elevators working, and public toilets usable (Heynen/Perkins/Roy 2007; Strebel 2011; Krinsky/Simonet 2017). By giving centre stage to labouring bodies, this work emphasises urban space as being in a state of flux, and highlights the role of gendered, racialised, poorly paid, precarious work in holding the urban fabric together.

By focusing on human bodies at work, however, such work risks overlooking the role of other-than-human agencies in forming and maintaining infrastructures. Not unlike social science and the humanities at large, urban research has undergone something of a posthuman turn, emphasising the multiple ways in which nonhumans dwell in and shape urban spaces often too readily described as human productions (Hinchliffe/Whatmore 2006; Barua/Sinha 2019). More recently, these nonhuman agencies have become a feature of urban environmental management itself, with tree alignments recast as green infrastructures for rainwater management and air pollution mitigation, and oyster reefs deployed as wave breakers (Wakefield 2020), for example.

For scholars of maintenance work, these new ontological foundations of infrastructural design and management must raise at least two questions. First, what happens to maintenance work when it is redirected towards nurturing not hard networks of concrete and steel but lively ecologies? How do the required skills change, and what implications does that have for the distribution of knowledge, expertise and power within the maintenance workforce? Second, when, say, flood mitigation or air pollution reduction infrastructures are made of living trees, their relations, and their dynamics, do trees themselves actually constitute the infrastructure, and therefore the object-target of maintenance work (the latter consisting for example of pruning, watering, leaf-blowing)? Or should they qualify as infrastructural workers, piecing together gutters, soils, and reservoirs through their metabolism, their relations, and even their communication? Indeed, efforts to en-rol nonhuman capacities in attempts to revitalise urban parks, regenerate the air, and capture rainwater call for the inclusion of nonhumans within understandings not only of infrastructures themselves but of infrastructural work.

Against this backdrop, I use the notion of ecological labour to designate a par-ticular form of maintenance labour, whose raison d'être is keeping nonhuman life alive and setting the right conditions for it to contribute its agencies to urban life. As an analytical device, the notion of ecological labour helps to shed light on the ways in which the ecological redesigning of urban space transforms urban mainte-nance labour and redefines the place that nonhumans play within it. I contend that conceiving of nonhumans as maintenance workers offers a fruitful way of bringing together the insights of more-than-human modes of inquiry with more conven-tional understandings of the social relations at work in maintenance labour.

In Geneva, the centrality of human labour to park work is explicitly being ques-tioned. After Geneva's green space service had laid off over ten per cent of its labour force, its adjunct director highlighted how "vegetal intelligence" was becoming an actionable force within maintenance efforts:

> On the one hand, we are optimizing resources and materials. On the other hand, we are now giving more room to vegetal intelligence [...] [which] contributes to the reduction of our maintenance tasks. (Geneva's green space service adjunct di-rector, cited in de Weck 2016)

Throughout its decades-long existence, the service had become renowned for its roses and its fine-grained mosaiculture – the delicate sculpting of elegant mas-sifs of annual flowering plants. The *Horloge Fleurie*, for instance – Geneva's largest and finest piece of mosaiculture – remains one of the most iconic landmarks of the city. This traditional approach to urban flowers had largely been predicated on creating arrangements of horticulturally bred, disposable annual and biannual plants, uprooted and replaced at the end of each season. From 2011-2012, the green space service started removing flower mosaics and rose bushes and replacing them with new flowery designs described as "livelier", "lighter" and "more fluid". Ser-vice employees noted how "new", "radical", or "provocative" these new perennial-and grass-based arrangements were, and how much they contrasted with Geneva's "very Swiss" horticultural tradition (Figure 5.1). Perennials' lifecycle and the quality of their growth starkly distinguish them from annuals: they survive the passing of seasons and years, producing more of themselves as time passes. It is not anec-dotal that the French word for perennial is *vivace* – a noun which has 'life' as its root. Highlighting the relevance of this connotation, a gardener made a pun when describing the difference perennials were making to her work: "[when we first in-troduced perennials] I kept asking myself: is this plant a perennial [*vivace*] or a deadennial [*crevasse*]?"

Figure 5.1: A new perennial border on the shores of Lake Geneva.

Image: SEVE, 2012.

The use of perennials and mobilisation of their capacity to produce more of themselves, to grow, and to occupy space, owed to new legislation about the safe-guarding of biodiversity and to a ban on chemical herbicides in public space. It was also linked to the translation of concepts of landscape ecology into green space design. In the francophone green space sector, designer and writer Gilles Clé-ment for instance played a key role in experimenting with and advocating plant-led park design (Clément 2006). As for the use of the term "vegetal intelligence", it reflects the adjunct director's own personal interest in permaculture and plant phi-losophy. Although much debated within plant sciences, several best-selling books have recently popularised the notion of plant intelligence and brought ideas about plants' communication, sensitivity, and even intent to a non-specialist audience (Ernwein/Palmer/Ginn, this volume).

However, attempts to rationalise material and human resources mattered just as much in the production of Geneva's new vegetal landscape, and the definition of "vegetal intelligence" within the service is marked by this (Ernwein 2021). Perennial plants were specifically discussed in terms of their capacities, and the potential they held to decrease gardeners' work: for instance, because perennials do not require uprooting at the end of their flowering season like annuals do, there is no need to fertilise and rake the soil before replanting other annuals, to drive the uprooted plants to a composting site, or to organise the transfer of new plants from the horticultural production centre. In planning documents accompanying the changes, the service's top managers even insisted that gardeners should now "stop gardening" altogether. Gardeners were quick to identify the contribution of perennials to the transformation of their work:

> This is now the first year that we introduce perennials into flowerbeds. Big novelty. So let's see what comes out of it. We'll observe the changes. But it also contributes to the reduction of work. A planted perennial doesn't require to be planted anymore. You have to take care of it, of course, but you don't need to plant it anymore. [...] Clearly, we need to do our job with fewer people. So, solutions have to be found. After optimizing the workforce, our tasks are now changing. (Anonymised Gardener, 2013)

The perennials introduced not only have the capacity to store their energy away during winter and spring to life again in the warmer season, but also to display other types of growth, allowing them to prevent the spread of unwanted species (for example through ground-covering dynamics) or to hide said unwanted species (with bushier growths, and modes of planting as loose groups rather than in lines), therefore reducing weeding tasks as well.

Yet perennial plants did not merely render redundant some of the most labour-intensive tasks that Geneva's gardeners would otherwise focus on; they were also called upon to perform new tasks. For instance, when service managers took the decision to green Geneva's cemeteries (where, traditionally, gravel covered most of the grounds), they decided not to follow the conventional path, that is, removing a layer of gravel, adding top soil, sowing lawn seeds, regularly watering them and keeping away until the lawn is strong enough to withstand being trod on (Figure 5.2). Instead, to both spare resources and experiment with a new greening paradigm, they seeded some areas with a mix of perennial ground-covering plants that did not need soil preparation and were trample-resistant, and designated others as areas that 'weeds' were to reclaim (see Ernwein 2020). In other terms, knowledge about different species' capacities was used to turn a process ordinarily reliant on intensive human labour into an experimental, plant-labour-based one.

Figure 5.2: Plants reclaiming gravel in Geneva's St-Georges cemetery, 2016.

Image: Marion Ernwein.

On plant labour: a feminist reading of nonhuman work

Having set the context of the chapter, in this section I move to a theoretical discussion of the notion of plant labour and its place in ecological work. The section first introduces existing writings on nonhuman labour and their contribution to rethinking the place of nonhuman agencies in the processes of value creation, exchange, accumulation, and reproduction. It then highlights the limits of this literature for capturing the specificities of plant labour and highlights how feminist theories of work can help to think about plants specifically.

If more-than-human geographies and multispecies studies could still be accused, not so long ago, of overlooking political economic questions, discussions within these subfields over the role of vibrant materiality and lively nonhuman agencies in value generation and capital accumulation are clearly changing the terms of the debate. In a way, what might be termed the second generation of more-than-human inquiry might in fact have more in common with the materialist revolution within resource geographies, and its efforts to re-enliven political economic analysis (Bakker/Bridge 2006). Resource materialists have, for instance, long argued that matter identified as resource has a tendency not to allow itself to be smoothly turned into commodities; material stuff poses challenges, and sometimes constitutes a barrier to capital accumulation, leading scholars to foreground its inherent "unruliness" (Bakker 2013). However pertinent within scholarship focused on the extraction of non-organic matter, this view of nonhuman materiality as barrier, or obstacle, to capital accumulation, is of limited analytical import in fields seeking to problematise bio-based economies. Within research on biocapitalism in a broad sense, living matter, lively capacities, and various expressions of life are precisely described as that which is sought to be captured, harnessed, valued, and exchanged (Helmreich 2008). The concept of the lively commodity, for instance, highlights the key role played by the capacity to display expressive signs of life in generating exchange value within the exotic pet trade (Collard/Dempsey 2013). Nonhumans, however, contribute to processes of value generation in many more respects than as commodities, however fictitious,[2] including, an increasing number of scholars argue, as labourers.

Marx's famous comparison of the bee and the architect (Marx 1976 [1867]) is a recurring trope within efforts to rethink the place of nonhuman life in the production of value (Ingold 1983; Clark 2014; Kallis/Swyngedouw 2018). That Marx sought to distinguish the type of contribution made respectively by humans and nonhumans certainly suggests that the question of the nonhuman is less incongruous to critical political economy than it might seem at first sight. Marx holds that all living animals share a fundamental metabolic condition: the fulfilment of their physiological needs requires them all to labour to transform their environment. That human work stands out, is for Marx, clear: it is guided by intent. That there are uniquely human forms of labour, however, does not directly translate into the notion that labour is itself uniquely human: there remain forms of 'instinctive' or 'primitive' labour that are shared across the living board. In the past years, this insight has been expanded through research seeking to reposition animals within analyses of capitalist modes of production, from fixed capital to labour. For instance, charismatic pandas engaged in commodified encounters with zoo visitors are more than objects of display, they are engaged in an affective performance that Barua (2020) describes as work. In much the same way, the role of animals within the film industry isn't simply that of performance machines, conditioned into performing semi-automated acts through coercion or feeding: they learn the tricks of the job, and acquire professional capacities, contributing their active labour to films (Estebanez/Porcher/Douine 2017). Spurred by improved knowledge about animals'

---

2   Polanyi (1944) and others working in his wake use the term "fictitious commodities" to describe anything that is treated as a commodity even if it does not have all the necessary qualities of one, such as being a discrete entity that can be alienated from its context. See also Castree (2003b), Li (2014).

intelligence – which complicates old distinctions between those living creatures endowed with intentionality, and those that are not – this research suggests the difference between human and nonhuman labour is much less self-evident than decades of Marxist writings had suggested.

The contributions of nonhumans to circuits of capital are not restricted to the first circuit – the production of commodities – they also contribute to the second circuit, that is, the circuit of reproduction (Perkins 2007, this volume; see also Heynen 2006). In Marxist parlance, the second circuit of capital refers to that part of monetary capital gained through producing and selling commodities that is not reinjected directly into more means of production, but in the quotidian rejuvenation of the workforce, through for instance investments in the built environment (the consumption fund). Although conventionally defined in terms of fixed capital, maintenance theorists have reappraised the role of labour in maintaining and reproducing this secondary circuit over time. Perkins (2007, this volume) has likewise argued that trees, in fact, also contribute their labour within that circuit. Planted to provide workers with enjoyable areas of shade and cool air, street trees are not just the ossified dead labour (Kirsch/Mitchell 2004) of tree surgeons, but they also perform the work of growing.[3] Should they cease to live, the secondary circuit of capital would break down, and the recuperation of the labour power of the workforce would be compromised. While urban parks work as fictitious commodities within cities' efforts to compete for 'green' or 'most sustainable' status, or by accruing more value to real estate within processes of gentrification, trees' metabolism is always-also part of a circuit of reproduction.

The view, however, that the concept of nonhuman labour is relevant for trees, and plants more broadly, is not uncontested. For some, labour is precisely a site of subjectivation, where labourers explicitly engage their subjectivity in a collaborative endeavour. For animal theorist Jocelyne Porcher, for instance, animals become labourers at the point where they engage their subjectivity in a meaningful collaboration with their humans (Porcher 2015). Without that subjective engagement within a collective task, there is no work to speak of. In the plant realm, however, the notion of intentionality is a topic of debate, and the very possibility for intersubjective encounters between humans and plants poses deep questions about the meaning of subjectivity, the temporality of encounters, and what counts as one when the protagonists speak such vastly different languages. In the rest of this section, I show that feminist theories of work can help us to overcome the obstacle of intentionality. For the purpose of this chapter, their strength precisely resides in their decentring of intentionality in delineating work from non-work, and in

---

3   The phrase 'dead labour' refers to the idea that commodities embody, or ossify, the work necessary to produce them, which includes "any number of discrete processes, often occurring over vast stretches of space and time" (Kirsch/Mitchell 2004: 697).

their inclusion of an ever-growing number of aspects of life itself into the politics of work. I now delve into two contributions of this scholarship to theorising plant labour.

First, trees' labour of reproduction has much in common with Marxist feminist notions of domestic labour. Focusing on the injection of capital within regenerative infrastructures as the main avenue through which the workforce is reproduced, Marxist feminists argue, obscures the role played by women within private space in achieving just that. Describing the achievement of chores within the household as – mostly feminine – labour, Marxist feminists argue, forces to question why that labour is not valued and remunerated in the same way as its masculine counterpart (Federici 1998; Simonet 2018). Marxist feminism in fact has a special place in efforts to re-theorise the role of nonhuman nature in reproducing the conditions under which capitalism flourishes. Alyssa Battistoni, for instance, advances the concept of hybrid work as an alternative to the vocabulary of ecosystem services, pervasive within environmental management spheres (Battistoni 2017). Understanding trees' cleaning of the atmosphere as the labour of reproducing conditions of life, she argues, calls into question why that labour is less valued than the equivalent productive labour of crops growing food. Therefore, by describing trees' metabolism as labour, the potential role of collective bargaining and social organising in defining the value of their life is foregrounded, taking the question of valuation away from the instrumentalist perspective of ecosystem services.

Feminist theory's other powerful contribution to thinking of plants as labouring is its problematisation of intentionality. For feminist theorists of work, that women often do not conceive of their domestic tasks as labour is precisely that which allows it to be exploited (Simonet 2018). In that respect, feminist technoscience studies probably have the most provocative insight to contribute, with their contention that not just domestic tasks constitute a form of – reproductive – labour, but intimate bodily functions themselves. "[M]any forms of labor highlighted by feminist theorists have been overlooked precisely because they do not produce material goods in a traditional sense", but healthy bodies, good spirits, and working capacities, writes Battistoni (2017: 17). Further challenge is yet posed when the end product of labour is not other people's good spirits or healthy bodies, as in the case of domestic work, but the development of one's own tissues. Recent work indeed suggests physiological processes themselves, and not just reproductive tasks, have in fact become the scale at which labour is enrolled within a range of settings including clinical trials and the tissue trade. "[P]articipation in clinical trials", Melinda Cooper (2008: 90) suggests, "invalidates any distinction between labour power and the body of the labourer" and forces us to reconsider labour as "the experience of self-transformation – commodified" (ibid: 76). When enrolled within a process of value creation, what could otherwise simply be one's metabolic activity, is turned into physiological, or metabolic, labour. This conceptual proposal is taken up by Beldo (2017) to reconceptualise the life of industrial broiler chicken. Through the concept of metabolic labour, Beldo seeks to capture the central role of chicken's excessive vitality in the creation of exchange value. As much as chickens are bred and enhanced, and even genetically engineered, the creation of value out of their lives is predicated upon the capacity of their liveliness to exceed all the inputs that humans put into their life.

Through their problematisation of reproduction and regeneration as work, feminist writings therefore highlight the role of labour other-than-productive (at least in the conventional sense of productive) in holding together the infrastructures of life in capitalist economies. Through their emphasis on the exploitation of vital processes, they also force us to reconsider the role of intentionality in defining work. Contemporary forms of exploitation are precisely pernicious because they are not limited to those singularly conscious types of work that conventional Marxism has insisted on. Of particular import for this chapter are two contentions: that a given activity need not be experienced as work to qualify as such, and that metabolic processes may play no less important a role in certain forms of work than conventional tasks. These insights are of particular relevance for thinking about and with plants, when notions of consciousness, intentionality, and intersubjectivity prove problematic. Should we, therefore, talk about labour when the intelligence of plants is enrolled in efforts to spare humans work? My view is that we should, precisely because their capacities could be recognised and nurtured otherwise. As I discuss in Ernwein (2020), the mobilisation of plants' capacities in ecological labour furthermore leads to a radically distinct mode of valuing their existence, from disposable, undead commodities whose exchange value results from their circulation within an international horticultural market, to largely decommodified, yet active contributors to park maintenance, whose value resides in the equivalence of their capacities with human work. Whether one mode of valuation is more desirable or ethical than the other, however, is debatable, as the next section will show.

Plant labour: always-also social

Because nonhuman labour literatures attempt to shift our attention away from social agency in the creation of value, they tend to verge on erasing human workers altogether. In contrast, in this final section I contend that the institutional context in which work is distributed, organised and remunerated needs to be included more centrally in discussions of nonhuman work. This is particularly important given the gendered, racialised, and classed dimensions of maintenance work, which cannot be simply left aside when discussing plant labour. I therefore discuss how describing plants' enrolment in park maintenance as labour helps to shed a new light on the production of uneven social relations of work. In other terms, this section seeks to provide a – necessary partial – answer to the question: "what becomes of communities of human workers after nonhuman vital capacities are enlisted to intensify, reduce, or modify labouring actions?" (Besky/Blanchette 2018: np). In this final section I weave empirical observations back in to highlight why these theoretical discussions are important in the context of urban maintenance labour.

Les Beldo's definition of metabolic labour exemplifies the backgrounding of the politics of human labour in nonhuman work writings. His definition, as that "which remains after human labour is subtracted from the equation of the 'production' of animal flesh" (2017: 112), implies that pure forms of labour – either human or nonhuman – do exist. This, I suggest, limits our understanding of the types of relations that make up work, and of the contributions of nonhumans to their politics. In fairness, mentions of nonhuman labour's place within a broader "enrol[ment of] forestry labourers, equipment, and trees into associations conducive to social (re)production" (Perkins 2007: 1156), or into a "whole collective of laborers (both social and nonsocial)" (ibid: 1157) are to be found in Harold Perkins's work. Likewise, Jonathan Clark (2014: 160) suggests that work is in fact neither human nor nonhuman, but distributed: "one approach […] is to stop thinking of labour as something that is done by individuals, whether human or nonhuman, and start thinking of it as a manifestation of […] the distributive agency of heterogeneous assemblages of human and nonhuman actants". Despite these mentions, however, in neither work is there a clear sense of how human and nonhuman agencies interact, how different labourers find their place within the workforce, and how the latter is governed as a collective entity.

Jocelyne Porcher stands out again, with her explicit focus on the human-nonhuman relations necessary to put animals to work. As an anthropological invariant, Porcher contends, work is a social institution through which subjectivities are formed and social relations forged:

> To work is not merely to produce; to work is to invest one's intelligence, one's affects, one's subjectivity, into the production of a use-value. To work is to live together; to work is to act upon the world and to act upon oneself. Work is therefore a process of subjectivation. (Porcher 2017: 30 – my translation)[4]

Reflecting on her research with small-scale livestock farmers in France, she notes:

> Living with animals is the first rationale for their vocation for most of the farmers that I have encountered. Economic rationales serve this purpose, and not the other

---

4   Original : "Travailler, ce n'est pas seulement produire, c'est investir son intelligence, son affectivité, sa subjectivité dans une production à valeur d'usage. Travailler, c'est vivre ensemble ; travailler, c'est agir sur le monde, mais c'est aussi agir sur soi-même. Le travail est ainsi un processus de subjectivation".

way round. Animals do not serve just to generate income; it is income that serves cohabitation with livestock. (Porcher 2014: 4)

With relations themselves as the single most important rationale for working, Porcher approaches interpersonal collaboration as the fundamental analytical scale. A focus on relations can clearly help to illuminate what the integration of plants as workers entails for human labourers in Geneva. Indeed, as a result of plants being allowed to use more of their metabolism in order to produce, reproduce, and maintain dynamic landscapes, the embodied interactions between gardeners and plants changed dramatically, with an increase in observational work:

> We used to plant flowers in lines, with specific distances. Now lines are over. We had to change our mental program. It was difficult at first not to make lines any-more, it took us some time. Then, it happened that a plant would take over another one, that some plants would die asphyxiated. At the beginning, there were some reactions, our colleagues said: 'that's not possible, it won't work', but that's just how nature works. If one plant risks taking over another one, we let them do. And we wait to see what happens. (Anonymised gardener, 2013)

The notion of putting trust in plants and "waiting to see what happens" is partic-ularly radical when compared to previous, more conventional ways of conducting work. In the decades prior to the 2011 restructuring, Geneva's gardeners had been working within what might be termed a fixed chronological logic. In that logic, each of the 52 weeks of the year harboured its own pre-defined series of tasks. For in-stance, for logistical reasons, and regardless of the likelihood that plants could have lived a bit longer, the uprooting and replanting of flowerbeds always took place in the same weeks. When working with plants expected to re-seed themselves, gar-deners had to learn to spend more time observing dynamics. Seeds might reach their desired maturity any time between, say, week 30 and week 35. The objective of letting plants enact their metabolic potential therefore guides the temporalities of work, replacing a series of temporally predetermined maintenance tasks, and requiring the adoption of a radically different professional posture (on this point see also Brice, this volume).

However, with its focus on intersubjective encounters, this kind of approach leaves little, if any, explanatory role to the broader structures that organise social relations of work. How is knowledge about how to identify maturity in grassy plants transferred to field employees? How is the employees' work kept under control by a bureaucracy that always-also has to be accountable to the public and to municipal accountants? As Heather Paxson cautions:

> When organic agencies are foregrounded in labor theories of value, the enabling and constraining forces of market demand, safety regulations, tax structures,

and mortgage-holding banks are obscured. Ecologies of production include those forces as well. (Paxson 2018: np)

Marxist-feminist descriptions of work as a site structured by wider social structures, therefore, must retain a hold if we are to understand the relations of work as always-also, even though only ever partly, scripted through power relations and social structures.

As outlined above, Geneva's parks workforce underwent an unprecedented decrease. That decrease, however, was not experienced evenly across the board. The size and organisation of teams changed, new management hierarchies were introduced and managers recruited, and new planning and design posts were created. To ensure that the service had the right expertise to implement its new approach to design and maintenance, that is, state-of-the-art knowledge about plants and their dynamics, the recruitments were focused on individuals holding degrees in landscape architecture, garden history and nature management. In other terms, resources were redirected from some sections of the workforce – field workers with technical horticultural degrees – towards new ones – design workers with university degrees.

Within the field crews themselves, the adoption of new greening practices also created new specialisations and distinctions. Before the restructuring, the service had been described as fairly decentralised, with small teams of workers in charge of their respective park.[5] In contrast, decision-making underwent a process of re-centralisation, and larger teams were formed, within which individuals were rendered more specialised and more mobile. Training was provided to those members of the workforce expected to work with perennials and grassy plants, with service managers insisting on shifting from a generalist to a specialised workforce. Whilst many enjoyed the skills upgrade, others had to re-focus on more explicitly maintenance-oriented tasks: some of those who had been performing tasks as diverse as rubbish-picking, flower watering, bush trimming, and grass cutting, saw their work refocused on cleaning-only, or mowing-only, tasks. Therefore, park maintenance was made more 'ecological', but that entailed creating a divide between those doing conventional maintenance tasks and those who could become ecological workers.

Plant labour itself, finally, was conceived as a means of streamlining human labour. The case of planting is particularly telling. For several weeks, between the end of May and the start of June, teams used to pause their maintenance work to focus their energy on uprooting and replanting flowerbeds. For the new annuals to be delivered in the right place, and at the right time, foremen needed to coordinate

---

5   Archives de la ville de Genève (2017) *Notice d'autorité - Service des espaces verts et de l'environnement (SEVE)*, p. 5.

with the service's production unit, to book lorries, and to schedule the transfer of plants from the polytunnels – located outside of town – to flowerbeds. With perennial-based flowerbed design, the labour of changing flowerbed appearance at the start of each season is largely devolved to plants themselves. Furthermore, the human labor required to nurture them requires less logistics; instead of disrupting the normal flow of labor, it can be built into it, therefore decreasing disruptions in the workflow and rendering work processes seamless.

In sum, the turn to plant intelligence marked a novel approach to workforce management, one that shifted agency back up to designers and planners, that specialised workers, and that attempted to streamline their work. This highlights that understanding how work is distributed among humans and nonhumans also requires us to examine the forms of workforce management that allow plants to labour, and the contribution of that labour to the governing or disciplining of the workforce.

When plants don't work

In this chapter, I have argued that although conventionally conceived as a human intervention on the materiality of urban infrastructures, maintenance work can be fruitfully expanded to include nonhumans, whose capacities to form and maintain infrastructures are increasingly harnessed within what I have called an ecological regime of urban maintenance. Having thus set the scene, the chapter then specifically examined the role that plants play as ecological workers. It positioned this argument within a broader set of reflections on nonhuman labour and acknowledged the challenge that plants' lack of intentionality and their incapacity to engage in intersubjective exchanges pose to extending nonhuman labour to plants. Feminist writings on reproductive and regenerative labour were then deployed to argue that intent should in fact be decentred, for otherwise invisible forms of exploitation in unorthodox work settings to become tangible. As for intersubjectivity, the last section highlighted the new forms of collaboration required for humans to share their labour with plants. The relations might not have the same speed and intensity as human-animal intersubjective exchanges, but for plants to work, workers have to deploy new modalities of attention. The chapter, however, highlighted the need to take into account the structural-institutional setting in which more-than-human relations and modalities of attention are organised and governed. It cautioned that plants are not merely contributing their labour to new more-than-human collaborations, but also to structural transformations of working conditions, which are neither all equalising nor all empowering.

So, what difference does the ecological turn in urban planning and design make to maintenance labour? Who counts as a worker within the ecological labour force?

It should now be clear that the ecological is more than a new object on which maintenance is applied. Efforts to make maintenance labour ecological require new knowledges and skills as well as the transformation of the tasks at the core of maintenance work. Yet they also rely on new understandings of the nature of work and of workers themselves, with vegetal capacities increasingly integrated within work collectives and contributing to the production of uneven social relations of work.

Despite being the focus of this chapter, it is important to note that the enrolment of vegetal capacities is but one of the modalities through which a new maintenance workforce, inclusive of a higher proportion of unpaid labour, is being constituted under contemporary austerity urbanism. In Newcastle's parks, it is not plants, but volunteers, who are providing the bulk of the maintenance labour power. During research conducted in 2017, Newcastle's park rangers noted how, in the absence of both park-keepers and landscape architecture thinking at the top management level, maintenance had become more "reactive than proactive", and certainly not more "ecological". In the absence of design and planning, rangers and their volunteers were "fighting fire" and trying to avoid park closure, rather than helping communities of human and nonhumans thrive together. The volunteers joined for "wildlife-y type of stuff", but instead of working with plants, they often found themselves exceeded by them. That plant metabolism can exceed work relations might offer a glimpse of hope, pointing to the possible reclamation of life outside of work relations (Weeks 2007). Except that volunteers and rangers know very well that uncontrolled spread of plants can eventually lead to site closures and communities being deprived of access to their local park.

As conventional, municipal maintenance labour is being dismantled from all sides, labour unions are in desperate need of new concepts that can engage with the diversity of new forms of work that co-exist with waged labour. At the same time, they must engage with increasing urban environmental vulnerabilities and with the necessary transformations of work that more 'ecological' approaches to urban infrastructures bring about. When observing the response of the public workers' union to the changes described in Geneva, one quickly realises that these are clearly not easy tasks. After the decrease in workforce was announced in Geneva's parks, the public workers' union organised a campaign, which included strikes, marches and sit-ins. The union's public communication contested that any of the changes in the parks' vegetal composition had to do with rewilding, and press releases described the removal of flowerbeds, rose bushes and other horticultural features as a form of 'de-greening' of urban parks whose sole objective was to allow the workforce to be compressed. Plants' labour, in other terms, remained entirely invisible in these conventional union narratives. I want to end by suggesting that the absence of nonhumans in union struggle limits their ability to formulate a response that simultaneously defends the rights of workers and recognises the entangled and distributed nature of ecological work in the Anthropocene. What might the union's struggles and claims look like if it were to be attentive to the way plants' and humans' labour-power is jointly managed and disciplined? This question is of crucial importance if we are to creatively think about the futures of maintenance work within an urban context that is increasingly marked both by the discipline of austerity and the challenges of the Anthropocene.

Acknowledgements

This work was funded by the Swiss National Science Foundation, first through a project grant for the "(Re)naturalising Cities" project (PI: Prof. Juliet J. Fall, 2011-2015), and second through an Early Postdoc.Mobility fellowship (2016-2017). I am grateful to my interviewees in Geneva and Newcastle for their time and generosity. Many thanks also to Jeremy Brice, James Palmer and Franklin Ginn for their comments on a previous version of this chapter.

Chapter 6 - Vegetal labour and the measure of value: Reckoning time and producing worth in capitalist viticulture

Jeremy Brice

The story of capitalism is increasingly recognized as a story of the labour processes, modes of valorization and accumulation strategies which have grown up around working plants which inhabit productive spaces from farms to plantations and laboratories. The Atlantic plantation ecologies and slave economies which pioneered the alienated and commodified labour relations that would later underpin industrial capitalism owed their existence in part to sugar cane's propensities to reproduce asexually and asocially (Tsing 2015), while appropriation of the metabolic surpluses furnished by the crops and forests of the freshly colonized Americas subsidized early capitalist economic expansion (Moore 2015). The fossil fuels which later powered the industrial economies out of whose critique Marxist political-economic theories originated, and which remain the predominant energy source of contemporary late liberal capitalism, are the residue of millions of years of photosynthetic accumulation performed by ancient forests and algae (Mitchell 2011). Even attempts to staunch contemporary capitalism's appetite for fossil fuel carbon often enrol contemporary 'working forests' into biofuel production (Palmer 2021). Everywhere vegetal life entwines itself with both capitalist accumulation and its critique, making it difficult to account for either historical or contemporary capitalist political economies without addressing plants' part in their formation and operation.

A growing body of research therefore questions orthodox political economy's longstanding depiction of nonhuman organisms including plants as inert resources which affect the organization of capitalist economies only insofar as their material or reproductive peculiarities impede capital's efforts to intensify the application of, and the extraction of surplus value from, human labour (see Haraway 2008; Beldo 2017; Johnson 2017). Building on animal studies researchers' arguments that efforts to "frame animals as co-constitutive actors in the production of social life [...] need to be extended to their equally important status as labouring subjects within processes of valorization" (Barua 2016: 726), scholars such as Ernwein (2020, 2021), Palmer (2021) and Perkins (2007) propose that:

> plant metabolism (in the form of photosynthesis, growth, and carbon sequestration) might usefully be conceptualized as a distinct form of nonhuman – in this case, vegetal – labor in its own right. (Palmer 2021: 142)

The concept of vegetal labour opens up valuable space for critical engagement with the part played by working plants' efforts and energies in constituting and configuring capitalist production, exploitation and accumulation processes. However, it also raises awkward questions about whether such radically other-than-human beings can be accommodated within conceptualizations of labour configured around a specifically human capacity to produce and valorize objects through reshaping matter into a form which corresponds to a preconceived design (Marx 1982 [1867]). The difficulties which such anthropocentric conceptualizations pose for animal labour scholars are well documented (Barua 2016; Beldo 2017; Wadiwel 2018), yet the impediments to speaking of labouring plants are arguably considerably more formidable. Unlike animals, plants possess few means of evading or resisting capture and appropriation by humans. Moreover, their photosynthetic metabolisms – which generate an energetic living through translating and incorporating unruly environmental influences from sunlight to rainfall rather than through pursuing, capturing and consuming food – give them a propensity towards pervasive corporeal entanglement in and dependence upon their environments. Such radical openness to the forces which animate their metabolic processes seemingly leaves plants few means of acting autonomously to appropriate or reconstitute an external nature, which historically has often led philosophers to portray vegetal life as being intrinsically passive (Brice 2014a; Head et al. 2014; Fleming 2017). In what sense might beings with so little capacity to appropriate the means of their subsistence voluntarily be considered to 'labour', much less to participate in the processes of value production which underpin contemporary capitalist economies?

In this chapter I address this question through returning to Marx's (1993 [1939]: 361) depiction of labour as a process of worldly transformation identified with "the transitoriness of things, their temporality, as their formation by living time". Arguing that Marx depicts labour as an activity which generates change and thus produces time, the following section re-examines his argument that under industrial capitalism the quantity of human labour-time expended in producing a commodity defines its value. Suggesting that human labour becomes positioned as the sole agency capable of producing value only through modes of time-reckoning premised upon an abstract and context-invariant (or sidereal) time, I propose that examining other timekeeping practices may disclose orderings of value production which redistribute the capacity to generate worth across species boundaries. In the third section I draw on ethnographic fieldwork within one of Australia's largest wine companies to illustrate how viticultural practitioners reckon the passage of seasonal time through attention to the photosynthetic exertions of grape vines, enabling these working plants' metabolisms to pattern the rhythms of human labour. In the fourth section I argue that translating these task-specific rhythms of labour into the sidereal time which choreographs the industrial production processes that transform grapes into saleable wines enables grape vines to participate actively in processes of capitalist valorization. The penultimate section examines what happens when this translation between grape vines' metabolic rhythms and the sidereal time of wine production is disrupted, arguing that failure to commensurate and coordinate these different temporalities can *de*valorize the fruits of workers' labours and thus rob both vegetal and human labour of its capacity to produce value. I conclude by suggesting that the labours of working plants and humans alike acquire the capacity to generate capitalist value only when they become the focus of the time-reckoning technologies which choreograph more-than-human labour processes. Attending to the means by which time is reckoned can thus provide critical insight into whose labour is valued (and whose is rendered worthless) within specific regimes of capitalist valorization and commensuration. It may also stimulate experimentation with time-reckoning technologies which might yield more egalitarian distributions of the capacity to produce value.

Time, labour and value

> Labour is [...] a process by which man [*sic*], through his own actions, mediates, regulates and controls the metabolism between himself and nature. He confronts the materials of nature as a force of nature. He sets in motion the natural forces which belong to his own body [...] in order to appropriate the materials of nature in a form adapted to his own needs. Through this movement he acts upon external nature and changes it, and in this way he simultaneously changes his own nature. (Marx 1982 [1867]: 283)

Plants appear distant indeed from Marx's famous depiction of living labour as a self-willed and intentional force which endows the materials upon which it works with value (and specifically with a use-value) through reshaping them into a desired form (Postone 1993; Johnson 2017). Yet plants' photosynthetic metabolisms possess prodigious capacities to effect material transformation (Palmer 2021), and for Marx labour was nothing if not a metabolic process which transforms both labourers and the environments in which they work (Battistoni 2017). Indeed, Marx's formulation defines labour through its unique capacity to alter the world, and to produce conditions which differ from those which preceded its occurrence. On this basis Gould (1981: 57) situates Marx within a philosophical lineage stretching back to Aristotle which takes such differences between 'befores' and 'afters' as the stuff of which the temporal distance between past and future is made, arguing that: "For Marx [...] the constituting activity that introduces time is labor". In Marx's view, then, the material transformations effected through productive labour not only imbue its objects with value but generate time.

This suggests that the technologies and practices which register productive transformation as temporal distance – and thus lend form, intensity and duration to labour – also define (and are defined by) the magnitude, social relations and authorship of value production through the labour process. Indeed, Marx's own analysis of capitalist value production expresses this reciprocal relationship through its argument that capitalism alone casts all concrete labour processes as instances of an abstract labour-time, necessary to all productive activity, in whose reckoning:

> We consider the labour of the spinner only in so far as it [...] is a source of value, that [...] differs in no respect from the labour of the man who bores cannon [...] Here we are no longer concerned with the quality, the character and the content of the labour, but merely with its quantity. (Marx 1982 [1867]: 296)

Once conceived as a homogeneous and fungible quantity, abstract labour-time may be construed as the sole input common to all commodity production and utilized as a universal equivalent in terms of which the relative worth (or exchange-value) of otherwise dissimilar goods may be commensurated (Postone 1993; Castree 2009). Comparing the quantities of socially necessary labour-time required to produce two commodities which afford different use-values, Marx argued, thus makes it possible to calculate their value. Through this process "the measure of the expenditure of human labour-power by its duration takes on the form of the magnitude of the value of the products of labour" (Marx 1982 [1867]: 164), in turn recasting the fabrication of commodities for exchange as the sole endeavour which renders concrete labour valuable and productive. In order to understand capitalist modes of valorization and valuation, then, it is necessary to examine the *temporal technologies and conventions* which create an abstract measure of duration which is applicable across all labour processes.

This universal equivalence between differing types of labour is often depicted as having emerged in part through the widespread use of mechanical clocks to choreograph complex manufacturing processes in the industrializing societies of early modern Europe (Adam 1998). Such accounts emphasize the clock's capacity to divide time into units of a standardized, context-invariant length determined by shared social convention, in contrast to earlier timekeeping practices which registered change and assessed duration through reference to local environmental rhythms and specific tasks (Ingold 2000; Moore 2015). Utilization of clocks, it is often argued, created a 'sidereal' temporal framework which disentangled the measure of time from the activities or events which might transpire within it (Thompson 1967; Castree 2009; Glennie/Thrift 2009), enabling qualitatively distinct kinds of concrete labour to become different but comparable quantities of abstract labour "measured by its duration [...] on the particular scale of hours, days, etc." (Marx 1982 [1867]: 129).[1] Through this delegation of the reckoning of time to – and the reorganization of productive activity around – devices which were themselves products of commodified labour, the magnitude of material transformation came to be measured against capitalist wage-labour relations themselves. As a result, under industrial capitalism the measurement and distribution of value:

> does not express directly the relation of humans to nature but the relations among people as mediated by labor. Hence, according to Marx, nature does not enter directly into value's constitution at all. (Postone 1993: 195)

I would therefore argue that Marx's positioning of human labour as the sole agency capable of valorizing materials emerges from his value theory's basis in the analysis of a historically specific encounter between the social relations of production characteristic of industrial capitalism and a very particular set of techniques for reckoning and measuring time.[2] Situating and provincializing Marx's value theory in this fashion suggests that the capacity to produce change and to generate value might be distributed differently within other practices of production, and specifically within those which employ alternative ways of reckoning time's passage. Indeed, analyses of financialization which argue that the locus of contemporary capitalist value production is shifting away from wage labour disciplined by the clock and towards speculation upon possible future changes in asset prices, enabled by various promissory and probabilistic technologies of anticipation, arguably diagnose

---

1   This argument should not be mistaken for a technologically deterministic assertion that the invention of clocks alone triggered the abstraction of time and the commodification of labour. Postone (1993) and Moore (2015), for instance, both argue that abstract time initially became socially salient, and the development of mechanical timekeeping technologies was stimulated, through disputes within the medieval European cloth industry over the duration and intensity of work performed by wage-earning weavers. Only several centuries later would techniques of time-reckoning and time-discipline forged through these struggles be incorporated into a package of social, legal and organizational innovations which extended the wage labour relation and the commodity form to other spheres of production.

2   This interpretation suggests that Marx's own treatment of the capacity to labour as a uniquely human trait may result as much from the framing of his analysis of capitalist value production in terms of the sidereal time that is so integral to the wage labour relation as from any more general humanist bias in his thinking (see for instance Haraway 2008; Barua 2016; Johnson 2017). In so doing it perhaps provides a more parsimonious explanation for Marx's sometimes ambivalent stance on the nonhuman world's role in value production, which: "acknowledges that the earth 'is active as an agent of production' in creating use value – though he is nevertheless adamant that exchange value could only come from labor" (Battistoni 2017: 16).

just such a mutation in the relationship between time-reckoning and value production (for a critical review see Christophers 2018). However, while such accounts of financialization broaden discussions of capitalist value production beyond classical political-economic concerns with the relation between sidereal clock-time and wage-labour, their account of value generation remains grounded in specifically human (albeit socio-technically augmented) capacities to form, and to act purposively upon, expectations about the future. This chapter makes the different move of suggesting that examining alternative ways of reckoning time may also disclose orderings of value production which redistribute the capacity to generate worth across species boundaries. This reasoning suggests that plants, animals and other creatures may participate actively in performing value-producing work in settings where nonhuman activity precipitates the transformations through which the passage of time is constituted and measured. Recent scholarship on nonhuman labour often hints at this possibility, arguing that nonhuman organisms should be recognized as performing value-producing work in part because:

> temporalities of nonhuman labour emerge from the labouring activities themselves, rather than being dictated by sidereal and chronological divisions of the working day into work and leisure (cf. Marx 1976 [1867]). They are contingent on 'sensuous multi-temporal' rhythms of nonhuman participants. (Barua 2017: 283)

Such arguments imply that working animals, plants or microbes become empowered to produce value when, through asserting their ethologies, habits and routines, they oblige their human co-workers to attune and synchronize their labours with rhythms of nonhuman activity. In so doing, they precipitate more-than-human labour processes whose pace and duration emerge through mutual attention and response across species boundaries and whose products derive their value as much from the propensities and sensitivities which entice working creatures to lend their energies to labour processes as from capitalist logics of exploitation and accumulation (Barua 2016, 2019).

I draw from this argument the broader implication that differing attributions of the capacity to engage in value-producing labour are entwined inextricably with contrasting approaches to registering the passage of time. Thus, if plants can be shown to participate as actively as do labouring humans and working animals in constituting the passage of *time* then this will suggest that their activities are likely also productive of *value*. In the following section I therefore examine the time-reckoning practices of humans who work closely alongside the grape vines cultivated by capitalist viticultural and winemaking enterprises in Australia. Through examining how the photosynthetic metabolisms of these working plants pattern the seasonal temporalities of wine production, and thus animate the labour of viticultural and oenological workers, I begin to tease out how plants' capacities are enrolled actively in the productive labour which underpins capitalist agricultural commodity production.

Seasons and sugar

Wine grape production provides a promising setting in which to explore how the activities of plants might order the temporalities of capitalist labour, for viticultural work is organized around specialist calendars of working seasons (illustrated in Figure 6.1) characterized by changes both in grape vines' physiological development and in the pace and content of human labour (Ulin 1996). Seasonal change thus entails multiple intermingled transformations in the more-than-human labour processes which produce grapes suitable for winemaking – grapes whose value becomes the object of especially intense concern as vintage (the grape harvesting and winemaking season) approaches.

Figure 6.1: This diagram loosely illustrates the calendar months corresponding to each season of the southern hemisphere viticultural working year.

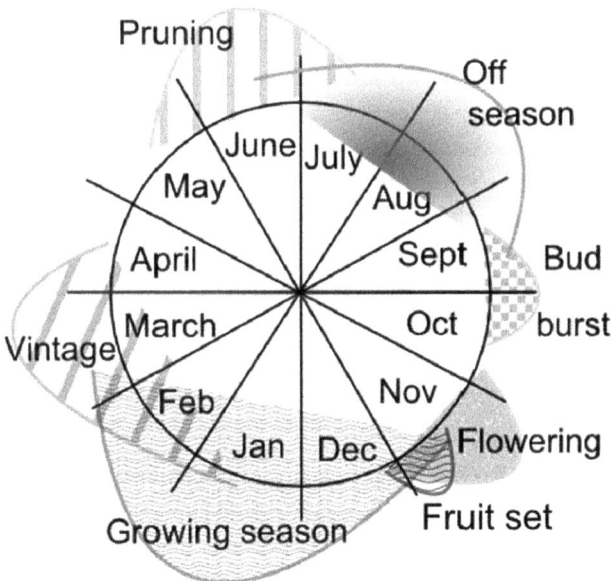

The onset of vintage, which typically occurs between mid-January and mid-March in Australia's viticultural zones, precipitates radical changes in the tempo of work for grape growers and winemakers. During the growing season which precedes vintage, full-time grape growers and vineyard managers observe a regular routine of leaf thinning and pesticide spraying while winemakers, having usually already bottled the previous year's wine, often have minimal work commitments. However, as vintage commences the ripening of grapes increasingly dictates the tempo of their labour, for the harvest must be timed precisely if the crop is to meet the stringent quality specifications set by the multinational wine companies which purchase most of Australia's wine grapes. Grapes must not be picked until they ripen. However, they must then be harvested quickly (before bad weather, disease or overripening can damage them), then crushed and processed within a few hours before their flavour can deteriorate (ibid). The grapes' price will depend upon their maturity and quality, so for grape growers a year's income is at stake in delivering their crop to the winery ripe and unspoiled. The growing season's regular working hours therefore give way to a frenzied race to pick grapes just as they attain their optimum ripeness and to convey the crop quickly to the winery. Grape growers using mechanical harvesters are often obliged to supervise picks which begin at 1am or 3am so that the fruit may reach the winery by the following morning, while winery staff must work until the day's grape intake is safely processed – a task which may on occasion require working days twelve or more hours long.

I witnessed the painstaking work required to achieve this precise synchronization between viticultural labour and grape maturation during six months of ethnographic fieldwork within one of Australia's largest wine-producing corporations (referred to in this chapter as 'The Company'). During this time I repeatedly workshadowed and interviewed Company vineyard managers, winemakers and grower relations managers who were responsible for deciding when to harvest grapes, for organising and timetabling picks, and thus for ensuring that the vintage produced wine suitable to be sold under one of The Company's numerous brands. During a visit to one of The Company's vineyards its manager, John,[3] demonstrated how maintaining a close attention to the material transformations effected through grape vines' metabolic activities facilitates the precise synchronization of human labour and vegetal development required to produce grapes suitable for wine production.

Fieldnotes, mid-February 2011: This morning is different from my previous visits to John's vineyard. Vintage is fast approaching and John's staff have begun carrying out maturity tests on the grapes. Twice a week they collect twenty bunches of

---

3   The names of all Company employees mentioned in this chapter have been replaced with pseudonyms in order to preserve their anonymity.

grapes from each block (a discrete management unit of vines whose fruit is grown to supply one particular wine product) which visual inspection suggests[4] may be approaching ripeness. On returning to the vineyard's small field laboratory they crush these grapes and conduct several analytical tests on the juice. They test its sugar concentration in degrees Baume, its pH and its titratable acidity (both measures of the juice's acidity). But they pay most attention to its sugar concentration, which will determine the resultant wine's alcohol content – an important influence upon its marketability. After completing each test, John's staff upload the result to The Company's computer network so that the winemaking team can view the data and incorporate it into their planning for vintage. Once today's tests were complete John printed out a spreadsheet of test results, freshly updated to include today's data. He pointed out its key feature: a predicted harvest date for each block, calculated automatically from the test results obtained so far...

Changing sugar and acid concentrations hold significance for John and his colleagues because they express a critically important vegetal metabolic process. Throughout the growing season grape vines photosynthesize, converting carbon dioxide and water into sugar and waste oxygen, meaning that sugars accumulate in grape juice over time while the acids found there early in the season break down. These biochemical transformations are central to many forms of vegetal labour (Palmer 2021), but they are particularly important to John and his colleagues because the alcoholic fermentation which converts grape juice into wine requires sugar. Testing sugar and acid concentrations repeatedly and regularly therefore enables Company staff both to establish approximately how close their grapes currently are to becoming ripe enough to be processed into wine and to assess how quickly they are approaching readiness for harvest. Practices such as Baume testing thus empower the material transformations effected through grape vines' metabolic activities to mark and express the passage of seasonal *time*, rendering the speed at which the growing season elapses contingent upon their exertions. As Company employees like John use techniques such as Baume testing to measure the duration of tasks and processes, and to coordinate their firm's operations, techniques of attentiveness to working plants' photosynthetic metabolisms transform into time-reckoning practices (Munn 1992).

---

4   Such initial signs of impending ripeness tend to be registered relatively informally by the practiced eyes of Company vineyard managers and of viticulturists performing regular vineyard maintenance tasks such as checking the vines for signs of damage or disease. While performing such tasks, employees may take note of signs of change in the grapes, from increases in the size of the berries or changes in flavour to more obvious indicators such as the onset of *veraison* – the process during which the skins of red grape varieties darken and gain their characteristic hue.

Figure 6.2: A Company employee records maturity test result data in between testing juice samples contained in plastic flasks.

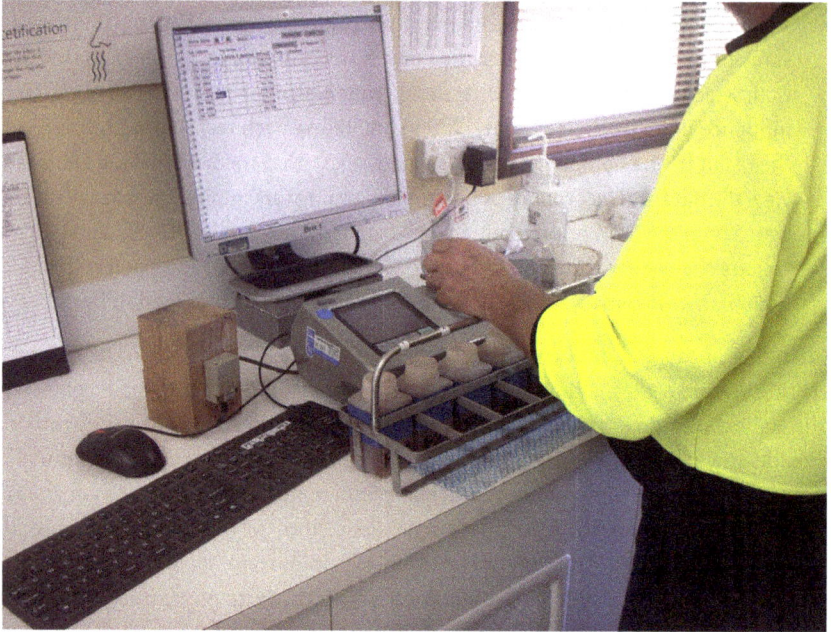

Image: Jeremy Brice.

In the process, the vines' metabolic activities are empowered to structure, stretch and compress the seasonal time which organizes the labour of vineyard and winery workers. Through calibrating their work schedules to the projected pace of sugar accumulation – a tempo influenced by the grape variety and clone cultivated in each block, as well as each vineyard's aspect and microclimate – Company employees attempt to synchronize their labour (and most especially the act of harvesting) with the ripening of their grapes. In this regard Baume testing exemplifies a suite of techniques – from chemical tests to sensory assessments of the grapes' flavour-ripeness performed by highly trained and experienced winemakers – through which The Company attempts to coordinate its workers' activities ever more precisely with the ripening of grapes as the harvest approaches (as discussed further in Brice 2014a). Yet despite such painstaking efforts, achieving such fluent coordination remains difficult, for grape vines' metabolisms are notoriously sensitive to changing environmental conditions and are easily prompted to behave quite differently than such tests might predict.

Fieldnotes, mid-February 2011: … after printing out the test results, John showed me how to read the spreadsheet. How each row held sugar and acid test results, grouped by test date, for one particular block. How each block's sugar concentration increased as the test dates advanced. But not very much. John explained that in a 'normal' year the grapes would be riper by now. But this year's growing season had so far been unusually cool, wet, and overcast, and sugar accumulation had proceeded surprisingly slowly. John shrugged and explained that this was why he didn't set much store by the predicted harvest dates shown on the spreadsheet. When planning for vintage he usually checked the weather forecasts and then reinterpreted the raw test data himself. And the weather forecasts were currently making him anxious. Eyeing the clouds visible through his office window he described how, if it rained heavily over the coming weeks, his vines might absorb enough water from the soil to dilute their grapes' juice – cancelling out the small increase in sugar concentration that he had so far observed. How this might actually leave the grapes *further away* from ripeness, delaying vintage by a week or two. This uncertainty, John told me, made him nervous and agitated – always alert for the onset of a vintage that never quite arrived.

John's dismissive attitude towards the predicted harvest dates illustrates something important about the form of time reckoned through techniques such as Baume testing. The growth of vegetation and the ripening of grapes are not fixed in any stable relationship to the sidereal time of calendars and clocks, meaning that sugar time may speed up, slow down, or occasionally even run *backwards* in relation to calendar dates depending on environmental events in the vineyard. While heat-waves may accelerate the onset of vintage, stormy weather may delay the grapes' development – leaving harvesting contractors and Company winemakers waiting listlessly for weeks for the work of picking, crushing and fermenting grapes to commence. In such situations, idle picking gangs and cellar hands illustrate the capacity of vines' metabolic activities not only to set human bodies and machinery into productive motion, but to impede or delay the labour processes and material transformations out of which valuable grapes and wines emerge. Crucially, such events illustrate that the pace of these labour processes (and thus of value production within The Company) is not solely, and perhaps not even primarily, defined by the familiar capitalist imperative to maximize the application of and extraction of surplus value from human labour. They instead disclose a form of capitalist valorization characterized by continual adjustment of the tempo of human waged labour and commodity production to mirror the metabolic rhythms of *working plants*.

Translating temporalities

Reckoning time, and ordering the pace of labour, in this fashion is a less idiosyn-
cratic practice than it might initially appear. Recent accounts of park management
(Ernwein 2020) and arboriculture (Gibson/Warren 2020; Palmer 2021) emphasize
both the considerable responsiveness to vegetal temporalities which these forms of
labour demand of human workers and the importance of close attention to changes
in key plant species in achieving this temporal attunement. In this respect they re-
semble anthropological studies of time-reckoning among non-western cultivators
and pastoralists, which have long portrayed skill and success in raising crops as
depending upon techniques of environmental attentiveness to engender a fluent
temporal coordination between human labour and the development of key productive organisms (Evans-Pritchard 1969; Munn 1992). This striving after coordination is often argued to render the pace of social and economic activities so thoroughly contingent upon seasonal changes in crop plants that the passage of time
becomes inseparable from sequences of concrete agrarian tasks, leading some commentators to characterize such regimes of time-reckoning as being 'task-oriented'
(Thompson 1967; Ingold 2000; Glennie/Thrift 2009). Intriguingly, recent scholarship on nonhuman labour sometimes draws indirectly on such accounts of task-
oriented time-reckoning to argue that working animals (and perhaps plants):

> are situated at the centre of their productive activity when conducting tasks, tem-
> poralities of which are rhythmic, intrinsic to and emerging from movement itself,
> not sidereal or chronological. (Barua 2016: 729)

This inventive piece of reasoning suggests that working nonhumans like John's
vines play an active role in generating value because they co-constitute the temporalities immanent to the *tasks* which compose more-than-human labour processes.
However, as Ingold (2000: 324) notes, the temporalities which emerge from task-
oriented time-reckoning practices have "no existence apart from the tasks themselves [...] and cannot be separated or abstracted from [them]", implying that the
forms of time and value precipitated through nonhuman labour are inseparable
from particular, concrete trans-species engagements. The temporality generated
through one more-than-human labour process would therefore seem to be neither
equivalent to that of another nor amenable to conversion into the abstract and
fungible measures of labour-time typically taken to underlie the calculation and
commensuration of value under capitalism.

　　Studies of the working plants and animals which labour in sites of indus-
trial-capitalist commodity production from intensive poultry farms to industrial
forestry enterprises often appear to support this argument. In such settings, political-economic analyses often argue, techniques ranging from rigidly timetabled
livestock feeding regimes (Beldo 2017; Wadiwel 2018) to the cultivation of fast-

growing hybrid tree varieties (Boyd/Prudham/Schurman 2001; Gibson/Warren 2020) are employed to accelerate and standardize nonhuman metabolic processes. Such interventions seek to minimize 'unproductive' periods such as those described in the previous section – during which the production and realization of surplus value must await material transformations wrought primarily through nonhuman biophysical processes – through reshaping rhythms of animal and vegetal reproduction, metabolism and death to facilitate the continuous application of human wage-labour (Adam 1998). As the timescapes of nonhuman life and labour are reconstituted, through the mediation of calendars and clocks, around the sidereal time which organizes and measures capitalist value production, the temporalities of nonhuman life become subordinated to (and subsumed under) those of capital accumulation. Such techniques of temporal abstraction and economization are therefore frequently depicted as erasing the beastly temporalities whose expression within the labour process enables nonhumans to define the tempo of production and to generate value – transforming working creatures into fixed capital incapable of either co-constituting or disrupting the temporal logic of capitalist production.

Taken together, these arguments seem to suggest that while the exertions of working animals and plants do effect meaningful material transformations, these may be recognised as constituting productive work only if the task-specific rhythms of the labour processes which they animate stand apart from the sidereal time which underpins capitalist modes of value production, commensuration and exchange. This view of nonhuman activity as being productive of material transformations which hold worth within particular more-than-human taskscapes, but nevertheless remain illegible and external to the modes of commensuration which constitute capitalist value, perhaps underwrites Barua's (2019: 653) contention that: "animals are workers in the shadows of capitalism: their unwaged labours are rendered invisible". However, such an analysis leaves relatively little room for nonhuman labour to participate actively in capitalist valorization processes, permitting it do so only in 'niche industries' insulated from imperatives to maximize surplus value production (Gibson/Warren 2020) or when experiences of attunement to nonhuman temporalities themselves become desirable commodities[5] (Haraway 2008;

---

5   Notably, considerable scholarship on the traffic in charismatic fauna set up by eco-tourism, the pet trade and competitive animal sports suggests that synchronous co-presence with creatures such as dogs, horses and lions may in itself sometimes generate an 'encounter value' for the paying customers who experience it (see for instance Haraway 2008; Collard/Dempsey 2013; Barua 2017). As such, the value of sharing such animals' space, and perhaps some aspects of their *time*, may exceed that of the remuneration provided to the humans and nonhuman workers who labour to orchestrate inter-species encounters. Access to spectacular beasts and companion animals may thus become the focus of promissory economies in which breeding stock, locations and assets associated with charismatic crea-

Collard/Dempsey 2013; Barua 2019). Against this backdrop, the reckonings of seasonal time performed through The Company's Baume testing programme acquire a new significance. For the measurements of sugar concentration produced through Baume testing may, if tests are conducted and interpreted carefully, be translated into the calendar dates according to which labourers' working hours, grape deliveries, and the entire organization of vintage are scheduled. In the process, the task-specific rhythms of the vines' photosynthetic metabolisms are rendered intelligible within the systems of temporal and economic commensuration which underpin capitalist labour relations and are thus enabled to influence the temporal organization of value production.

This capacity for temporal translation makes Baume testing especially useful to Company viticultural managers, who must somehow coordinate their winery's processing schedules with the ripening of hundreds of blocks of grapes dispersed across the viticultural regions of South Australia if they are to produce palatable and saleable wine. This means that picking, crushing and processing grapes requires meticulous advance planning – much of it performed by grower relations managers like Mark, whose words in an interview illustrate some of the logistical and temporal complexities involved in choreographing a successful harvest:

> So we get all this Baume data, sugar ripeness and things like that – we have predictive models of when we think things are gonna be ripe. We then say to the winery 'We'd like to pick this much, this is what we think'. Then, I guess, differing priorities are taken into account. For instance, if the canopies are failing in a region and they're running out of water, well, that might take priority over another region that's not so hot. Or if there's a disease issue [...] So perhaps we'd like to pick 3,000 tonnes of Barossa Valley Shiraz over this week. But we might be limited by the amount of trucks we have, 'cause that's all external. We might be limited by the amount of harvesters, so then that's got to be taken into account. And then the winery only has so many crusher slots available. So [another grower relations manager] gets his allocation of slots for the Barossa and Clare, I'll get my slots for Langhorne Creek, McLaren Vale, the Southeast. [...] And then it's a matter of me, based on what I saw with the winemakers, sort of going down a list from ripest to less ripe, although there's also idiosyncrasies in that. [...] And then [the projected harvesting dates] get sent out to the growers, they'll confirm that's OK to happen, and generally there's sort of a 7-10 day [wait] period. So if we're sitting here on Monday morning, we're probably looking at picking [the following] Monday, Tuesday onwards.

---

tures acquire exchange-value by virtue of their potential to yield a future revenue stream even as these animals' temporalities remain aloof from capitalist modes of timekeeping and commensuration.

Knowing exactly when grapes will attain optimal ripeness is crucial partly because the contractors who own most grape harvesting machinery lack sufficient staff and vehicles to harvest every block simultaneously and therefore work to exacting timetables, while successful picks also require the timely provision of trucks (usually owned by separate contractors) to transport the grapes to the winery. These hauliers and harvesting contractors, like the cellar hands who need to be available to crush the grapes as soon as they arrive at the winery, don't schedule their shifts according to changing sugar test results. Instead they work according to the hours and dates in which their work engagements and pay are calculated. Maintaining the meticulous coordination between varied human and nonhuman actors which enables grapes to be harvested and processed successfully into wine therefore requires a constant, painstaking oscillation between the task-specific rhythms of the vineyard and the sidereal time which organizes intensively mechanized contract labouring and industrial production. As such, Baume testing's most valuable contribution lies in its capacity to keep work in the winery 'in time' with events in the vineyard through drawing the vines' metabolic rhythms (at least temporarily) into a calculable relationship with sidereal time.

Figure 6.3: A harvester (right) prepares to disgorge freshly picked grapes into a plastic bin carried by a tractor (left). After the bin is filled, the tractor driver will load it onto a waiting truck for transport to the winery.

Image: Jeremy Brice.

Crucially, this means that articulating grape vines' metabolic rhythms with the sidereal time of the clock does not, in this setting, erase them. Instead, it enables events in the vineyard to accelerate, or hold in check, the industrial processes through which The Company converts ripening grapes into wine. It thus plays an indispensable role in facilitating the seamless flows of productive labour through which The Company valorizes these materials. In this sense, Company employees' struggles to synchronize the wildly different temporalities of photosynthesising vines, harried contractors and inflexible winery machinery exemplify Bear's claim that within contemporary capitalism labour often generates value precisely through:

> [...] attempting to reconcile various technological devices, temporal rhythms, and representations into a productive act of work. It reflects the ways in which technological devices open people up to non-human pressures and forces. (Bear 2014: 74)

Mark's words chime with Bear's argument, for they highlight that it is through holding together multiple contrasting temporalities that Company staff effect the material transformations which enable them to produce commodities fit for exchange. However, Bear's analysis could perhaps be taken a step further. Although the heroic acts of time-synthesis which she describes may require attunement to various nonhuman forces, the capacity to produce value through reconciling these clashing rhythms belongs in her view ultimately to skilled and attentive human workers whose "labour strains to bring together these incommensurable temporalities" (ibid: 80). My argument, by contrast, is that through opening up the constitution of time to vegetal agencies such as photosynthesising grape vines, techniques of attentiveness such as Baume testing enable the exertions of working plants to choreograph and co-constitute the capitalist labour processes through which Company employees endow commodities with value. This means that the capacities to produce value which 'make work productive' in Bear's sense arise only through the careful alignment of human labour with the metabolic exertions of grape vines, transforming the vines into active participants in capitalist valorization processes. As such, while these working plants may produce capitalist value only through the mediation of human labour, Company workers' capacities to valorize commodities are also contingent upon socio-technical arrangements which synchronize their work with the vines' exertions. Yet despite the best efforts of Company staff such coordination always remains fragile and, as the following section explains, if the different temporalities brought into relation through practices such as Baume testing desynchronize then this can profoundly imperil the modes of valorization which depend upon them.

Desynchronization and devalorization

Fieldnotes, mid-April 2011: Today The Company's viticulture division has invited me to accompany Mark and Joe (a winemaker) as they assess the ripeness and quality of grapes at vineyards belonging to external grape suppliers. Unlike John, these growers are independent contractors from whom The Company purchases grapes, so a winemaker must assess each block's quality and agree a price for its grapes before the crop may be harvested. I arrive at Mark's office with high expectations, but my enthusiasm dissipates quickly when I find him reading through a spreadsheet with a look of resignation. Each row on this spreadsheet represents one block of vines whose ripeness and quality Joe is supposed to assess today. The list is long enough to cover three sheets of A4. Or it *used* to be. Most of the entries have been crossed out in yellow highlighter. Mark explains that we won't be visiting the highlighted blocks. Since he compiled his list yesterday The Company has rejected these grapes as too damaged by disease to be suitable for wine production. Only the six blocks which remain un-highlighted are still sufficiently 'clean' for Joe to assess them.

I have become wearyingly familiar with such situations. For some weeks viticultural regions across South Eastern Australia have been experiencing extremely heavy rainfall. The storms have created terrible conditions in which to harvest grapes, turning solid ground to mud – meaning that mechanical grape harvesters tend to become stuck if driven into a vineyard. However, pathogenic fungi which feed off the sugars that accumulate in ripening grapes thrive under these conditions, especially a green mould called *Botrytis cinerea*. Botrytis can, if infected grapes aren't picked within the first few days after a storm, rapidly turn whole blocks' (and whole vineyards') crops of grapes into mouldy-smelling bags of pulpy mush which disintegrate during picking. The speed of this process means that growers who rely on machine harvesting must often stand by and watch their crop rot on the vine. So Mark and I both know what each yellow highlighter mark means: that he will have to inform another grape grower that part of their crop has just become worthless, and that they will lose a portion of this year's income.

Mark's spreadsheet makes the workings of valorization, or rather of *devalorization*, within The Company starkly visible. Through marking out blocks whose fruit has become worthless for winemaking purposes from those whose grapes might still hold value, it illustrates how badly awry value production can go when coordination between the photosynthetic temporalities of the vineyard and the sidereal time of contract harvesting and winery work breaks down. It thus highlights the extent to which Company employees' ability to produce valuable commodities depends upon mediating between these different ways of reckoning time, and between the contrasting labour processes which they coordinate. For the complexity of choreographing such temporal translations, and of managing the frictions generated by encounters between differing enactments of time (see Brice 2014a), makes it all too easy for events in the vineyard to drift dangerously out of alignment with The Company's picking and processing schedules.

Figure 6.4: Grapes infected with Botrytis cinerea. Grapes in the centre of the top left bunch display the characteristic grey-green 'fur' or 'felt' of a mature, sporulating grey rot infection.

Image: Jeremy Brice.

Botrytis outbreaks such as those depicted by Mark's spreadsheet are potent instigators of such desynchronizations, in part because *Botrytis cinerea* shares with numerous other fungal species a propensity (described in Perkins 2007; Tsing 2015) both to infiltrate the processes of vegetal metabolic labour which facilitate capitalist value production and to subvert them to its own advantage. These metabolic entanglements between vine and fungus, which render the temporalities of a botrytis mycelium's own life cycle contingent upon sugar accumulation in infected grapes (see Brice 2014b), mean that the pace at which a botrytis infection proceeds depends heavily upon rates of photosynthesis among infected vines and by extension on the temperature and humidity of their surroundings. As a result, like sugar time, the pace of a botrytis infection's development bears no fixed relationship to the passage of sidereal time. Indeed, given the right conditions, such infections could spread fast enough to spoil the vast majority of the blocks on Mark's itinerary within a day of his drawing up his list. And despite Mark's and his colleagues' best efforts it is difficult, if not impossible, to recalibrate the schedules of harvesting contractors and winery workers to match such rapid and radical nonhuman metabolic transformations when the meticulous management of scarce workers and machinery requires that grape harvesting, delivery, and processing be timetabled up to a week in advance.

Importantly, this means that the value of botrytis-damaged grapes did not evaporate because the vines in question had ceased to perform their photosynthetic labour. Instead, The Company's elaborate procedures for coordinating the passage of sugar time in suppliers' vineyards with the work of wine production regularly became ineffectual as the proliferation of botrytis frequently rendered grapes irredeemably mouldy before they could reach the standards of sugar ripeness which it normally prescribed. The unruly metabolic rhythms of botrytis thus created a fateful mismatch between contrasting temporalities and the labour processes which they organized. Bear (2014: 82) suggests that such dramatic clashes between incommensurable temporalities often precipitate "a terrifying collapse of [...] agency" which robs labour of its capacity to effect productive transformation. Indeed, growers and winemakers faced with botrytis outbreaks such as that described above often experienced a sudden and unnerving evaporation of the capacity to generate value through their work. Pickers often still laboured to harvest botrytis-damaged grapes, winery workers sometimes agreed to crush and ferment them and, as prospects for the harvest grew increasingly bleak, some growers even engaged contract winemakers to vinify grapes which their usual buyers had rejected as hopelessly diseased in hopes of replacing lost revenue through selling the resultant wine. However, performing the labour of wine production so hopelessly out of time tended to yield only discoloured and mouldy-smelling liquids worth a fraction of the price that a 'clean' wine would have commanded (see Brice 2014b). Botrytis' interference with the temporal relationship between vineyard labour and winery work thus not only rendered the time and effort invested in such materials by winemakers and cellar hands unproductive of value but retrospectively devalued the labour expended over the preceding year by growers and vineyard workers to raise such grapes. The temporal tensions induced by botrytis shattered not only the delicate translation of sugar time into sidereal time but also the conversion of photosynthetic production into exchange-value.

Examining these catastrophic devaluations both of wine grapes and of human labour makes it all too clear that while the metabolic work performed by working plants such as grape vines can sometimes play an indispensable part in generating capitalist value, these plants – like human workers – do not produce value *alone*. Their ability to do so is contingent upon delicate apparatuses of time-reckoning, measurement and translation which can, under the right circumstances, transform rising sugar concentrations into dates and times. Yet it is also conditioned by, and subject to disruption from, metabolic entanglements with microbes and micro-climates which hold the potential to disturb these fragile temporal translations. Should these multi-species vineyard rhythms become alien to the techniques of abstraction and commensuration which render both time and value fungible then the work performed by plants, and the material transformations which they effect, can easily become decoupled from the sidereal time which organizes capitalist ab-stract labour. In the process the ability to valorize materials dissipates, rendering the labours of both vines and human workers as worthless as botrytised grapes rotting on the vine.

Conclusions

Early in this chapter I asked in what sense beings as seemingly passive as plants might be considered to labour, and to produce value, within contemporary cap-italist economies. In response I have argued that working plants engage actively in value-producing labour within settings such as The Company because they are, at least in these contexts, empowered to contribute to the generation and reckon-ing of *time*. Close observation of work in The Company's vineyards illustrated that vegetal metabolic processes such as photosynthesis, as measured through changes in the material composition of grapes, define the pace and the seasonal rhythm of labour for human viticultural workers. Mediated through measurements and forecasts of sugar accumulation, the vines' metabolic activities may stretch, com-press and rearticulate the tasks and schedules of vineyard workers and harvesting contractors. They thus choreograph human labour into rhythms of productive ac-tion that transform unripe grapes into palatable and saleable wines. Vines may not themselves engage in the "free, conscious activity" which defined productive labour for Marx (1988 [1844]: 76), but they nevertheless partake in capitalist valorization processes through calling forth (or holding back) such activity among their human co-workers.

This argument disturbs the self-referential circuit of capitalist time- and value-commensuration posited by orthodox Marxist political economy, which positions commodified human labour-time itself as the sole measure of the abstract value which underwrites commodity exchange. However, it does not attribute any in-nate capacity for value production to working plants such as grape vines. Instead it implies that these plants' value-producing propensities are constituted through and contingent upon time-reckoning technologies such as Baume testing, which render task-specific rhythms that arise through productive engagement between humans and plants convertible into (and capable of patterning) the sidereal time which organizes the capitalist valorization processes performed by harvesting contractors and winery workers. As the previous section illustrates, if this translation of temporalities should falter then the more-than-human labour processes organized through it will lose their power to produce value. Yet breakdowns in temporal coordination such as those induced by botrytis infections do not simply prevent the material transformations effected through *vegetal* labour from producing capitalist value. They can also rob the labour of winemakers and vineyard workers of its capacity to transform grapes into saleable wines, suggesting that the value-producing capacities of human labour are (at least in this setting) as contingent upon the mediation of these time-reckoning technologies as are those of working plants.

This analysis does not imply that there is no difference between the work performed by humans and the labours of working plants (see Battistoni 2017; Palmer 2021). Instead, identifying that the activities of humans and plants alike become productive of capitalist value only when the transformations that they engender come to order the passage of time shifts the grounds of debate over whose work may valorize materials and thus qualify as productive labour. For this argument implies that the capacity to effect the passage of time and to produce value is not apportioned once and for all to species which possess characteristics such as consciousness or metabolism, but is instead attributed contingently through the mediation of particular modes of time-reckoning and temporal translation. In so doing, it suggests that each way of reckoning time expresses a particular distribution of the capacity to produce value – one which endows certain agencies and forms of labour with the capacity to imbue materials with worth, but also renders others unproductive, inconsequential and ultimately worthless.

This observation positions the time-reckoning arrangements through which the activities of certain plants, and of other nonhumans, are incorporated into capitalist value production processes as a central site of enquiry and political problematization for posthumanist political economy scholarship. It implies that attending critically to the specificity, variety and fragility of the temporal apparatuses whose mediation renders the work of plants productive (or unproductive) offers a means of understanding how and why the toiling of some creatures comes to matter within, and to affect the organization of, capitalist economic formations while the labours of other nonhumans are devalued. Moreover, the account of value production outlined in this chapter implies that enquiry into the technologies and practices of time-reckoning which coordinate more-than-human labour processes may also explain how the work of some humans who toil with and alongside plants comes to be positioned as productive of value while other workers' efforts are dismissed as worthless. It thus opens up the possibility of comparing the ways in which different forms of both human and nonhuman labour come to be valued (or devalued) through contrasting time-reckoning practices, of developing a critical accounting of their elisions and exclusions, and of excavating the uneven economic formations which condense around different ways of keeping time.

In foregrounding the role of both interdependencies and tensions between the temporalities of human and nonhuman labour in value production, such an analysis adds nuance to calls for the work of nonhumans to be recognized within contemporary political economies, whether through payments for ecosystem services or through political struggles for nonhuman labour to be compensated with care (see Collard/Dempsey 2013; Battistoni 2017). For it incorporates a recognition that, just as the organization of industrial production processes around the sidereal temporalities of capitalist wage-labour has often disrupted animal and plant rhythms in ways that harm both nonhuman labourers and the ecologies that they inhabit, so valorization processes choreographed by nonhuman temporalities may expose human workers to considerable (and unequally apportioned) economic insecurity. As discussed above, while attunement to the metabolic rhythms of grape vines may yield commercial rewards for grape growers and wine producers, it also makes their products' worth contingent upon – and their enterprises vulnerable to economic disruption by – unpredictable environmental events and often imposes fragmented, unsociable and highly disruptive working patterns on their workers.

Both wage-labourers and the owners of vineyards are exposed to such devalorization events, yet their impacts are also differentiated not only according to the varying attachments to labour processes which attend unequal distributions of ownership but through the temporal logics of contemporary capitalist accumulation itself. The forms of time-economy characteristic of contemporary shareholder capital, with their focus upon the regular reporting of short-term returns to investors, are deeply implicated in pressuring firms such as The Company to reduce costs through minimizing investment in the expensive machinery involved in wine production and maximizing its utilization. In so doing, they play a prominent role in generating the chronic scarcities of harvesting equipment and winery processing capacity which places such acute pressure on workers to ensure the precise temporal coordination of grape harvesting and transportation (and thus renders these processes so vulnerable to disruption when different temporalities clash). Through drawing attention to such vulnerabilities and contradictions within the temporal arrangements which underlie value production within contemporary capitalism, exploring the work of plants (and of other nonhumans) critically might perhaps propel experimentation with alternative ways of keeping time. In so doing, it may contribute to fashioning time-reckoning techniques and timescapes which are less prone to devalue the labours of both human and nonhuman workers, and more predisposed towards the cultivation of inter-species care and solidarity.

Acknowledgements

I wish to thank John, Mark, Nathan and their colleagues at The Company whose generosity, hospitality and patience made this research possible. I am also grateful to the editors of this volume and to Emilie Letouzey for their insightful feedback on earlier drafts of this chapter, which improved the manuscript immensely. The research on which this chapter is based was supported under ESRC postgraduate studentship ES/G019576/1, with supplementary funding from Jesus College, Oxford.

SECTION III
Future-making with plants

Chapter 7 - Shady work: African mahogany (*Khaya senegalensis*), cyclones and green urban futures in Darwin, Australia

Jennifer Atchison

Research from across the physical and social sciences focusing on green infrastructure emphasises the role of trees and other plants in provisioning humans (Benedict/McMahon 2012). The expansive and multidisciplinary field of ecosystem services, for example, has inspired thinking about how trees and other plants might be brought into the discourse and the frameworks of capital in order to make more apparent their value and contributions to human health, wellbeing and quality of life (Coutts/Hahn 2015; Bayles et al. 2016). Such scientific assessments and valuations of the services that trees provide has helped to shift debates in subtle but important ways beyond the false choice of economy versus environment, and enabled decision makers to govern and make choices about biodiversity within cities, via accessible frameworks (Braat/de Groot 2012). They have also prompted a wider set of conversations suggesting that to make future cities habitable in the context of climate change, cities should be greener (Gill et al. 2007; Gaffin et al. 2012; Demuzere et al. 2014).

Explicit in many greening agendas is the link between urban trees and the provision of shade. In the tropical city of Darwin, Australia, calls to green the city are prompted by already high ambient temperatures which at times exceed 60°C (Thompson 2018a). Combined with high average humidity, there are real fears that parts of Darwin will soon become uninhabitable. Heat is becoming such a problem that it has prompted the Northern Territory Government and the city council to install shade structures along at least one main thoroughfare (Lawler 2018; Santamouris et al. 2018). The installation of constructed shade has not been without controversy in a city where trees are also being cleared for urban redevelopment and industrial expansion (Neild 2018). And such structures are not exactly viable alternatives for greater Darwin. Given the spatial area involved and the expense, trees remain the most viable option to green and to shade cities, including Darwin.

As much as we might agree that shade is important, shade itself is not a straightforward thing; its changeable, ungraspable qualities render it as always something shifty, vague and indeterminate. Inherently related to and affective of materials, but not itself material, shade can be imprecise, dubious and incomplete. Edensor and Hughes (2019) have recently argued that shade is a critical part of how we see landscapes and how they are constructed. It reflects the "critical agency of light in landscape's vitality" and its interplay with surfaces allow us to perceive and distinguish everyday embodied visual experiences which "anchor us in place" (Edensor 2017: 617). Further, Edensor argues, our relationship with shade needs recalibrating since shade is value laden, hinting at the perceived negative qualities of darkness in urban areas and "the relationship between light and dark" (Edensor 2015: 423). Edensor's provocation to rethink the relationship between shade and value is significant in the context of contemporary climate agendas focused on increasing shade in urban areas, in the sense that shade may not necessarily or straightforwardly be a universal good. Likewise, the distribution of shade as something important for human health and wellbeing has important justice dimensions where it is unevenly distributed. But this provocation also raises the question of who or what does the work of shade provision, and does this matter?

Accounting for the different kinds of work that plants might do in relation to shade – how they might participate in or even push back in the doing of this work, or the new ways in which plants are being enrolled into systems of value and exchange to green and shade cities, are prescient questions at the centre of this volume. In relation to shade, trees and other plants are commonly understood in a vernacular, if not a technical sense, as having a role to play in providing for or contributing to human wellbeing in urban areas. But are they shade workers or labourers? If human frameworks for labour and economy are utilised, are trees also active participants in a work force, and what would it mean to think of them in this way? Conversely, as this volume asks us to consider, might the definitions of labour and work both need rethinking if we are to acknowledge multispecies worlds?

In this chapter, I consider urban trees as green infrastructure in the service of cities. The chapter is inspired by the material and political implications of agendas to get more plants into cities, but also by the contradictions presented by the risky business of living with urban trees and the way they complicate, stimulate, and provoke the life of the city in both mundane and profound ways. In this regard, it is also motivated by efforts to tell stories about trees as part of the history and development of cities. Specifically, I examine Darwin's changing relationship with African mahoganies (*Khaya senegalensis*) in the context of increasing urban heat effects, which demand more shade for human wellbeing, but also recurrent and increasingly severe tropical cyclones, which challenge historical planting choices and present planting dilemmas. Thinking through the implications of tree shade as shady work, I explore the idea that plant work and plant labour are vital but also precarious – more-than-human labour constituted by the material world, but which sits somewhere indeterminate in the scheme of work and labour geographies, not quite graspable.

The shadow work of trees

Interrogating work and labour has been a core and expansive project of human geography and the social sciences for decades (Castree et al. 2004). Broadly, themes have included the relation of work within and beyond capitalism, the uneven distribution of work and labour with attention to inequality and justice, and the affective agencies of those who work (Castree 2007). More recent scholarship has turned to the relationship between work and ecological crisis, responding to compelling evidence of radical environmental change and the multiple ethical dimensions and troubling trajectories of who works for what ends (Barca 2015; 2017). Unpaid work, precarity, forced migration in the pursuit of work, as well as new forms of exploitation, saturate the contemporary time/spaces of work in the context of climate and extinction emergencies. But there are also critical stories of more diverse and heterogeneous economies beyond.

For instance, Carr and Gibson (2016; 2017) have examined the geographies of making, drawing on feminist scholars. Their consideration of making as embodied and central to identities, legacies and futures challenges economic orthodoxies of work and labour in capitalist economies as simply the means by which stuff is generated, towards multiple ways of working with materials and sustaining lives. Even within the industrial heart of cities for example, can be found everyday micro-scale alternatives, such as craft and thrift, which open up new possibilities of responding to volatility. Likewise, Cretney (2017), drawing on Gibson-Graham, has examined how places are rebuilt after disaster and how disasters might provide possibilities for re-creating or re-negotiating the norms by which societies operate. In her hopeful treatment of disaster recovery, rights and responsibilities might be reframed outside the confines of western economic standards for growth.

The abstraction and commodification of nature has been a key part of theorising capitalist economies (Battistoni 2017; Moore 2018), meaning that for the most part, the workers or labourers in question have, nearly always, been human. This is not to say that nature does not work, but that, as posited by Mazen Labban (quoted in Kay/Kenney-Lazar 2017: 300) a distinction has commonly been made about the power of that labour as value in the market. The extent to which labour may have been recognised as more-than-human has often relied on metabolic analysis in the production and disposal of energy and waste, and yet as Kay and Kenney-Lazar note (2017: 307), Marxian approaches, upon which many analyses rely, are often limited with respect to 'the matter of nature'. However, cultural scholars have recently taken up questions of unrecognised and undervalued nonhuman labour and animal work against the long history of these concepts as the effort of humans alone (Colombino and Giacarria 2016; Barua 2017, 2019; Huber 2018; Narotzky 2018; Dashper 2019). Drawing from Haraway, Barua (2019: 653), for example, asserts that nonhuman work cannot be thought through human frameworks, offering descriptions of animal labour as "porous, performed relationally with a suite of other actors crosscutting animal-human divides". His typology of nonhuman work as metabolic, ecological and affective points toward the hidden exploitations of capitalism, whilst also illuminating that not all nonhuman work is part of capitalist modes of production.

While Barua has recently provided a lexicon for exploring and re-examining both how nature-capital relations have come to be and also how they might be reconfigured, the multiplicity of human-nature relations, more-than-human agencies and "changing material realities" require new ways of thinking about the "diverse living beings which push back" (Kay/Kenney-Lazar 2017: 307). At the centre of this volume are plants, photosynthetic organisms whose unique capacity to materialise the sun's energy underpins their success and utility in multiple worlds of relations. Plants are fundamental to the functioning of all terrestrial ecosystems and have also played key roles in the construction of contemporary economic systems. For example, wheat stored as grain can be moved and exchanged, facilitating its transformation into fungible, material commodity and enabling stock to be valued and traded across space and time (Head et al. 2012). Such material contributions to economies are now more commonplace, but accounting for plants as organisms which 'push back' is not simple. For example, while plants as providers feature prominently in recent attempts to value or recognise unrealised ecosystem services which might also benefit people – for example in the provision of recreational and aesthetic value or the mitigation of pollution or of heat in the form of shade (Coutts/Hahn 2015) – plants, and the roles envisaged for them, often remain passive.

In placing plants into contemporary debates about the place and nature of more-than-human work, I am inspired here by the recent work of Sonja Dümpelmann (2019) and her compelling empirical account of the way street trees have been backgrounded, and yet have also been vital material and discursive forces within urban life. According to Dümpelmann, to situate trees is to see them: how they are contested and examined; how they join in acts of displacement and social justice activism; how they partake in crisis and disaster, as well as within acts of national building. Even their death, she argues, "has saved them from becoming truly obsolescent in our cities and has enabled them to persist" (Dümpelmann 2019: 248). In sum, they are tenacious. Seeing trees, or bringing trees and other plants out of the shadows, to recollect Plumwood's (2008) notion of shadow places, reflects ongoing efforts within human geography and elsewhere explicitly to consider and account for the ways in which plants and their capacities make a difference to more-than-human worlds (Jones/Cloke 2002; Head et al. 2012; Head et al. 2015). Scholars have considered plants in diverse environments and contexts as active and consequential within and beyond their relations with humans (Head et al. 2015). In part, this emergent body of work is an effort to bring the diverse agencies of plants to light but it is also directed toward deconstructing a "false consciousness of place" (Plumwood 2008: 140), rematerializing the places that sustain capitalist societies such that the "illusions of our [human] independence of nature and the irrelevance of nature" (ibid: 142) are undone.

The contemporary interest in urban greening provides an opportunity to see and consider cities and the creation of liveable urban places as more-than-human work (Phillips/Atchison 2020). Returning to the questions of 'the work that plants do' and 'why this matters', in the following section I turn to the issue of shade and the critical need for more shade, particularly in tropical urban environments. To do this, I trace the controversy surrounding African mahoganies (*Khaya senegalensis*), cyclones and assessments of risk in the aftermath of tropical cyclones in Darwin. Drawing on analysis of media articles and arborist and government scientific reports tracing the tree destruction following Cyclone Marcus in March 2018, I consider the emerging difficulties of providing shade in Darwin in the context of recurrent tropical cyclones. African mahoganies have played a key role in rebuilding Darwin but are, more recently, problematized as risky objects.

African mahoganies in Darwin

According to Instone (2009: 827), Darwin is a place saturated in the "unconscious, subtle and pervasive reach of the frontier" and which is "reinventing itself as the new urban north". Concrete, durable surfaces and steel fences are the solid and indomitable face of settler frontier boundary making practices. They separate Indigenous, settler colonialist, migrant and refugee and mark out the territories of belonging and exclusion. In Instone's account, infrastructure performs a kind of relational work that implicates particular material relations between groups of people, and between those groups and nonhuman worlds. As physical material infrastructures, the built environment not only stands in the place of human work that might be done, such as the policing of boundaries, it also works to hold or fix in place particular white colonial visions for and narratives of Darwin.

So what of the green infrastructure? African mahoganies have been planted in Darwin since at least the mid-1950s but were planted in earnest after Cyclone Tracy – a category 5 event which struck on Christmas Eve 1974. The damage to vegetation from Tracy was significant and included defoliation, uprooting, limb fall and impact damage from flying debris. Scientific surveys conducted soon after suggested that trees were destroyers of property (Cameron et al. 1983). Significant damage to houses was attributed to trees, and the practice of parking caravans under trees contributed to their almost total destruction. However, tree work is not always as it first appears; trees could also protect property and the break provided by trees, including African mahoganies, was argued to have immobilised debris and reduced damage in key instances (Cameron et al. 1983: 101). Indeed, this was so obvious that it was suggested that had more vegetation been protected or left in the suburbs during their initial construction, the damage sustained in Darwin might have been reduced (Cameron et al. 1983).

The rebuilding of Darwin after Cyclone Tracy was, and in many ways continues to be, a key moment in the city's and nation's psyche, in terms of responding to disaster (West 2000). As Walters (1978: 59) recorded, the predominant response to the "catastrophic events wrought by nature" within rebuilding efforts took the form of the "engineered city". The reconfiguration of planning policy and building codes was fundamentally to change building practices and structural engineering requirements for high wind conditions (Walker 2010). But it also set the scene for the redesign of greenspace and the urban forest. As anthropologist Tess Lea (2014) records, the building of the new nearby satellite centre of Palmerston was one of the first Australian urban areas to be co-designed with entomologists:

> To reduce insect bites to tolerable levels (calculated as no greater than one bite per minute) they [entomologists] advised a network of mown parklands and shady trees on one side of arterial roads and a buffer of privately owned rural blocks on the other, creating open windswept areas that separated suburbs from breeding grounds. (Lea 2014: 97-98).

Lagoons were reconstructed and tree planting replaced cyclone-damaged scrub with shady, airy boulevards (Figure 7.1).

There was also specific attention given to the new tree species that were planted. A year after Tracy, D.A. Hearne wrote in *Trees for Darwin and Northern Australia* that the main considerations in selecting trees for the 'new Darwin' included habits of growth and form which could be "loosely defined [...] as erect, pendulous, columnar, spreading, mallee, fastigate or bushy" (1975: 1). A street tree, for example, should have a "clean, upright, narrow trunk, a shady ornamental crown [...] and perhaps a show of flowers" (ibid: 1). Amongst other species, African mahogany, a large tree growing to approximately 17-28 meters in height with "a dense crown of dark foliage" (ibid: 79), was planted in earnest. As Hearne noted, they were valued at the time for their quick growing potential, the perceived lack of maintenance they required, their drought and pest resistance, and their "most desirous feature" – a "large evergreen crown and the deep shade it creates" (ibid: 79). Mahoganies have a "round dense crown of dark green leaves" (ibid: 79);

underscoring the significance of this feature, mahoganies were commonly referred to as 'shade trees'.

Figure 7.1: Road and park verges deeply shaded by African mahoganies in Casuarina, Darwin, 2017. Although the shade of individual trees is also welcome, the broad and interconnected canopy of avenues and mass plantings link up to provide more continuous shade along thoroughfares and footpaths. Exposure to higher wind speeds through open spaces was also a factor contributing to the damage of many trees during Cyclone Marcus.

Image: Jennifer Atchison.

Many of the attributes Hearne noted in his volume contributed to the widespread success of African mahoganies in timber plantations across Northern Australia in the following decades, and much was learnt about how mahoganies had to be managed and monitored to ensure optimal timber growth (Nikles 2006). Records and accounts related to the urban tree plantings after Tracy are sparse, but it is likely, given what was learnt from forestry contexts, that the earlier predictions about the lack of maintenance required were premature. By the 2000s, many urban African mahoganies had grown to semi-maturity and were now very large trees; some were proving problematic. In one case brought to public attention in media coverage following the unexpected death of a man struck by a fallen limb in 2014, arborists called to the court to give evidence differed in their expert opinions. One put forward arguments that African mahoganies were more problematic to maintain in Darwin than in the African contexts he had worked (reported in Lawford 2016a). He perceived that they grew faster in Australia with unusually large and longer limbs, attributing this to Darwin's tropical climate (reported in Lawford 2016a), echoing other concerns that although they had provided the city with a fast treescape, they had "outgrown many of their locations" (quoted in Palin 2015). Another expert was quoted asserting that "pruning wasn't a viable option to remove the risks [...] because of the species characteristics" (quoted in Lawford 2016a). Further media coverage of the judicial inquiry also recorded that another arborist and a council staffer called to the court had specifically avoided describing mahoganies as dangerous (reported in Turner 2016). The coroner in the case described, with some annoyance, that extracting this description of mahoganies as dangerous, was like "extracting a sore tooth" (quoted in Turner 2016). This arborist had refused to concede the tree in question was the problem, arguing instead that the dangers related to a lack of pruning and maintenance rather than something inherently structural. The coroner found that despite the risks being previously known as early as 2006 due to a prior inquest, a regular maintenance and inspection program had not been put in place, and made specific recommendations that the Council make such provisions (reported in Lawford 2016b).

These discussions of tree risk and maintenance underscore how shade can become a form of plant work. First, the incidents above allow us to see beyond the ontological notation of mahoganies as shade, to a sense of shade being and becoming something trees have the capacity to make. As 'shade trees', mahoganies were assumed to be the thing that they do – to produce shade both deep and desirable, without human assistance. Yet over time, and as trees became very large, the production of shade and its value to people comes with increasing risks. As the provision of shade becomes precarious, it becomes more possible to see mahoganies separately from their shade, and shade as something produced rather than innate. Indeed, mahogany trees were only perceived to have provided safe shade when they were disciplined through maintenance. The controversies noted above thus also hint at a second condition of shade as work – the wider scope of labour beyond the tree required to produce quality shade. The tropical climate, for example, is important in producing and shaping trees as marked rainfall variability means that trees must often be watered through the dry season, at least until established. Human labour is also required in maintaining trees through pruning, trimming, inspecting for damage and attending to their health, and this interplay of plant growth and human activity is critical in order to render shade safe. Trees must be monitored and maintained to provide shade that services people. They must be reduced, controlled and managed in particular forms and expressions, indeed Hearne (1975: 79) had noted that they could be "lopped, pollarded or coppiced with no apparent ill affects". In other words, shade work without people is not reliable, uniform or consistent. This is often controversial in urban contexts when municipal authorities radically prune trees that shade suburban streets that intersect with above ground power lines. To work at shade and to be enrolled in the service of humans, African mahoganies had to be inspected and then shaped, ordered and restrained – without which they became risky, over and above the value of the shade they might otherwise provide.

The arrival of Cyclone Marcus in March 2018 as a category 2 event significantly amplified this situation, as controversy over African mahoganies erupted soon afterward. According to the Bureau of Meteorology, Marcus was the strongest cyclone to hit Darwin since Tracy in 1974 (BOM undated). Council reports noted damage to over 10,000 trees on public land alone (CODa undated) and that only 40 per cent of trees in the municipal area showed no damage (Clark et al. 2018). Although the post-cyclone scientific surveys showed that exotics as a broad category of introduced trees were more damaged than natives, this was not a universal feature, as particular natives were also highly susceptible and had been damaged. Concurrently, some introduced trees had performed very well. African mahoganies featured prominently in the follow-up scientific assessments; large semi-mature mahoganies had the highest rate of damage of any species and 66 per cent of these had significant damage to the point of complete uprooting (ibid). Mahoganies alone were estimated to have contributed to approximately 20 per cent of the total damage in financial terms (ibid).

However, it is also significant that the planting context was again seen to be crucial in relation to the severity of damage outcomes. For example, in council damage assessments, watering histories – the tendency for trees to have received frequent rather than deep watering – and soil profiles which differentially affected root ball development, were both identified as being influential with regard to the extent of damage (ibid). Planting situation and context were also noted. For instance, while narrow or small parks afforded protection and trees recorded less damage, trees in parks with large perimeter exposure to roads and open spaces, and increased exposure to the flow of air, recorded high rates of damage (ibid). City features including historical aspects of design to limit insect problems in the 1970s (noted in Lea 2014) may have contributed to increased wind speeds around trees subsequently increasing their susceptibility.

It is significant then that post-cyclone damage assessments after Marcus were accompanied by a rapidly changing public discourse and increasing rhetoric about the threat that mahoganies posed as a dangerous species. Articles from the same press that had initially referred to decades-old trees as 'victims' after the storm (reported in Williams 2018) quickly shifted; mahoganies became 'towering monsters' and a threat to critical infrastructure in an editorial opinion piece only five days later (NT News 2018). Mahoganies and other exotics feature prominently in nearly every media article following Cyclone Marcus and public commentators, such as those featured in the NT News (2018) highlight the description of African mahoganies as out of place, specifically 'unsuitable' (reported in Zwar 2018a). Related public media was more measured but emphasised that past planting choices were the mistakes of the past.

As the media shifted its attention to the category of species as a specific measure of risk, less obvious was the de-emphasis and omission of context and maintenance surrounding individual trees. Although in the scientific assessment "a large exotic tree (species not specified) growing in an irrigated park in saturated deep massive earths with minimal management" emerged as having the highest risk likelihood (Clark et al. 2018: 6), what seemed to surface in the public discourse and media coverage more broadly was quite simplistic messaging about the suitability or unsuitability of species and their incompatibility with seemingly fixed watering practices. While one councillor argued "you can't have a blanket rule and go out and cut down a species of tree" (quoted in Zwar 2018a), the Lord Mayor was re-emphasising the unsuitability of this African species in Australia, referring to their habit of shallow rooting in response to frequent watering (reported in Vanovac 2018). Tree maintenance – or rather the lack of it – was what had initially attracted Darwin to African mahoganies after Cyclone Tracy and yet the lack of maintenance, and the lack of appropriate watering regimes that would come over time to undermine root development, were key risk factors. In the weeks that followed, the city council responded to the issue of maintenance responsibility by focusing on efforts for recovery, producing a tree re-establishment list including a not-to-be planted list (CODb undated) – featuring mahoganies as a key problem species.

Clearly, the material presence and work of trees is spatially and temporally contingent, but this is not necessarily how it is imagined. Scientific and arborist assessments both pre- and post- Cyclone Marcus consistently identified site contextual factors and the multiple human and more-than-human labours of maintenance (watering history, soil profile, positioning and pruning) as being significant in determining how unsafe specific trees might be. Spatial or even temporal contingency might seem like a truism for all plants, however, following Cyclone Marcus certain tree species, African mahoganies in particular, came to be perceived as inherently risky regardless of context. They came to be understood as 'out of place' – detached or unhinged from the perceived 'proper' native African context and as growing with unusually heavy and therefore unstable limbs. In other words, they were re-categorised as risky regardless of context and the historically situated position of their growth. No mention was made of the protection that trees, including mahoganies, had afforded during Marcus, as had been done post Tracy; site conditions and individualised tree histories are present in analysis but disappear from the discourse. In this regard, the work of trees might not be so different from labour geographies more broadly, in that the spatialities of their labours articulate a politics of belonging but that the plight and conditions of workers often disappear from view.

Recasting tree work

In this chapter I have sought to bring to light the work of African mahoganies in the remaking of Darwin post cyclone Tracy. Arguably, seeing African mahoganies in this way moves us forward in terms of recognising their agency in contributing to liveability and wellbeing. Their shade was critical in making the city habitable for people, and other nonhumans, as much as the new buildings and infrastructures that were gradually rebuilt. As maturing trees, mahoganies worked, albeit quietly in the shadows, providing deep and welcome relief for the decades in between the two cyclones. In this sense, their shade was valued in that it allowed the city and its inhabitants to get on with new life and living. As living infrastructure, these trees served in the fundamental transformation of the city into the 'new Darwin', taking expression in different spatial configurations as city blocks and backyards were rebuilt. Ironically, however, it is the controversies over particular mature trees and the event of the second cyclone – Marcus – that brings their work to light and provides a different lens on the work of African mahoganies and the work of trees in city scapes more broadly. As fallen trees, African mahoganies were a significant part of the discourse of Cyclone Marcus as disaster; statistically they incurred significant damage, and certainly they fell from grace in public and expert acceptance as an appropriate urban tree. This example of the changing relationship between African mahoganies and the city of Darwin offers us at least three implications for thinking about the more-than-human work or labour of plants which together I argue, speak to the idea of tree work as *shady* – never straightforwardly perceived, reproducible or accepted.

First, the coproduction of tree shade, and the tendency of context to be overlooked, means that this labour is often imagined as replaceable, or even interchangeable. This is problematic. The very language of 'replanting' and 'regeneration' suggests that trees are switchable, interchangeable or substitutable in some way – easily replaced by planting new specimens of the same species, or even replaced with other species. Aside from the problem that this presents to the contribution that trees make to a material or relational sense of place, the danger of thinking about trees as replaceable is that the multiple ecological worlds and the multiple labours of plants in the service of others are overlooked. The subterranean work of root ball development and its stabilizing effects in association with watering histories is just one example of the unseen, and under-appreciated, work of relevance. A more distributed sense of plant agency (Marder 2012; Head et al. 2015) and indeed labour itself (Clark 2014) is required to capture the affective dimensions of this work across time and space. Replanting as replacing shade is a simplification that ignores the time frames involved; perhaps upwards of ten years is required to recover an equivalent canopy cover to that lost to Marcus (reported in Ashton 2019). Evidence has also emerged that due to widespread changes to habitats in northern

Australia, the remaining African mahoganies in Darwin are now critical roosting sites for raptors including the endangered Brahminy kite (Riddell 2017). These multiple dimensions of tree work are not immediately replaceable and pose governance and planning challenges to interests seeking to remove every mahogany tree from the city.

Second, recalling Hearne (1975), although the preferred attributes of trees may have shifted in Darwin, the selection of species post Marcus is still influenced, habitually, by an imaging of the future shape and structure of trees, as though they might simply be put in their place, as though they will perform, conform, and occupy a space irrespective of context, time and the care work it takes to maintain them. The work and labour of mahoganies has been partly recognised, but it is also understood to be entirely replaceable, recalling Ernwein's (2020) notion of plants as the undead. Such treatment of trees is predicated on a view of plants as objects, structures, material services or devices detached from their social and cultural roots, detached from the connections, relations and politics they will inevitably make and remake beyond life and into death. Ongoing assertions that green infrastructure is good stand in contrast to the often risky and sometimes anxious relations that develop between people and plants, and overlook the specific nature of the work that trees do in context; in Perkins' (2007: 1160) terms, they overlook the "emergent contradictions based in the politics of labouring nature". This view of plants as green infrastructure is an attempt to seize and structure the future, and requires, I argue, a bio-politics that recognises and goes beyond the notion of disposable plant labour wrought in the form and function of plants as a platform for urban development, or a botanical recipe for the salvation of urban problems. Drawing on feminist notions of making and maintenance, as Carr and Gibson (2016; 2017) have done, might provide a productive way to examine such politics.

Third, trees and other plants are only perceived to labour when they are alive, if at all, and yet, echoing Perkins (2007) and Dümpelmann (2019), some of the most valued contributions from urban trees occur after death. For instance, lessons from elsewhere show that cyclones often produce decades worth of green waste in a day, and green waste infrastructure is now understood as a part of transforming critical infrastructure in adapting to increased cyclonic frequency (Thummarukudy 2012). Following Cyclone Marcus, dead trees also created work, opportunity, business and momentum – a material and bio-capital transformation (Colombino/Giaccaria 2016). Some three months after the cyclone, crews of workers were still clearing fallen trees, chipping mulch, repairing roofs and broken fences. Public art installations were being made where fallen mahoganies lay (reported in Thompson 2018b). An entire parking lot was being pulled up and resurfaced; everywhere the city was activity and repair. This slow and generative work beyond death is not readily attributable to any effort or intention by trees as we might perceive it, and yet it is the accumulation of their industry over time – the laying down of cellulose through the work of photosynthesis, and its contribution to the lives of others through decay – that persists and resists complete abstraction. A labour after death provides scope to consider and appreciate the material transformation of trees into timber, wood and waste, coproduced with human others, as also part of how they continue to work, akin to Barua's (2019) notion of metabolic work. In this instance, trees and other plants, through their material transformations, labour through temporal frames that challenge traditional notions of work's relationship to time.

As much as it is in critical need of shade, the city of Darwin is now in the process of detaching itself from African mahoganies. The city council wrote of Cyclone Marcus as an "arboreal cleansing process" (Clark et al. 2018: 6). As soon as ten months after the cyclone, it put forward an urban forest management plan aiming for natural canopy shade by 2030, re-invigorated through native plant sales (reported in Zwar 2018b; CODc undated); the trope of nativism is a persistent exclusionary device. While the problematic lack of tree maintenance was noted in post-cyclone reports and assessments, debate is ongoing over the selection of more appropriate species based on shape, size, aesthetics and the provision of shade, all against changing climatic conditions and increasing heat. Tension remains over the urgent need for shade and the desire for rapid growth, versus larger long-lived trees that provide greater canopy cover and biodiversity benefits over time. It is also unclear how governance preferences for stable species and community preferences for native plants might intersect with the reconstitution of Darwin as a liveable tropical city into the future. And yet, removing remaining mahogany trees is proving both difficult and expensive; their ongoing presence in the life of Darwin continues. For now at least, it is clear that African mahoganies are still present – resistant and working in ways, as yet, unaccounted for.

Acknowledgments

An earlier version of this article was presented at the Nordic Geographers meeting in Trondheim, Norway, 2019, in a session titled the 'Politics and Places of Plants'. I thank participants at that session for constructive feedback. I also thank Professor Gunhild Setten and the Department of Geography, Norwegian University of Science and Technology, for hosting me while there and providing support. In pulling this volume together during the 2020 Covid-19 pandemic, I am grateful to the editors, who have provided immense care and academic collegiality.

Chapter 8 - Forest fuels: Vegetal labour and the reinvention of working forests as carbon conveyors in the US South

James Palmer

Forest covers 46 per cent, or roughly one million square kilometres, of the thirteen states that make up the US South region, stretching from Texas in the west to Virginia and North Carolina in the east, and from Kentucky in the north to Florida in the south (Oswalt et al. 2019). This is not only the most heavily forested region of the United States, but also the most intensively used for commodity production; around 70 per cent of all planted timberlands in the US are today found in this so-called "wood basket of the Nation" (ibid: 4). American forests have of course been viewed and utilised as economic resources for centuries, dating back at least to the time of the continent's colonisation. Yet today's forest landscapes have been radically transformed from those which greeted initial European settlers. Particularly from the late 19th century onwards, swathes of old growth forest were effectively liquidated, as a "wave of essentially extractive forestry" (Prudham 2005: 96) swept across the US, beginning in the Northeast but progressing quickly through the Great Lakes, down into the South and Southeast, and eventually up to the Pacific Northwest (Williams 1989). Where that old-growth has been replaced, especially in the South, it has often been with so-called 'working forest' stands planted and managed expressly for the purpose of producing wood-based commodities. Indeed, close to 30 per cent of all the world's forest products today come from the US, despite the country possessing just eight per cent of all forests globally (Oswalt/Smith 2014: 6). But if these products are emerging predominantly from working forests, what *kinds* of work are being performed by the trees that grow in them, and how exactly is that work linked to the production of particular forms of value?

In seeking to offer answers to these questions, this chapter will examine the rapidly expanding use of working forests of the US South to produce a commodity that was almost unheard of until the mid-2000s: compressed wood pellets for energy generation. The manufacture of such pellets – a combustible biomass fuel which can act as a renewable alternative to coal in the electricity sector – represents an increasingly significant component of forest-based economies in this region to-day. While American forests have been apprehended and used as energy resources in the past, the recent emergence of wood pellet manufacturing is unprecedented in at least two critical respects. Firstly, this new industry's growth is primarily a response not to any domestic demand for energy, but rather to policy incentives originating a long way outside the US, most notably in the UK and European Union (EU) (Abt et al. 2014).[1] Indeed, in 2018 almost five million metric tonnes of wood pellets were exported directly to the UK alone, where – as in many other Euro-pean countries – energy companies are entitled to receive government payments in exchange for burning such fuels (USDA Foreign Agricultural Service 2019).[2] In-ternational demand has grown so precipitously that the US South region now plays host to more than 20 industrial wood pellet mills, with an estimated combined out-put of close to ten million metric tonnes in 2017 (Oswalt et al. 2019: 47). Intensifying efforts to replace coal with bioenergy in the EU, Japan, South Korea and elsewhere, meanwhile, are driving the construction of still further mills, with seven new facil-ities expected to begin operating before 2025, adding a further five million tonnes to regional production capacity.

A second key difference between wood pellet manufacturing and historical ef-forts to exploit American forests as energy resources is this new industry's fun-damental entanglement with policy and political processes linked to the goal of climate change mitigation. As the chapter will show, the growing use of working forests in the US South to produce fuel is being legitimised not strictly by reference to compressed wood pellets' ability to generate renewable electricity, so much as by their broader potential to render electricity generation itself into a climate change mitigation tool. In that context, forests of the region are no longer being viewed merely as "nature's warehouse", offering up wood for various forms of tangible commodity production.[3] Much more ambitiously, these forests are being depicted as dynamic and productive entities wherein the very provision of wood promises,

---

1   There are no policies specifically encouraging or discouraging the burning of wood pellets to generate electricity in the US. Energy Information Administration figures indicate that less than one per cent of all US electricity was generated from burning wood or wood-derived fuels in 2019 (EIA 2020). In the UK, the equivalent figure was over ten per cent (BEIS 2020).

2   In the UK, the conversion of numerous formerly coal-fired electricity generation facilities to run on biomass fuels – most notably at Drax power station in Yorkshire – has been incen-tivised through two policy instruments: one enabling companies burning these fuels to sell tradeable certificates to other energy consuming organisations, and another guaranteeing a minimum price for the electricity generated through biomass combustion.

3   The term 'nature's warehouse' is paraphrased from a 1925 article authored by William B Gree-ley, Chief of the US Forest Service between 1920 and 1928 (Greeley 1925). Greeley specifically described virgin forests as "nature's undrained warehouses", in the context of growing con-cerns about timber famine. See Demeritt (2001) for a full discussion.

by itself, to render positive benefits to the global environment. Such changes are important not just because they enable new forms of economic value to be derived from working forests of the US South, linked both to energy production and to climate change mitigation. Just as crucially, the realisation of those new forms of value is being connected directly to the metabolic activities of trees, and specifically to the pace at which processes of photosynthesis and carbon sequestration can be made to take place.

Against this backdrop, this chapter draws on documentary analysis, data derived from site visits to wood pellet manufacturing facilities and forest stands in the US South conducted in 2018 and 2019, and interviews undertaken with 33 individuals – including industry representatives, expert scientific advisers and environmental campaigners – variously involved in debates about the socioecological impacts of forest-based bioenergy production in the region. The core argument of the chapter is that working forests of the US South are being quietly reinvented today not just as repositories of wood for tangible commodity production, but as finely tuned carbon conveyors whose contributions to climate change mitigation rely directly upon the enhancement of trees' metabolic efficiency. Moreover, building on recent posthumanist interpretations of Marx's labour theory of value (Battistoni 2017; Barua 2019; Krzywoszynska 2020), the chapter will contend that trees' metabolism – that is, processes of vegetal growth and carbon sequestration driven by photosynthesis – should ultimately be regarded as a form of labour that shapes these new forest-based economies. In the context of wider accounts of industrial forestry emerging from political ecology and resource geography, the present chapter's contribution is therefore to argue for a view of trees not simply as biological resources to be directed and shaped through various technoscientific and silvicultural means, but also as active players whose vegetal labour power serves to shape the remit of forest-based value production from the outset. While recognising the metabolic activity of trees as vegetal labour may seem unconventional, the chapter argues that this perspective can usefully serve to foreground the contingency and mutability of all resource-making practices undergirded by plant metabolism and growth (Palmer 2021). In so doing, the concept of vegetal labour may therefore serve as a starting point not strictly for optimising the sustainability of nature's ongoing integration into market relations, but rather for critiquing and redefining the fundamental values towards which nature-based production is oriented in working forests of the US South today.

"A forest is not like a mine": Loblolly pine trees as vegetal labourers

My first encounter with the working forests of the US South is hosted by Michael, an employee of a prominent company engaged in biomass wood pellet production in the region.[4] It is mid-April 2018, and Michael is driving us north along Louisiana State Highway 19, towards the border with Mississippi. Beyond lies a wood pellet mill employing roughly sixty workers, whose round-the-clock production serves to churn out around 500,000 metric tonnes of wood pellets each year. The forests which encircle the mill provide it with raw materials – or 'pellet furnish' – predominantly in the form of small-diameter tree stems, but also as wood chippings generated from the limbs and tops of larger trees as well. Between 100 and 120 lorry-loads of tree stems and chippings arrive at the mill on an average day; on busy days the figure can be closer to 180. It is midmorning and the weather is already unseasonably stifling and muggy. Mixed stands of tall trees – largely pines and assorted hardwoods – are pressed up against the highway for much of our journey. I've been forewarned that the sheer abundance of trees here will seem overwhelming. But my understanding of the landscape is rudimentary – I have no precise idea of how old these forests are, of the particular species that constitute them, or even of who owns them or how they are managed. Answers to the latter questions in particular are not likely to be straightforward either; not only are more than 80 per cent of the region's forests in private hands, but just one third of that proportion is owned by corporations – the vast majority of the rest is comprised of thousands upon thousands of small-scale, family-owned stands (Oswalt et al. 2019).[5] Despite the fragmented and enigmatic nature of the landscape however, I am reluctant to pose direct questions of my own at first; instead, what interests me is hearing Michael's own account of which are the right questions to ask about the increasing involvement of bioenergy producers in the region.

The first insight is that there will never be a single, correct vantage point from which to assess the health of the region's forests. The forces and processes involved – whether economic, environmental, political or cultural – are simply too dynamic for any given snapshot to tell a complete, unblemished story. That said, some forces and processes are more often overlooked than others. A particular bugbear, at least for Michael, is that assessments of the impacts of bioenergy production on forests often neglect to consider how the forest is itself altered through its enrolment into particular production networks and, by extension, economic markets. In making use of a forest, in other words, one does not simply deplete a reserve of inert matter,

---

4   Names of research informants have been altered to preserve anonymity. The subtitle phrase "a forest is not like a mine" is derived from Drax Group plc. (2017c).

5   By contrast, in the Pacific Coast region, 68 per cent of forests are under public management (Oswalt et al. 2019).

as one would a coal mine. Instead, one alters the already complex landscape of incentives within which tens of thousands of individual landowners must ultimately
take decisions – some autonomously, others on the advice of forestry consultants,
timber companies, or other actors – about how best to intervene in their stands,
about whether to fell or not fell particular trees at any given moment, and about
whether and how to replant, or even expand, their forests in the future. Unsurprisingly perhaps, for Michael, the use of forests tends continuously to improve them by
rendering them more productive and efficient. A healthy demand for forest products acts benignly, he explains, to "rejuvenate the forest cycle after cycle," bringing
benefits which "you don't get if you close the forest gate". Far better, in short, to
have industry keep the forest *as* forest, than to see tree cover lost altogether at the
hands of creeping urbanisation or shiny new commercial development projects.

To an extent, Michael's perspective is well-supported by historical data examining relationships between forest productivity and demand for wood-based products. According to one prominent US Forest Service report, for example, while the
South experienced population growth of 88 per cent between 1970 and 2010, and
disposable incomes more than doubled, the volume of timber products derived
from the region's forests also more than doubled in the same time period, even as
forested area itself underwent a moderate contraction (Wear/Greis 2012: 2). Today,
private forests of the South account for almost 60 per cent of all annual timber
removals taking place in the US (Oswalt et al. 2019: 9), and the region has long sustained diverse industries making use of this wood, whether by processing large-diameter saw-logs into furniture or construction materials, or by converting smaller-
diameter, so-called 'pulpwood' trees into paper, packaging, or other fibre-based
commodities. A key part of this story, and one well studied in forests elsewhere
in the US (Prudham 2003), has been the preferential cultivation of fast-growing
trees, and especially deliberate attempts to 'improve' the vigour of commercially
important species through industrial programs based on selective breeding. Accordingly, old-growth Southern forests dominated by the longleaf pine – thought
to have covered as much as 370,000 square kilometres at their height (Oswalt et al.
2012) – have not typically been replaced with stands of the same species, but rather
by dense plantings of a faster-growing, hardier relative: the loblolly pine (*Pinus
taeda*). Recent estimates suggest that there are around 22 billion individual loblolly
pine trees growing in the US South today, meaning that the species accounts, by itself, for approximately 20 per cent of all the region's above-ground biomass (Oswalt
et al. 2019: 28).

One may of course quite reasonably take issue with an account of industrial
actors – not just bioenergy producers, but the entire wood products sector – as the
gallant protectors of hundreds of thousands of square kilometres of forest. After
all, however impressive the figures, statistical accounts of historical productivity
gains still ultimately constitute a crude form of "reduction", in Demeritt's (2001:

439) terms, which ignores "everything about forests except the potential quantity of merchantable timber within them". Yet the seeds of an effective counterargument to this view might nonetheless be unearthed, this chapter contends, by scrutinising the nature of the ongoing work through which productivity is increased in working forests in greater detail. Within political ecology and resource geography, accounts of the nature-capital dynamic in industrial forestry have often regarded forests themselves as presenting a range of barriers or obstacles to seamless value production. Prudham (2005), for instance, suggests that capital must continuously grapple not only with forests' innate spatial extensiveness and requirement for land, but also with the bounded pace of tree growth, and the diverse material properties of trees themselves. Among the various strategies developed to overcome these obstacles (not just in forestry but in all nature-based industries), particular attention has been given to those which seek to enhance biological productivity itself, thereby achieving the so-called "real subsumption of nature" to capital (Boyd et al. 2001). In the forestry sector specifically, aforementioned industrial tree improvement programs constitute a classic example of this strategy, acting in effect to gradually tailor the genetic profile of specific trees and thus make them "work harder, faster, and better" over time (Boyd et al. 2001: 564). Yet this chapter contends that there are additional techniques by which nature's "real subsumption" has historically been achieved in industrial forests, operating not at the level of genetics, but rather at the level of the forest landscape itself.

Some of these techniques are certainly more rudimentary than others. As Michael explains en route to the Mississippi wood pellet mill, native hardwood species, such as oak, hickory, gum and maple, "come back in all the time" across much of the US South – the region's soils tending to be rich with their residual seed stock – and so must be kept continuously in check if landowners are to successfully "hold things in this pine position". Yet if loblolly pine is to excel, and not merely prevail against competing species, there are also subtler forms of work to perform. A visit to a recently thinned forest stand serves to illustrate the point well. Here Michael and I have been joined by Belinda, a former Mississippi Forest Service employee who now works in the wood pellet manufacturing industry. As background for what I am about to see, Belinda explains that working loblolly pine forests are typically over-planted with many more trees than can be supported through to full saw-log size; after ten or twelve years of rapid growth, when the trees are beginning to encroach upon their neighbours, the stand is thinned out – this not only generates intermediate income for the landowner (in the form of small-diameter roundwood and other material which can be sold to pulp or wood pellet mills), but also leaves the remaining trees with greater quantities of space and light to exploit, thereby maximising their growth. In stands which are thinned effectively, those loblolly pines which remain will grow into larger and better-formed individuals, with the ultimate reward being the production of final raw materials – in the form of large-diameter roundwood bound for saw-mills – capable of commanding the highest possible prices on the local market. It is worth emphasising that the designation of a tree's 'full' or 'final' size in this context is determined entirely by the needs of industrial production processes, and not by the innate limits of loblolly pine growth *per se*. Pines harvested after 25 or 30 years for saw-logs can often be 30 metres tall, but the trees have been known to live for over 200 years, and to grow to heights of around 50 metres in exceptional cases (Baker/Langdon 1990).

Figure 8.1: A loblolly pine stand where thinning has been enacted later than would have been ideal, April 2018, Mississippi.

Image: James Palmer.

The stand of trees that Belinda and Michael have taken me to see was thinned a few weeks prior to our visit, but is publicly owned and therefore not being managed intensively for timber production (Figure 8.1). The loblolly pines it contains nonetheless appear healthy and, at least to my untrained eye, already very large. My hosts, however, quickly identify two flaws; first, the spacing between the remaining trees is inconsistent, and second, the pines' live crowns – the upper portion of the tree playing host to needle leaves where photosynthesis takes place – are smaller than they should be for trees of this height. The diagnosis is unequivocal; the stand was almost certainly thinned later than would have been ideal, after the point at which 'crown closure' – where tree tops merge to form an unbroken canopy – had already occurred, and the trees' growth rates had thus been suppressed by excessive competition with their neighbours. While the thinning operation has now reduced that competition and restored sunlight to the forest floor, the remaining trees nonetheless lack what Michael calls "a big enough engine" to "achieve full saw-log size". For my own part, it is not until I have the opportunity to visit other, more intensively-managed working forest stands that these inadequacies – at least from the perspective of efficient saw-log production – are brought into sharper relief. In the corporate-owned stand shown in Figure 8.2 for example, located in North Carolina, the recently-thinned loblolly pines are not only more evenly and generously spaced, but also possess denser and more voluminous live crowns, and find themselves less encumbered by interloping hardwood species (marked by lighter coloured, broader leaves).

Figure 8.2: A recently thinned stand of loblolly pines in North Carolina, May 2019.

Image: James Palmer.

My initial visit to Mississippi is notable not only for the thermodynamic metaphor deployed by Michael to describe the function of the live crowns of the loblolly pines around us, casting them in effect as engines putting solar energy to work. It is also revealing in that it highlights mutual interdependencies between the complex, non-uniform growing dynamics of trees as they play out in real-world forests, and the forms of human labour which are brought to bear on those trees in pursuit of effective stand management and, ultimately, value maximization. Belinda and Michael are both adamant – there is much more to thinning than simply entering the forest and slashing down a few trees. Instead, this is a skilled form of labour that relies upon "affective ways of knowing nature" (Peltola/Tuomisaari 2015: 1), demanding not only a clear sense of when the moment is right to thin, but also a close attunement to the spatiality of the interactions in which trees are engaged with each other, as well as a "very good feel" for how decisions about which trees to remove and which to leave in place will carry forwards over subsequent years. Word of mouth thus plays a crucial role in enabling landowners across the region to procure the services of forestry professionals who can be trusted to thin their forests astutely, and not to do a substandard job.

By examining the intricacies of thinning it becomes clear that efforts to enhance the overall productivity of working forests involve not only working upon loblolly pines (whether by altering their genetic characteristics, or simply by cutting them down), but also working *with* these trees as dynamic, living entities. Far from being able to plant, thin and harvest trees according to whim, the forms of human labour brought to bear upon any given forest stand are unavoidably shaped by the situated performances of trees themselves – that is, by the specific temporalities and spatialities of the vegetal metabolic activity and growth that the trees exhibit in situ. That the metabolic performances of trees fundamentally shape processes of value production in industrial forestry – entwining trees and humans effectively in a "multidirectional process of enrolment" (Perkins 2007: 1156) – is a fact quite unrelated to the recent emergence of wood pellet manufacturing in the US South, of course. Yet, as the next section will show, the attribution of value to forest-based bioenergy is distinct from other forest product industries in that it is related not just to the amount or quality of timber produced within working forests, but also to the work that trees do to sequester carbon dioxide while they are growing. Tree metabolism, in short, takes on a new role in forest-based bioenergy economies – responsible no longer just for producing wood, but also for altering the composition of the global atmosphere. In light of this shift, silvicultural practices like thinning can be interpreted not strictly as efforts to overcome innate 'obstacles' or 'barriers' presented by nature, but rather as attempts to instantiate more synergistic *working* relationships between trees and humans, where both the former and the latter are explicitly acknowledged as sources of labour power. Moving to recognise and name trees as vegetal labourers may be perturbing to conventional views of labour as an exclusively human capacity, dependent upon intentionality and preconception (Barua 2017; Kallis/Swyngedouw 2018), but it is not merely a conceptual move. Rather, as the remainder of the chapter will seek to outline, accepting the idea of vegetal labour may itself be vital to illuminating the wider, political implications of wood pellet manufacturing for broader shifts in societal understandings of forests and their potentials, particularly in the context of climate change.

From "nature's warehouse" to dynamic carbon conveyor: Reinventing the Southern working forest

While techniques like thinning have been a silvicultural staple in the US South region for decades, until recently their principal function was to furnish forest product industries concerned with tangible commodity production with larger quantities of better quality wood feedstocks. The success of thinning operations is ultimately to be judged, from this perspective, by the extent to which they enhance the ability of multiple forest product industries, with diverse resource input requirements, to derive value from the vegetal productivity of the same stand of trees. And indeed, over the course of the second half of the 19th century, landscapes of the US South have been characterised by an abundance of both sawmills and papermills, the built hallmarks of two distinct but equally thriving industries, predicated on the availability of large-diameter saw-logs on the one hand, and smaller-diameter pulpwood, as well as other low-value forestry residues, on the other. The global financial crisis of 2008 and its associated recession, however, saw a steep downturn in rates of house building, and subsequently in demand for high-grade construction timber (Hodges et al. 2011). The rise of e-commerce and broader demographic shifts, meanwhile, has seen demand for conventional paper products decline significantly. The impacts of these last changes in particular – both in the sense of mill closures and job losses, but also reduced demand for the kinds of small-diameter roundwood typically extracted during thinning operations – would appear nothing if not propitious for the newly-emergent bioenergy industry. And, perhaps unsurprisingly, while there has recently been some consolidation of pulpwood-based manufacturing facilities (as demand for cardboard packaging and other fibre-based commodities grows to partly offset declines in conventional paper production), wood pellet manufacturers have not been shy to point to a keenly felt need for economic revitalization – in at least *some* parts of the US South – when underscoring the benefits they purport to bring to the region as a whole (Drax Group plc. 2017*a*).

Even where it has occurred however, the apparently straightforward shift from paper production to wood pellet manufacturing does not quite represent a like-for-like swap in all respects. Certainly, both industries generate much-coveted employment opportunities, and the kinds of feedstocks arriving at pellet mills do overlap almost perfectly with those that would in the past have arrived more frequently at mills producing paper. The precise pathways through which the bioenergy industry's use of those feedstocks serves to generate value however, are more complex, and distinct, from those which would have applied in the economy of paper manufacture. At the most fundamental level, these differences arise from the industry's discursive positioning of wood pellets as a resource commodity capable not only of meeting global demand for energy, but also of responding to environmental and political imperatives, particularly in the UK and EU contexts, for the fulfilment of that demand to also contribute positively to climate change mitigation. As a result, value generation in the wood pellet economy relies not strictly upon optimising working forest stands to produce the greatest possible quantity of saleable raw materials, but rather on optimising them to sequester the greatest possible volume of carbon dioxide from the atmosphere.

With this imperative in mind, wood pellet manufacturers operating in the US South region must do more than simply demonstrate the ability of their industry to slip, almost unnoticed, into a pre-existing industrial forestry regime, thereby further perpetuating the well-oiled symbiosis of manufacturing industries with a taste for smaller- and larger-diameter roundwood respectively. Instead, they must demonstrate why that regime of production is itself more effective, as a means of enabling working forests to contribute to climate change mitigation, than alternative forms of management predicated around less intensive or more infrequent harvesting, or simply the active protection of forests from industrial use altogether. Yet, somewhat paradoxically, industry actors do not pursue this objective through recourse to official carbon accounting methodologies for bioenergy production. Carbon accounting in forestry contexts is already notoriously contestable in any case – not least because the counterfactual scenarios against which the effects of specific interventions must be compared cannot themselves be empirically verified (Carton/Andersson 2017). But in the case of bioenergy specifically, the legitimacy of such accounting has been undermined further still by a regulatory insistence, enshrined in EU law, that combustion emissions can safely be counted as zero, on the assumption that they will be cancelled out by further plant or tree growth in the future (European Union 2018).[6] In light of the urgency with which meaningful greenhouse gas emissions reductions must be achieved if 'dangerous' levels of climate change are to be avoided before the end of this century, there has been particular dismay in the scientific community that current regulatory frameworks incentivise all forms of bioenergy production equally, despite the fact that some – particularly those predicated on forestry – might well generate an effective "carbon debt" which could take several decades to eradicate through subsequent tree growth (Searchinger et al. 2018: 2; see also Schulze et al. 2012).

Acutely conscious of this controversy, bioenergy interests operating in the US South have therefore – in seeking to affirm the climate benefits of their activities in the region – tried to turn the focus of debate away from calculative technologies of carbon accounting, and back towards the on-the-ground, metabolic activities of trees themselves. At the heart of this alternative approach lies the establishment of a moral economy of vegetal life which, crucially, distinguishes not between trees

---

6   Annex VI of the EU's Renewable Energy Directive declares that "emissions of CO_2 from fuel in use [...] shall be taken to be zero for biomass fuels" (European Union 2018).

according to the volume of carbon dioxide that they physically hold in place (stored up in the form of wood), but rather according to the ongoing rate at which they draw carbon dioxide down from the atmosphere over time. According to this moral economy, younger loblolly pine trees, whose relative growth rates – and hence their relative rates of carbon sequestration – are greater than those of more established trees, come to be regarded as more virtuous and more beneficial for climate change than their larger, more mature counterparts, explicitly on the basis of their superior capacity for metabolic work. Paraphrasing Marx (1976 [1867]), such trees might be said to appeal to bioenergy capital because they help to reduce the 'climate change mitigation necessary labour time' of the working forest as a whole. As one energy company, the UK's largest consumer of wood pellets produced in the US South, explains, "older trees will have more carbon stored (after a 'childhood' spent absorbing it), but if these are not harvested [...] their carbon absorption plateaus" (Drax Group plc. 2017b). Consequently, a forest playing host to "a steady-stream of CO_2-hungry young trees" is depicted as innately more advantageous for climate change than one populated by larger but ultimately more moribund vegetal lifeforms (Drax Group plc. 2016). And the ultimate proof of bioenergy's climate benefits will thus be found, the argument goes, not in any lofty greenhouse gas life cycle analysis or similar calculative methodology, but rather in the more tangible, and hence verifiable, existence of vegetal lifeforms metabolising – indeed, working – that much harder for capital than they were before.

What counts most about bioenergy production from this perspective is thus not strictly its distinct carbon footprint, measured in isolation from those of other industries making use of forest resources. Rather, what is to be welcomed is the ability of that industry to incentivise the optimisation of a set of working arrangements – or what Alyssa Battistoni (2017) would term a hybrid labour regime – predicated upon dense overplanting, vigorous initial tree growth, and astute, well-timed thinning. To understand the benefits of forest-based bioenergy, in short, one must grasp the dynamics of the working forest as a whole, and not merely the specific tree-harvesting and manufacturing processes associated with biomass wood pellet production. Industry actors, accordingly, have sought to defend their activities in the US South not simply by explaining the various stages of bioenergy production, but by positioning those activities as a harmonious component of the broader life-cycle of the working forest itself, depicting it in effect as a finely-tuned, almost self-perpetuating system for producing wood and sequestering carbon dioxide. Under this view, a better-calibrated hybrid labour regime brings benefits to the global climate by enabling working forests more efficiently to convey carbon dioxide out of the atmosphere and into the form not only of biomass wood pellets, but a whole array of other commodity forms as well, including items as diverse as tissue paper, cardboard boxes, roof beams and writing desks. The forest, in other words, constitutes a valuable climate change mitigation tool not because of its ability to function as a gradually accumulating carbon sink, but rather because of its capacity to act as a vigorous, high-throughput carbon conveyor.

Despite being a longstanding silvicultural practice then, in the hands of the bioenergy sector well-timed thinning gains the capacity to add use value not only to those trees which it leaves in place to continue growing in working forests of the US South (by enabling them to maximise their own potential growth rates and eventually become larger, better-quality sawlogs). It also becomes a means of adding surplus value to those trees which are removed and converted into wood pellets themselves, since those pellets come to be understood – by investors and policy-makers[7] – not merely as tangible energy carriers, but also as material signifiers of an increase in the overall work rate of the forest carbon conveyor from which they were derived. The very existence of biomass wood pellets, in other words, can from this perspective be regarded as evidence of the increased efficiency of other forms of commodity production based upon working forests of the US South as well, and thus of an increase in the rate at which carbon dioxide is locked up in those other commodities, existing *elsewhere*. One important consequence of this view, of course, is that it effectively circumvents debates about the 'true' carbon footprint of forest-based bioenergy, by insisting that the climate change impacts of wood pellet manufacturing cannot meaningfully be disentangled from those of the wider production system that animates the working forest – the socioecological whole must be understood, in short, as greater than the sum of its parts. At a more fundamental level however, this approach also acts subtly to normalise particular ideas about how forests – and perhaps, how vegetal life more broadly – might best contribute to climate change mitigation efforts, centred most obviously around the notions that hard work, efficiency and productivity are environmentally benign and virtuous achievements. In this context, the affordances of the concept of vegetal labour – as an idea which appears, on the surface at least, to reinforce logics of work, efficiency and productivity – demand more sustained and critical interrogation.

The ends of vegetal labour: Towards post-work forest futures?

What ends, and whose interests, are ultimately served by contending that the metabolic activity of loblolly pine trees – that is, their continual photosynthesis, growth, and carbon dioxide sequestration – might usefully be recognised not

---

7   Policy mechanisms such as those described in footnote one effectively acknowledge this surplus value by financially rewarding energy providers for burning biomass fuels. Drax Group plc., owner of the UK's largest power station, received a total of around £900 million of public funds in 2019 explicitly in exchange for using wood pellets to generate electricity (Drax Group plc. 2020).

merely as a natural biological process, but as a form of labour in its own right? Certainly the purpose cannot be to insist that all forms of labour undertaken by humans can also be performed by plants; emotional and other immaterial forms of labour especially would seem to be far more difficult to ascribe to nonhuman workers (Gill/Pratt 2008).[8] Nonetheless, at least where the vital capacities of both human and vegetal lifeforms to "change the form of matter" (Marx 1976 [1867]: 133) are concerned, the concept of vegetal labour compels us to leave human exceptionalism out of our efforts to parse the various "living potentials that capital parasitizes upon in its quest to expand and reproduce" (Barua 2019: 656). Indeed, since for Marx labour should properly be understood not as a thing, but rather as a relational, metabolic process linking nature and society (Robertson/Wainwright 2013), perhaps the more fundamental theoretical insight afforded by the concept is that plants' potentials are never brought into contact with fully formed economic processes (whether in forestry, agriculture, or other industries reliant on vegetal activity). Rather, those potentials – as a form of labour – fundamentally co-constitute the realm of the economic from the outset.

Within analyses of the political economies of food and energy provisioning specifically, an advantage of the concept of vegetal labour is that it can "productively collapse" (Krzywoszynska 2020: 231) the conventional distinction between (natural) resources and (human) labour, thereby promoting an assessment of capital's exploitative tendencies which pays no heed to species boundaries. Indeed, a move to scrutinise more closely the terms under which nonhuman lifeforms – whether loblolly pine trees, dedicated energy crops, or even soil biota – are put to work by capital, is arguably long overdue in an era characterised not only by ongoing efforts to ramp up forest-based bioenergy production, but also by influential scientific, policy and practitioner discourses advocating the potential benefits of ecological intensification in agriculture (Kleijn et al. 2019), and of 'nature-based solutions' to a range of environmental challenges in other fields as well (Kotsila et al. 2021). In this broader context, the act of labelling the metabolic activities of plants and trees as vegetal labour – rather than as ecosystem services or a form of natural capital – is more than a glib metaphorical shift. To reduce plants' capacities to mere ecosystem services is after all to subordinate the vegetal world tamely to the perpetuation of existing forms of economic organisation, while to insist that plants are a form of capital positions them as just one among many "materialised forms" of value in motion, without questioning the terms on which value itself comes to be defined (Marx 1976 [1867]; Postone 1993). By contrast, the idea of vegetal labour

---

8   That said, one might argue that in certain economies (such as tourism or carbon offsetting markets), value production is achieved partly through the enrolment of the aesthetic properties of forests into spectacular images designed to generate demand. Whether this can be said to constitute "immaterial labour" on the part of forests is a moot point.

brings to the table a dose of humility about the wider purposes of both vegetal *and* human existence, since labour itself can only ever be "a partial descriptor of lives, relationships, and activities" (Battistoni 2017: 24).

From this perspective, the real strength of the concept of vegetal labour is arguably its capacity to highlight the contingency and mutability of the continual regenerative work that must go into producing all elements of the biosphere (cf. Cooper/Waldby 2014), and – in so doing – to affirm the ongoing potential for that work to be harnessed in the pursuit of alternative ends. Where the forests of the US South specifically are concerned, the concept therefore serves not only to illuminate the logics by which the bioenergy industry seeks to generate value from the work of loblolly pine trees. Equally important it its ability to question the hierarchies through which capital depicts particular species – and particular kinds of vegetal activity in forests – as more valuable sources of work than others. As Myers (2015: 19) points out, forestry management predicated "only on carbon cycling contradicts well-established scientific evidence on the role of old-growth forests in maintaining biodiversity, plant and animal habitat, water and nutrient cycling, and soil stability". That the work of (some) trees in working forests can be harnessed to help convey carbon dioxide out of the atmosphere more efficiently, in short, does not preclude alternative configurations in which the work of (other) trees – indeed, other forms of life existing in the forest more broadly – is harnessed to achieve other end goals. Even as it might seem, therefore, to play into the hands of productivist efforts to put nature to work more intensively – not least by implying that the vegetal kingdom constitutes a reserve of labour power yet to be put to work – the concept of vegetal labour could also be said to retain within itself the seeds of socio-natural relations set up to work against, rather than with, the grain of prevailing capitalist values.

The concept of vegetal labour must be deployed with care, of course. Unlike humans, plants cannot help but to respond to external stimuli; their photosynthesis, growth, and carbon sequestration – as well as the consequences of this metabolism, whether for humans, other plants, or the wider environment – occurs unbidden, and, for some at least, might just as well therefore be understood, and accepted, as a "free gift" (Moore 2015). Vegetal lifeforms, ultimately, unsettle the very distinction between production and reproduction; it would certainly not do to overlook the invitation thereby extended to us to reflect on the limitations of a worldview that positions productive work, however contestably defined, as the single most important basis for measuring the worth of a life, whether human or nonhuman (Federici 1975, Weeks 2011). Yet it also remains the case, as Besky (2019: 33) points out, that a "plant's ecology shapes the forms and, more importantly, the meanings of the labour necessary to produce it". And where wood pellet manufacturing in the working forests of the US South specifically is concerned, key aspects of the ecology of the loblolly pine – most importantly, its propensity to grow and sequester carbon more rapidly at a younger age – are serving to naturalise not only a fundamental link between energy and growth (with all its familiar connotations of progress and prosperity), but also a view of environmental remediation as achievable primarily through an intensification of work and consumption themselves. Against this backdrop, rather than contending simply that the life of loblolly pine trees cannot be reduced to a form of labour, there is arguably much to be gained from foregrounding instead the question of how else we might work collaboratively with these trees – indeed, with the forests of the US South as a whole – beyond simply towards the perpetuation of an energy economy that itself reinforces the pursuit of vigorous growth, efficiency and productivity at all costs (Daggett 2019).

Pursuing such questions may be worthwhile simply as a means of pushing back against the appeal of wider 'solutions' to global climate change that propose to enrol nature's own energies to compensate for the deleterious effects of our resource-intensive lifestyles. No less importantly, however, such questions also invite efforts to experiment, in Besky and Blanchette's (2019: 12) terms, with "locally specific ways to politicise capital's fragile and desperate hold over work". Indeed, in the case of the US South specifically, the need for such local experiments is arguably only intensified by the fact that the futures being carved out for the region's forests are prescribed not principally by local actors, but from the external vantage point of British and European climate change mitigation agendas. Given the neo-colonial dimensions of these expanding bioenergy economies, as well as a painful underlying history of forced and slave labour in the US South, one might of course quite reasonably call for forests of the region to be emancipated from the clutches of capitalist, market-based relations altogether. Yet such efforts would likely be rendered futile by the longstanding status of industrial forestry as a cornerstone not just of the US South's economy, but also its broader social identity. By contrast, a more explicit acknowledgement of the irrepressible labour power of trees might pave the way for the formulation of alternative imaginaries of future forest-based economies in the region, wherein the contours of collaborative, hybrid labour that enjoin trees and humans in these landscapes are reshaped to serve more creative, fully self-determined ends. Supplanting efforts to emancipate forests from capital with efforts simply to reclaim their vegetal labour power in this way may, for some at least, represent a dereliction of environmental and decolonial duties. Yet it is also the case that the disavowal of vegetal labour may not be a realistic option in a region so habituated to putting its forests to work. Far better, under these circumstances, to embrace actively the possibilities of restructuring hybrid labour in working forests around more progressive values than those which prevail today, than to relinquish control of forest futures altogether.

Acknowledgements

The research underpinning this chapter was generously funded by the University of Bristol's Vice-Chancellor's Fellowships scheme. I am indebted to all of the industry representatives, forestry professionals, scientific advisors, academics and campaigners who gave up their time to be interviewed, whether in the UK or the US. I would particularly like to thank Jennifer Atchison and Franklin Ginn for their constructive comments on an earlier draft of the chapter, and Marion Ernwein and Maan Barua for numerous helpful conversations that helped to give shape to the core arguments.

Chapter 9 - Latent capital:
Seed banking as investment in climate change futures

Can Dalyan

Seed banks are peculiar spaces of multispecies work and cohabitation. Against the backdrop of plant biodiversity loss, climate change and food security crises, plant-human relations come into sharp focus inside seed banks, and the work of seeds and conservationists takes on a vital significance. In line with the universalist underpinnings of biodiversity conservation (Lowe 2006; Choy 2011), popular narratives about this multispecies work are often framed in terms of ensuring humanity's survival at a time of global ecological ruination. In this piece, I will offer some critical remarks about the role that seed banking plays in the everyday geopolitics and biopolitics of climate change. Drawing on multi-year ethnographic fieldwork at the Turkish Seed Gene Bank (TSGB), I will first delineate how ex-situ plant conservation work is enlisted in novel configurations of power and knowledge in the Global South in ways that stand in stark contrast to the universalist tenets of biodiversity conservation, and that bring to surface fragmented visions of the Anthropocene. Second, I will explore how human and plant labor are intertwined in seed banking and what these entanglements may tell us about the nature of work in late capitalist ecologies of ruin.

Ethnographic attention toward plant labor is relatively new. While a robust body of work on animal labor (Blanchette 2015, 2019, 2020; Barua 2016, 2017, 2019; Coulter 2016; Beldo 2017; Parreñas 2018; Wadiwel 2018) and different aspects of plant being – such as plant intelligence (Myers 2015), plant sexuality (Hartigan 2017), and plant-human communication (Schulthies 2019) – has emerged in the last decade, the study of plant labor, especially in the context of conservation, is yet to find its place in this literature. Following a number of recent studies that have explored the inner workings of prominent international seed banks such as the Millennium Seed Bank at London's Kew Gardens and the Svalbard Global Seed Vault on the Island of Spitsbergen (Roosth 2016; Harrison 2017; Chacko 2019; Lewis-Jones 2019), this chapter turns its attentions to the life and labor of seeds inside the vaults of a national seed bank in the biodiversity-rich Global South. More specifically, it aims to explore how human and plant labor is managed in a conservation regime that banks on competitive climate futures.

In *The Mushroom at the End of the World*, Anna Tsing (2015) suggests it might be time to start imagining ways of achieving common, collaborative life without any guarantees now that capitalism's promise of progress – and postwar ideals of development – have been replaced by boundless precarity and never-ending trouble. Informed by the relationship between matsutake mushrooms that grow in blasted landscapes and mushroom pickers who reorient their lives and labors in search of the matsutake in order to survive the end of full-time employment, Tsing's proposal is arguably more salient than ever in light of the recent global coronavirus pandemic. The collaborative survival project of seed banking that I analyze in this piece is another capitalist endeavor that does not assume or seek modernist progress. In fact, it is a project built squarely upon the promise and premise of continued, worldwide environmental devastation. Unlike the indeterminacy that defines the relationship between the matsutake and its humans and that banishes their alienation from each other, however, seed banking holds fast onto technoscientific dreams of control and value extraction. In order to describe how the success of this enterprise rests on the biopolitical regulation and speculation of plant and human life, in the following pages I first lay out the legal and historical foundations of seed banking and then analyze the work that conservationists and seeds do inside the Turkish Seed Gene Bank.

Seed Banks after the Convention on Biological Diversity

Since 1993, when the Convention on Biological Diversity (CBD) granted nation states sovereign rights over nonhuman life and private parties intellectual property rights over modified varieties, national seed banks have functioned as regulatory spaces of more-than-human work where particular ideologies of conservation as well as notions of nature and nationhood are produced. By demarcating the legal sphere of national sovereignty from that of intellectual property, national seed banks carry out a dual task: they naturalize the nation on one hand by ascribing it a timeless quality; on the other hand they nationalize nature by marking nonhuman life with the stamp of sovereignty. In this process, conservation bureaucracies enlist the labor of civil servants as well as seeds to gain a foothold in competitive futures of climate change by ensuring that the latent potentialities of seeds are protected and kept viable in frozen storage.

The Convention's legal reconceptualization of nonhuman life constituted a radical break in plant biodiversity conservation. The CBD not only removed plant genetic resources from the global commons once and for all, but also allowed sovereign nationhood to be defined and instituted through plant life. This change in the ownership regime of nonhuman life emerged partly in response to the longstanding grievances of biodiversity-rich countries in the Global South regarding the extractive practices of international biomedical and pharmaceutical companies, whose fortunes had flourished in the 20th century along bioprospecting routes upon which imperial economies of the 18th and 19th centuries had themselves been built. In order to address these concerns while securing the continuity of research and commerce across borders, the CBD also invited signatory parties to establish a multilateral access and benefit sharing system that would ensure the "just and equitable" use, transfer, and research of nonhuman genetic material. However, this proposed system never came to full fruition due to the lack of disciplinary and retributory mechanisms regarding the potential misuse of shared materials (Roa-Rodríguez/van Dooren 2008).

The first comprehensive attempt to overcome this shortcoming of the CBD in plant conservation was the 2004 International Treaty on Plant Genetic Resources for Food and Agriculture (the Plant Treaty), which placed sixty-four essential crop species in a pool that would be regulated under its own multilateral system under the aegis of the Food and Agriculture Organization (FAO) of the United Nations. Subsequently, to provide a fuller and more concrete legal framework for access and benefit sharing under the CBD, the Nagoya Protocol on Access to Genetic Resources and the Fair and Equitable Sharing of Benefits Arising from their Utilization (the Nagoya Protocol) was adopted at the Conference of the Parties to the Convention on Biological Diversity in 2010. Today, even though a large portion of international material transfer arrangements are administered via the Plant Treaty and the Nagoya Protocol, these exchanges are often backed up by additional bilateral clauses to protect source countries and institutions. Moreover, the implementation and policing of these clauses vary across countries, since national conservation policies are often tied to changing local economic, scientific, and political considerations (Aistara 2011; Tamminen/Brown 2011).

As reports from the Plant Treaty governing body conventions continue to demonstrate (FAO 2019), historical anxieties that stem from colonial legacies of bioprospecting and the desire to capitalize on potentially valuable genetic material continue to give shape to protectionist conservation policies in the biodiversity-rich Global South, often leading seed banks like the TSGB to seal their collections off from international circulation and access and benefit sharing. Per the CBD, signatory parties can claim sovereign ownership of nonhuman life by certifying a species' native place of origin, and seed banks play a critical role in this process in the context of plant genetic resources. The first step of such certification is the collection, conservation, and research of targeted varieties – usually crops and medicinal plants – and seed banks act as a focal point for all these procedures. In addition to offering a quick technoscientific fix for biodiversity loss, one major reason for the proliferation of national and international seed banks in the last two decades is the centralizing impact they provide for conservation bureaucracies worldwide. While seed banks have been critical to plant biodiversity conservation for decades (Curry 2017), the need to centrally collect, codify, conserve and control biocapital in centralized institutions only emerged as a global imperative in the post-CBD landscape (Breithoff/Harrison 2018; Tamminen 2019).

Turkey joined this global shift in 2010 with the opening of the TSGB, the country's first 'national' seed bank. Tasked with the collection, conservation, and research of Turkey's rich crop biodiversity and the evaluation of botanical research permit applications received from foreign institutions, the TSGB was the Turkish conservation bureaucracy's attempt at institutionalizing its management of plant biodiversity in the post-CBD era. From its inception, the TSGB's task as a conservation institution seemed distinct from international seed banks with an openly universalist outlook. For example, at the 2008 opening ceremony of the now-famous Svalbard Global Seed Vault, the former President of the European Commission José Manuel Barroso tellingly called the vault "the frozen Garden of Eden", while the Norwegian Prime Minister Jens Stoltenberg labeled it "the Noah's Ark for securing biological diversity" (Schmidt/Meinhart 2009). In these two biblical references, Barroso and Stoltenberg not only universalized the mission of the seed vault, but also retraced the apocalyptic imagery that had garnered the institution worldwide financial and political support. In contrast, during the TSGB's opening in 2010 (Figure 9.1), the then-Prime Minister Erdoğan argued for "the global need for efficient use and fair distribution of resources" after citing the global import of Turkey's crop biodiversity and the country's perennial wisdom in plant breeding as the "birthplace of agriculture" (Hürriyet 2010).

The gulf between these narratives was not coincidental. The universalist rhetoric that accompanies projects like the SGSV and the Millennium Seed Bank frames climate change and biodiversity loss as issues that affect a universal subject, humanity, and thus as deserving of a global response (Colebrook 2016). At odds with the concerns of biodiversity-rich countries in the Global South, this rhetoric glosses over imperial histories of bioprospecting that facilitated the emergence of institutions like the MSB and their vast, global collections in the first place (Chacko 2019). At the TSGB, institutional narratives of loss often push against this universalist ideal that erases historical difference. Even though Turkey is party to both the CBD and the Plant Treaty, the TSGB has functioned in permanent tension with international bodies and regulations since its inception in 2010. It has not only been reliably reluctant to cooperate with foreign institutions requesting access to its collections, but it has also routinely denied the permit applications of foreign scientists wishing to conduct botanical research in the country. Turkey, of course, is not an outlier in this sense: the struggle to exercise vigilance against the threat of biopiracy has been a defining feature of conservation practices in the Global South since the 1980s (Hayden 2003; Kloppenburg 2004).

Figure 9.1: The opening ceremony of the Turkish Seed Gene Bank in 2010.

Image: Can Dalyan.

In the post-CBD biodiversity conservation paradigm, national seed banks like the TSGB operate as institutional hubs where potentially commodifiable plant genetic resources are secured for the future benefit of the nation state. And as conservationists in these banks are saddled with the task of being active gatekeepers of national biowealth in addition to carrying out mundane conservation duties, the nature of their labor transforms along with its political and temporal orientations. At the TSGB, this brand of protectionist conservation necessitates civil servants' rigid self-alignment with the bureaucracy's priorities and expectations. As such, adapting to and making meaning out of their own roles in preserving Turkey's plant biodiversity in the Anthropocene without any recourse to sharing becomes an essential part of conservations' everyday work.

Conservationists' labor

The bedrock of food security is crop genetic diversity (Westengen et al. 2018) and those in the Turkish conservation community are generally aware that as the home of many essential crop varieties and their wild relatives, Turkey's crop biodiversity is critical for the breeding of much-needed new varieties that can withstand novel soil and climate conditions. Turkey is one of the most crucial crop biodiversity hotspots worldwide in terms of species richness and the diversity of different genepools (see Figure 9.2), and the search for understudied Turkish crop wild relatives that may hold the key to the development of new breeds and resistances has only begun in earnest in the last decade. Scientists and civil servants in the Turkish conservation bureaucracy often cite the fact that Turkey has been a popular bioprospecting hub for European plant hunters since the 18th century (Baytop 2003, 2010) when discussing matters of policy. In addition to shaping the outcome of permit applications and access and benefit sharing decisions, this history also influences long-term policy commitments and the temporal politics and orientation of mundane crop biodiversity conservation practices at the TSGB.

Figure 9.2: Crop species richness world map

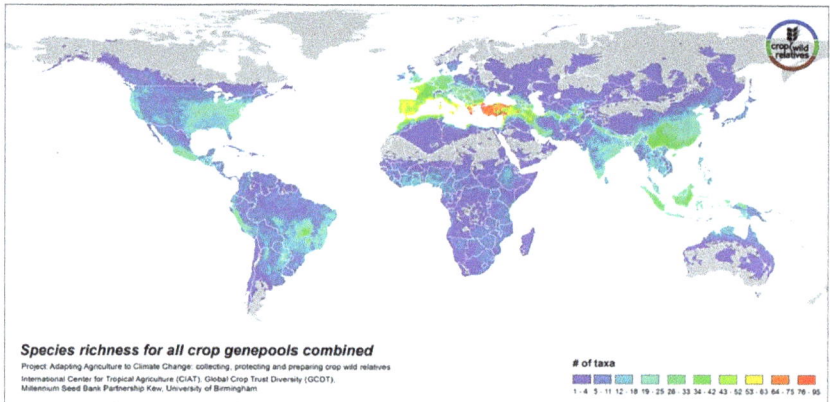

Source: www.cwrdiversity.org

The TSGB's global import rests on the potential commodifiability and value of its collections. The ownership of such material, predicated upon close guardianship against biopiracy, endows countries like Turkey with a type of power that exists in potentia. By granting nation states sovereignty over plant life, the CBD has set the course for state institutions to claim, conserve, and manipulate latent genetic potentialities in crops that may prove essential for sustaining global food security (Roa-Rodríguez/van Dooren 2008; Tamminen/Brown 2011). Yet, as those in the Turkish conservation community often point out, due to lack of funding and scientific infrastructure, it takes Turkish plant breeders years to conduct gene analyses, research resistances, and develop new varieties, let alone embark on the painstaking legal process of claiming sovereign rights over particular species through certifying their place of origin. Because the TSGB breeders are not able to research and economically benefit from the Bank's collection in the short term, the Turkish conservation bureaucracy has been opting to wait and make sure that the potential national biowealth locked up inside the TSGB's vaults is not shared and exploited elsewhere. And since the Bank's collection is mostly made up of crop landraces, bureaucrats and conservationists alike expect the latent potentialities in the Bank's vaults to increase in value due to the worsening effects of climate change and crop biodiversity loss on global food security. One outcome of this policy is the protracted signing process of the Nagoya Protocol in Turkey.

Since 2010, when the Protocol was first adopted by the Conference of the Parties to the Convention, Turkish bureaucrats have been offering similar narratives about Turkey's unwillingness to commit to the Protocol. Between 2013 and 2016 when I conducted the bulk of the interviews underpinning this research, the head bureaucrat in charge of the group who negotiated Turkey's signing of the protocol was the TSGB's manager. During our conversations on the state of the negotiations, he often stressed that neither he nor the Ministry had any objections to the text. Yet they were not in a rush either: they were essentially choosing to wait and observe the consequences in ratifying countries. A kindred sentiment was echoed by the manager of The Aegean Agricultural Research Institute Seed Bank – the old focal point of Turkish conservation bureaucracy – during an interview in 2015. In his narrative, it was disheartening to see Western countries create unjustifiable extra economic value out of the genetic biowealth of countries like Turkey, who remained at the mercy of their partners to do right by them when it came to benefit sharing. Much like the TSGB, the Aegean Institute shared materials almost exclusively with Turkish academic bodies and rarely with foreign institutions. And when they did, they did so only after inserting strict bilateral clauses in material transfer agreements. If Turkey were to ratify the Nagoya Protocol, not only would the Turkish government have to pass binding access and benefit legislation at some point, but both banks in question would also start receiving added pressure from the international conservation community to comply with the Protocol's regulations.

The perspectives of these scientists/civil servants who occupied two of the highest-ranking positions in Turkish conservation bureaucracy – and who managed the two seed banks that housed the better part of Turkey's plant biodiversity – were revealing in terms of the work expected from lower-level conservationists. Inside the TSGB and other government institutions, civil servants' individual readings of international biodiversity conservation often closely aligned with the protectionist sensibilities of the higher echelons of the conservation bureaucracy. When I talked with the TSGB staff about how they felt about the policy of collecting and preserving Turkish biodiversity without ever opening it up to the outside world, they cited the well-known species that Turkey had lost to Western plant hunters; likened the loss of biowealth to loss of land and independence after World War I; and drew parallels between bioprospecting and the flight of Greco-Roman antiquities from Turkey in order to legitimize the Bank's operating principles (Dalyan 2018). On the one hand, these narratives pointed to Turkey's singular position in the Global South as a former imperial force that lost imperial lands, wealth, and sovereignty to current suitors of its national biowealth. On the other, they helped the TSGB staff situate the meaning and significance of their work within a broader and ongoing history of loss while also highlighting the ever-expanding horizons of subjective alignment that their positions in civil service required of them.

Even though these narratives of loss and wrongdoing mostly targeted foreign actors, conservationists also saw Turkish citizens as potential threats to national biowealth, evidenced most clearly by the TSGB management's apprehension about local seed exchange festivals (*tohum takas şenlikleri*) that were borne out of the radical transformation that seed commerce went through in Turkey in the 2000s. In the wake of a decade-long push for privatization and monoculture in agriculture directed by World Bank planning (Karapinar et al. 2010; Keyder/Yenal 2013), the Erdoğan-led government banned the sale and purchase of traditionally grown varieties that lacked Ministry licensing in 2006, and then legalized the circulation of transgenic crops in 2010 (Atalan-Helicke/Mansfield 2012). Mirroring a broader turn toward mandatory licensing and the restriction of farmers' rights to save seeds that was observed in France (Bonneuil/Thomas 2009) and the European Union (Demeulenaere 2010) in the second half of the 19th century, this radical shift received adverse reactions from farmers associations, NGOs, and various political groups nationwide, and locally organized seed exchange festivals started to pop up along the western coast of Turkey in an act of protest and community building in the early 2010s. Taking advantage of a loophole that left non-commercial exchange of seeds out of the reach of the 2006 law, farmers, hobbyists, activists and environmentalists gathered together in these events to listen to seminars, attend workshops and, most importantly, exchange seeds that they independently owned.

Groups and individuals who organized, attended, or even supported these festivals aroused skepticism in the Turkish conservation bureaucracy, and when the seed exchange movement finally reached the capital of Ankara in 2013, the TSGB's manager decided to observe the festivities firsthand with three other Bank staff members. At the very first seminar that they attended, after listening to an agricultural commune representative recount how his commune exchanged seeds of endangered landraces with comrades from communes abroad to help the species' chances of survival, the Bank staff members started a heated exchange with the speaker that led to an early termination of the day's events. The contrast between the two battling conservation ideologies was drastic: while the commune member refused to concede that seeds could belong to a national or private body, the TSGB staff argued that the commune was not only committing a crime but also naively giving away precious national biowealth, which instead of propelling Turkish economy and agriculture forward, could now be patented abroad and sold back

to Turkey at exorbitant prices (Dalyan 2018). The TSGB staff's spirited defense of
the official stance of the conservation bureaucracy, again, pointed to the extent
of the intellectual and emotional work expected of civil servants as part of their
regular duties, the type of work that Hardt and Negri (2004) call "affective labor."

Plant labor

What can the articulation of seeds' and conservationists' labor inside a seed bank
tell us about the nature of nonhuman work in a damaged planet? From a distance,
it would be easy to characterize the seeds' capacities to stay viable at -18°C as labor
within the framework of ex-situ conservation. After all, the work of seed banking
simply cannot be achieved without the natural capacities and capabilities of seeds.
Indeed, in her work on the oil palm sector, Sophie Chao (2018: 442) notes that it
is possible to describe seeds as "nonwaged, extrahuman workers whose vitality is
appropriated and transformed by humans into capitalist value". In agreement with
Besky and Blanchette's (2019) arguments about 'the work of nature', however, I am
hesitant to conceptualize the (re)productive capacities of seeds as labor, since the
work of value creation in seed banking hardly seems reducible to the natural capacities of any one species. Wary also of extending the interpretive reach of work to
seeds and reifying work's seemingly natural hold over contemporary social imagi-
nation (Weeks 2011), I will instead point to how the latent existence of seeds in cold
storage makes possible and in turn holds together the expansive assemblage of
institutions, bureaucracies, markets, and laws built around plant biodiversity conservation. Because while the (re)productive labor and capacities of seeds that are
maximized via standardized processes of cleaning, drying, freezing, viability testing and regeneration are the very foundation of ex-situ plant conservation work,
this work gains its particular political and economic salience only within a certain
techno-legal and technoscientific configuration.

The fundamental role that frozen seeds perform within this assemblage is keeping the inherently messy categories of nature and nation pure and intact. Thom van
Dooren (2009) calls seeds "conservation proxies" since focusing on the preservation
of seeds alone signifies the prioritization of plant genetic material above all other
biosocial and evolutionary aspects of plants' lives. The international biodiversity
conservation community has pivoted towards the ex-situ conservation of genetic
material and information in the last three decades (Haraway 1997; Hayden 2003;
Bowker 2005), which in part was a reflection of a broader trend in life sciences
toward the commodification of organisms and life itself (Franklin 2003; Haraway
2003; Parry 2004; Sunder Rajan 2006). Moreover, the ownership regime set up by
the CBD that upholds the proprietorship of genetic information as the basis of legal
ownership has sped up the commodification of plant genetics worldwide. As plant

genetic resources move between the spheres of national sovereignty and intellectual property in the post-CBD legal landscape, concepts of nationhood and nature emerge and disappear as a function of this movement.

Marilyn Strathern (2001: 9) states that the paradigm of intellectual property itself perpetuates the idea of an untouched nature: "If technology in general creates 'nature' as a world of materials waiting to be used or of natural processes that carry on without human intervention, then patents create a domain of 'nature' in a very specific sense". In the particular context of the post-CBD plant genetic resources ownership regime, what is accepted to belong in the realm of national sovereignty is hence a very specific idea of nature that is pure and unblemished. To quote Strathern (2001: 10) again, "the rubric is that nature cannot be patented. Ipso facto, anything patentable is already out of the realm of nature". In this generative relationship between nature and intellectual property, a seed bank is more than a stopgap: the two legal and conceptual forms exist in embryonic and fully distinct states inside a seed bank at the same time.

The TSGB, for example, currently lacks the capabilities to research, sequence, patent and monetize the valuable varieties in its collection, and it also refuses to share these specimens using international access and benefit sharing arrangements. As a result, the Bank's cold storage rooms function as incubators for genetic nationhood (to emerge through certification of native origin) and intellectual property (to emerge through patenting). In a legal sense, these two spheres exist in embryonic form inside the TSGB. On a discursive level, however, they appear to conservationists as fully shaped and completely separated. The TSGB staff and the broader Turkish conservation bureaucracy talk about the Bank's collection exclusively in the idiom of national biowealth regardless of whether any varieties in the collection have been legally certified as native to Turkey or not. Nature, in other words, is readily equated with the nation in the course of everyday conservation work. As Sakari Tamminen (2019) demonstrates in his analysis of the Finnish conservation bureaucracy, the official certification process under the CBD that aims to establish the native origin of plant and animal species often ends up exposing the paradox of using the territorial frameworks of modern nation states to define the historical movement and biosocial existence of nonhuman life. The enduring ability of the technoscientific and techno-legal assemblage of international ex-situ plant biodiversity conservation to mark and maintain the spheres of genetic nationhood and intellectual property as separate from each other thus rests on the (re)productive capacities and latent potentialities of seeds in cold storage.

Frozen seeds also perform a global, world-historical function. Seed banking ultimately is an act of hope, and this hope entails the possibility of reintroducing conserved species back into the wild, as well as utilizing them to survive acute food security crises and radical ecological change through sharing and research. Even though reintroduction projects pose immense challenges (Williams et al. 2002;

Leger/Baugman 2015; Lewis-Jones 2019) and the sharing and research of plant genetic material across borders is always a politically charged endeavor (Dalyan 2018;
Hayden 2003), this hope springs eternal in the conservation community. In international conservation projects such as the SGSV and the MSB it presents itself as
a universal lifeline for the imperial subject of humanity, and in national endeavors
like the TSGB as a horizon that can be reached via national technoscience. In both
cases, it is again the latent potentialities of seeds that hold these neocolonial and
postcolonial assemblages of power and knowledge together. The various forms that
the hope of salvation, redemption, and value extraction takes all stem from the life
forces of seeds.

Conservation Work in the Anthropocene

In this chapter, I explored the assemblage of international biodiversity conservation governance and the work that conservationists and seeds do inside the TSGB
with a view to understanding the specific conditions under which we conceive and
manage climate futures today. In the context of plant biodiversity conservation,
I showed that this management takes place in a legal ownership regime that en-
courages both nation states and private bodies to see the commodification of plant
genetic resources as the ultimate goal of conservation. Through the example of the
TSGB, I demonstrated that the conservationists' and seeds' labors are enlisted in a
biopolitical (and geopolitical) conservation regime that not only monitors and con-
trols the life processes of seeds in frozen storage, but also the lives of civil servants
who work in a politically volatile bureaucracy.

The analytical framework of more-than-human or "hybrid" labor (Battistoni
2017) has been helpful in unpacking the assemblage of ex-situ plant biodiversity
conservation. The biopolitical management of life in cold storage – what some
scholars have called cryopower (Friedrich 2017; Peres 2019) – becomes meaningful
within this assemblage only when the labors of bureaucrats, scientists, and seeds
are arranged in a particular fashion, and only under a specific international legal
ownership regime that values and understands nonhuman life in terms of genetic
information. As Besky and Blanchette (2019) argue, the work is not done by anyone in particular in multispecies assemblages like seed banks: it is the specific
alignment of scientific, economic, and political interests – as well as human and
nonhuman infrastructures – that shapes the contours and configurations of work
in these spaces.

Inside the TSGB, the environmental futures that this work is meant to bring
to life are not conceived in universalist terms but in terms of capitalist futures. As
conservationists longingly and diligently wait for a time when the Bank will finally
be able to capitalize the seed collection that it has been working hard to protect,

they do not contemplate the bleak future of humanity in the Anthropocene, but the sorts of reparations that Turkey will be able to accrue from its collection in the future. In line with the parameters of international biodiversity conservation, the latency that conservationists enforce upon the lives of seeds at the TSGB is thus an investment in capitalism's futures in Turkey – an investment that banks on continued global capitalist and ecological ruination.

Acknowledgements

The research for this piece was made possible by a Dissertation Fieldwork Grant from the Wenner-Gren Foundation and a Luigi Einaudi Fellowship for Dissertation Research from the Mario Einaudi Center for International Studies at Cornell University. I would like to thank the editors of this volume for their generous comments on earlier drafts of this chapter.

Bibliography

Abt, Karen/Abt, Robert/Galik, Christopher/Skog, Kenneth (2014): Effect of Policies on Pellet Production and Forests in the U.S. South, General Technical Report SRS-202, Asheville, NC: USDA Forest Service Southern Research Station.

Adam, Barbara (1998): Timescapes of Modernity: The Environment and Invisible Hazards, London: Routledge.

Aistara, Guntra (2011): "Seeds of Kin, Kin of Seeds: The Commodification of Organic Seeds and Social Relations in Costa Rica and Latvia." In: Ethnography 12/4, pp. 490-517.

Alderman, Derek (2004): "Channing Cope and the Making of a Miracle Vine." In: Geographical Review 94/2, pp. 157-177.

Allen, Jonathan (2004): "Redefining the Network." In: Information Technology & People 17/2, pp. 171-185.

Anguelovski, Isabelle/Connolly, James/Garcia-Lamarca, Melissa/Cole, Helen/Pearsall, Hamil (2019): "New scholarly pathways on green gentrification: What does the urban 'green turn' mean and where is it going?" In: Progress in Human Geography, 43/6 pp. 1064-1086.

Aras, Bülent/Yorulmazlar, Emirhan (2018): "State, Institutions and Reform in Turkey after July 15." In: *New Perspectives on Turkey* 59, pp. 135-157.

Ashton, Kate (2019): "One Year on from Cyclone Marcus, A Darwin Tree-Planting Scheme Promises not to Repeat Past Mistakes." In: ABC News, March 15, 2019 (https://www.abc.net.au/news/2019-03-16/cyclone-marcus-new-darwin-tree-planting-scheme-greening-city/10907290). Last Accessed: June 5, 2019.

Atalan-Helicke, Nurcan/Mansfield, Becky (2012): "Seed Governance at the Intersection of Multiple Global and Nation-State Priorities: Modernizing Seeds in Turkey." In: Global Environmental Politics 12/4, pp. 125-46.

Baber, Zaheer (2016): "The Plants of Empire: Botanic Gardens, Colonial Power and Botanical Knowledge." In: Journal of Contemporary Asia 46/4, pp. 659-679.

Baker, James/Langdon, Gordon (1990): "Pinus Taeda." In: Russell Burns/Barbara Honkala (eds.), Silvics of North America: 1. Conifers; 2. Hardwoods, Agriculture Handbook 654, Washington, D.C.: U.S. Department of Agriculture, Forest Service, pp. 497-512.

Bakker, Karen (2013): An Uncooperative Commodity: Privatizing Water in England and Wales, Oxford: Oxford University Press.

Bakker, Karen/Bridge, Gavin (2006): "Material Worlds? Resource Geographies and the 'Matter of Nature'." In: Progress in Human Geography 30/1, pp. 5-27.

Balling, Robert/Gober, Patricia (2007): "Climate Variability and Residential Water Use in the City of Phoenix, Arizona." In: Journal of Applied Meteorology and Climatology, 46, pp. 1130-1137.

Banoub, Daniel/Martin, Sarah (2020): "Storing Value: The Infrastructural Ecologies of Commodity Storage." In: Environment and Planning D: Society and Space 38/6, pp. 1101-1119.

Barca, Stefania (2015): "Greening the Job: Trade Unions, Climate Change and the Political Ecology of Labour." In Raymond L. Bryant (ed.) The International Handbook of Political Ecology, Cheltenham: Edward Elgar, pp. 387-400.

Barca, Stefania (2017): "Labour and the Ecological Crisis: The Eco-Modernist Dilemma in Western Marxism(s) (1970s-2000s)." In: Geoforum 98, pp. 226-235.

Barca, Stefania (2020): Forces of Reproduction: Notes for a Counter-Hegemonic Anthropocene, Cambridge: Cambridge University Press.

Barua, Maan (2016): "Lively Commodities and Encounter Value." In: Environment and Planning D: Society and Space 34/4, pp. 725-744.

Barua, Maan (2017): "Nonhuman Labour, Encounter Value, Spectacular Accumulation: The Geographies of a Lively Commodity." In: Transactions of the Institute of British Geographers 42/2, pp. 274-288.

Barua, Maan (2019): "Animating Capital: Work, Commodities, Circulation." In: Progress in Human Geography 43/4, pp. 650-669.

Barua, Maan (2020): "Affective Economies, Pandas, and the Atmospheric Politics of Lively Capital." In: Transactions of the Institute of British Geographers 45/3, pp. 678-692.

Barua, Maan/Sinha, Anindya (2019): "Animating the Urban: An Ethological and Geographical Conversation." In: Social & Cultural Geography 20/8, pp. 1160-1180.

Battistoni, Alyssa (2017): "Bringing in the Work of Nature: From Natural Capital to Hybrid Labour." In: Political Theory 45/1, pp. 5-31.

Bayles, Brett R./Brauman, Kate A./Adkins, Joshua N./Allan, Brian F./Ellis, Alicia M./Goldberg, Tony L./Golden, Christopher D./Grigsby-Toussaint, Diana S./Myers, Samuel S./Osofsky, Steven A./Ricketts, Taylor H./Ristaino, Jean B. (2016): "Ecosystem Services Connect Environmental Change to Human Health Outcomes." In: Ecohealth 13/3, pp. 443-449.

Baytop, Asuman (2003): Türkiye'de Botanik Tarihi Araştırmaları, Ankara: TÜBİTAK Yayınları Akademik Dizi.

Baytop, Asuman (2010): "Plant Collectors in Anatolia (Turkey)." In: Phytologia Balcanica 16/2, pp. 187-213.

Bear, Laura (2014): "For Labour: Ajeet's Accident and the Ethics of Technological Fixes in Time." In: Journal of the Royal Anthropological Institute 20/1, pp. 71-88.

BEIS (2020): UK Energy Statistics, 2019 & Q4 2019, UK Department for Business, Energy & Industrial Strategy Statistical Press Release. https://assets.publishin g.service.gov.uk/government/uploads/system/uploads/attachment_data/file/877047/Press_Notice_March_2020.pdf (accessed August 17 2020).

Beldo, Les (2017): "Metabolic Labor: Broiler Chickens and the Exploitation of Vitality." In: Environmental Humanities 9/1, pp. 108-128.

Benedict, Mark/McMahon, Edward (2012): Green Infrastructure: Linking Landscapes and Communities, Washington, D.C.: Island Press.

Bergues, Martine (2004): "Dire avec des Fleurs: Manières de Jardins et Modèles de Cultures." In : Véronique Nahoum-Grappe/Odile Vincent (eds.), Le Goût des Belles Choses : Ethnologie de la Relation Esthétique, Paris: Editions de la Maison des Sciences de l'Homme, pp. 67-81.

Bergues, Martine (2011): En son Jardin: une Ethnologie du Fleurissement, Paris: Éditions de la Maison des Sciences de l'Homme.

Berque, Augustin (1986): Le Sauvage et l'Artifice: les Japonais devant la Nature, Paris: Gallimard.

Besky, Sarah (2019): "Exhaustion and Endurance in Sick Landscapes: Cheap Tea and the Work of Monoculture in the Doors, India." In Sarah Besky/Alex Blanchette (eds.), How Nature Works: Rethinking labor on a Troubled Planet, Albuquerque, NM: University of New Mexico Press, pp. 23-40.

Besky, Sarah/Blanchette, Alex (eds.) (2019): How Nature Works: Rethinking Labor on a Troubled Planet, Albuquerque, NM: University of New Mexico Press.

Besky, Sarah/Blanchette, Alex (2018): "Introduction: The Naturalization of Work." In: Cultural Anthropology. Online.

Besky, Sarah/Blanchette, Alex (2019): "Introduction: The Fragility of Work." In: How Nature Works: Rethinking Labor on a Troubled Planet." In: Sarah Besky/Alex Blanchette (eds.), Albuquerque, NM: University of New Mexico Press, pp. 1-19.

Blanchette, Alex (2015): "Herding Species: Biosecurity, Posthuman Labor, and the American Industrial Pig." In: Cultural Anthropology 30/4, pp. 640-69.

Blanchette, Alex (2020): Porkopolis: American Animality, Standardized Life, and the Factory Farm, Durham, NC: Duke University Press.

Bonneuil, Christophe/Thomas, Frederic (2010): "Purifying Landscapes: The Vichy Regime and The Genetic Modernization of France." In: Historical Studies in the Natural Sciences 40/4, pp. 532-568.

Bowker, Geoffrey (2005): Memory Practices in the Sciences. Cambridge, MA: The MIT Press.

Boyd, William/Prudham, W. Scott/Schurman, Rachel A. (2001): "Industrial Dynamics and the Problem of Nature." In: Society & Natural Resources 14/7, pp. 555-570.

Braat, Leon C./de Groot, Rudolf (2012): "The Ecosystem Services Agenda: Bridging the Worlds of Natural Science and Economics, Conservation and Development, and Public and Private Policy." In: Ecosystem Services 1/1, pp. 4-15.

Brancher, Dominique (2015): Quand l'Esprit vient aux Plantes : Botanique Sensible et Subversion Libertine (XVIᵉ-XVIIᵉ siècles), Genève: Droz.

Brasier, Clive (1990): "China and the origins of Dutch elm disease: an appraisal." In: Plant Pathology 39, pp. 5-16.

Brasier, Clive (1995): "Episodic selection as a force in fungal microevolution, with special reference to clonal speciation and hybrid introgression." In: Canadian Journal of Botany 73/S1, pp.213-221.

Brasier, Clive (2000): "Intercontinental Spread and Continuing Evolution of the Dutch Elm Disease Pathogens." In: Dunn, Christopher (ed.), The Elms: Breeding, Conservation, and Disease Management, Boston, MA: Kluwer Academic Publishers, pp. 61-72.

Brasier, Clive (2001): "Rapid Evolution of Introduced Plant Pathogens via Interspecific Hybridization." In: BioScience 51/2, pp. 123-133.

Brasier, Clive/Buck, Kenneth (2002): "Rapid evolutionary changes in a globally invading fungal pathogen (Dutch elm disease)." In: Biological Invasions 3, pp. 223-233.

Brasier, Clive/Kirk, Susan (2001): "Designation of the EAN and NAN races of Ophiostoma novo-ulmi as subspecies." In: Mycological Research 105/5, pp. 547-554.

Braun, Bruce (2005): "Environmental Issues: Writing a more-than-human urban geography." In: Progress in Human Geography 29/5, pp. 635-650.

Braun, Bruce (2006): "Environmental Issues: Global Natures in the Space of Assemblage." In: Progress in Human Geography 30/5, pp. 644-654.

Braverman, Irus (2015): Wild Life: The Institution of Nature, Stanford, CA: Stanford University Press.

Breithoff, Esther/Harrison Rodney (2018): "From Ark to Bank: Extinction, Proxies and Biocapital in Ex-Situ Biodiversity Conservation Practices." In: International Journal of Heritage Studies 26/1, pp. 1-19.

Brenner, Neil/Theodore, Nik (2002): "Cities and the Geographies of Actually Existing Neoliberalism." In: Brenner, Neil/Theodore, Nik (eds.), Spaces of Neoliberalism: Urban Restructuring in North America and Western Europe, Oxford: Blackwell, pp. 2-32.

Brice, Jeremy (2014a): "Attending to Grape Vines: Perceptual Practices, Planty Agencies and Multiple Temporalities in Australian Viticulture." In: Social & Cultural Geography 15/8, pp. 942-965.

Brice, Jeremy (2014b): "Killing in More-than-Human Spaces: Pasteurisation, Fungi, and the Metabolic Lives of Wine." In: Environmental Humanities 4/1, pp. 171-194.

Bridge, Gavin (2000): "The Social Regulation of Resource Access and Environmental Impact: Production, Nature and Contradiction in the U.S. Copper Industry." In: Geoforum 31/2, pp. 237-256.

Britton, Kerry/Jiang-Hua, Sun (2002): "Unwelcome Guests: Exotic Forest Pests." In: Acta Entomologica Sinica 45/1, pp. 121-130.

Budiansky, Stephen (1992): The Covenant of the Wild: Why Animals Chose Domestication, New York, NY: William Morrow & Co.

Bureau of Meteorology (BOM) (no date): "Severe Tropical Cyclone Marcus." (http://www.bom.gov.au/cyclone/history/marcus.shtml).

Callon, Michel (1986): "Some Elements of a Sociology of Translation: Domestication of the Scallops and the Fishermen of St. Brieuc Bay." In Law, John (ed.), Power, Action, Belief: A New Sociology of Knowledge, London: Routledge and Kegan Paul, pp. 196-233.

Cameron, David M./Rance, Stanley J./Lukitsch, P.J. (1983): "Tree Damage in Darwin Parks and Gardens during Cyclones Tracy and Max." In: Landscape Planning, 10(2), pp.89-108.

Campanella, Thomas (2003): Republic of Shade: New England and the American Elm, New Haven, CT: Yale University Press.

Carr, Chantel/Gibson, Chris (2016): "Geographies of Making: Rethinking Materials and Skills for Volatile Futures." In: Progress in Human Geography 40/3, pp. 297-315.

Carr, Chantel/Gibson, Chris (2017): "Animating Geographies of Making: Embodied Slow Scholarship for Participant-Researchers of Maker Cultures and Material Work." In: Geography Compass 11/6, e12317.

Carton, Wim/Andersson, Elina (2017): "Where Forest Carbon Meets Its Maker: Forestry-Based Offsetting as the Subsumption of Nature." In: Society & Natural Resources 30/7, pp. 829-843.

Castree, Noel (2002): "False Antitheses? Marxism, Nature and Actor-Networks." In: Antipode 34, pp. 111-146.

Castree, Noel (2003a): "Environmental issues: relational ontologies and hybrid politics." In: Progress in Human Geography 27/2, pp. 203-211.

Castree, Noel (2003b): "Commodifying What Nature?" In: Progress in Human Geography 27/3, pp. 273-297.

Castree, Noel (2007): "Labour Geography: A Work in Progress." In: International Journal of Urban and Regional Research 31/4, pp. 853-862.

Castree, Noel (2009): "The Spatio-Temporality of Capitalism." In: Time & Society 18/1, pp. 26-61.

Castree, Noel/Coe, Neil M./Ward, Kevin/Samers, Michael (2004): Spaces of Work: Global Capitalism and Geographies of Labour, London: Sage.

Castro, Teresa (2019): "The Mediated Plant." In: e-flux journal 102 (https://www.e-flux.com/journal/102/283819/the-mediated-plant/). Last Accessed December 4, 2020.

Chacko, Xan Sarah (2019): "Creative Practices of Care: The Subjectivity, Agency, and Affective Labor of Preparing Seeds for Long-Term Banking." In: Culture, Agriculture, Food and Environment 41/2, pp. 97-106.

Chamowitz, Daniel (2012): What a Plant Knows, Oxford: Oneworld Publications.

Chao, Sophie (2018): "Seed Care in the Palm Oil Sector." In: Environmental Humanities 10/2, pp. 421-46.

Choy, Timothy (2011): Ecologies of Comparison: An Ethnography of Endangerment in Hong Kong, Durham, NC: Duke University Press.

Christophers, Brett (2018): "Risking Value Theory in the Political Economy of Finance and Nature." In: Progress in Human Geography: 42/3, pp. 330-349.

Chrulew, Matthew (2017): "Freezing the Ark: The Cryopolitics of Endangered Species Preservation." In: Joanna Radin/Emma Kowal (eds.) Cryopolitics. Frozen Life in a Melting World, Cambridge, MA: The MIT Press, pp. 283-306.

City of Darwin (CODa) (undated): "Replanting Darwin – The Right Tree in the Right Place." https://engage.darwin.nt.gov.au/39605/documents/88715 (accessed February 20, 2020).

City of Darwin (CODb) (undated): "Tree Reestablishment Advisory Committee Consultation Report" FINAL. City of Darwin Community Engagement Team. https://engage.darwin.nt.gov.au/39605/documents/94843 (accessed January 20, 2020).

City of Darwin (CODc) (undated): "Establishing a Resilient Urban Forest for Darwin, Best Practice Guidelines." City of Darwin. https://www.darwin.nt.gov.au/sites/default/files/publications/attachments/trac_final_report-establishing_a_resilient_urban_forest_for_darwin.pdf (accessed July 17, 2020).

Clark, Jonathan (2014): "Labourers or Lab Tools? Rethinking the Role of Lab Animals." In: Nik Taylor/Richard Twine (eds.), The Rise of Critical Animal Studies: From the Margins to the Centre, London: Routledge, pp. 139-164.

Clark, Michael A./Hill, Jason/Tilman, David (2019): "Multiple Health and Environmental Impacts of Foods." In: Proceedings of the National Academy of Sciences 116/46, pp. 23357-23362.

Clark, Mike/McGregor , J./Parsons, B. (2018): "An Assessment of Tree Damage and Resilience in Darwin Parks Following Tropical Cyclone Marcus March 17th 2018." Darwin, City of Darwin. https://engage.darwin.nt.gov.au/39605/documents/88594). accessed: 20 January 20, 2020

Clément, Gilles (2006): Le Jardin en Mouvement: De la Vallée au Jardin Planétaire, Paris: Sens & Tonka.

Coccia, Emanuele (2018): The Life of Plants: A Metaphysics of Mixture, Medford, MA: Polity.

Cohen, Shaul (1999): "Promoting Eden: Tree Planting as the Environmental Panacea." In: Ecumene 6/4, pp. 424-436.

Colebrook, Claire (2016): "What Is the Anthropo-Political?" In Cohen, Tom/Hillis Miller, Joseph/Colebrook, Claire (eds.), Twilight of the Anthropocene Idols, London: Open Humanities Press, pp. 81-125.

Collard, Rosemary-Claire/Dempsey, Jessica (2013): "Life for Sale? The Politics of Lively Commodities." In: Environment and Planning A 45/11, pp. 2682-2699.

Colombino, Annalisa/Giaccaria, Paolo (2016): "Dead Liveness/Living Deadness: Thresholds of Non-Human Life and Death in Biocapitalism." In: Environment and Planning D: Society and Space 34/6, pp. 1044-1062.

Condic, Maureen (2014): "Totipotency: What it is and What it is Not". In: Stem Cells and Development 23/8, pp. 796-812.

Cooper, Melinda (2008): Life as Surplus: Biotechnology and Capitalism in the Neoliberal Era, Seattle, WA: University of Washington Press.

Cooper, Melinda/Waldby, Catherine (2014): Clinical Labor: Tissue Donors and Research Subjects in the Global Bioeconomy, Durham, NC: Duke University Press.

Coulter, Kendra (2015): Animals, Work, and the Promise of Interspecies Solidarity. New York, NY: Palgrave Macmillan.

Coupaye, Ludovic (2013): Growing Artefacts, Displaying Relationships: Yams, Art and Technology Amongst the Nyamikum Abelam of Papua New Guinea, New York: Berghahn Books.

Coupaye, Ludovic/ Pitrou, Perig (2018): "Introduction. The Interweaving of Vital and Technical Processes in Oceania." In: Oceania 88/1, pp. 2-12.

Coutts, Christopher/Hahn, Micah (2015): "Green Infrastructure, Ecosystem Services, and Human Health." In: International Journal of Environmental Research and Public Health 12, pp. 9768-9798.

Cretney, Raven (2017): "Towards a Critical Geography of Disaster Recovery Politics: Perspectives on Crisis and Hope." In: Geography Compass 11/1, e12302.

Cronon, William (1991): Nature's Metropolis: Chicago and the Great West, New York, NY: W.W. Norton & Company.

Cueille, Sophie (2003): "La Campagne à Portée de Jardin." In: Histoire Urbaine 8/2, pp. 129-140.

Curry, Helen Anne (2017): "Breeding Uniformity and Banking Diversity: The Genescapes of Industrial Agriculture, 1935-1970." In: Global Environment 10/1, pp. 83-113.

Daechsel, Markus (1997): "Military Islamisation in Pakistan and the Spectre of Colonial Perceptions." In: Contemporary South Asia 6/2, pp. 141-160.

Daechsel, Markus (2013): "Misplaced Ekistics: Islamabad and the Politics of Urban Development in Pakistan." In: South Asian History and Culture 4/1, pp. 87-106.

Daggett, Cara New (2019): The Birth of Energy: Fossil Fuels, Thermodynamics, & the Politics of Work, Durham, NC: Duke University Press.

Dagognet, François (1988): La Maîtrise du Vivant, Paris: Hachette.

Dalyan, Can (2018): Latent Lives: Genebanking and the Politics of Conservation in Turkey. Cornell University Library (https://doi.org/10.7298/X47H1GTJ).

Darley, Marshall (1990): "The Essence of 'Plantness'." In: The American Biology Teacher 52/6, pp. 354-357.

Darwin, Charles (1881): The Formation of Vegetable Mould, Through the Action of Worms, London: John Murray.

Dashper, Katherine (2019): "More-Than-Human Emotions: Multispecies Emotional Labour in the Tourism Industry." In: Gender, Work & Organization 27/1, pp. 24-40.

de Weck, Julien (2016): "Ôter du Béton pour Verdir Genève au-delà de ses Parcs." In: Tribune de Genève. August 30, 2016.

Demeritt, David (2001): "Scientific Forest Conservation and the Statistical Picturing of Nature's Limits in the Progressive-Era United States." In: Environment and Planning D: Society and Space 19/4, pp. 431-459.

Demeulenaere, Elise (2014): "A Political Ontology of Seeds: The Transformative Frictions of a Farmers' Movement in Europe." Focaal 69, pp. 45-61.

Dempsey, Jessica (2016): Enterprising Nature: Economics, Markets, and Finance in Global Biodiversity Politics, Malden/Oxford/Chichester: John Wiley & Sons.

Demuzere, Matthias/Orru, Kati/Heidrich, Oliver/Olazabal, Eduardo/Geneletti, Davide/Orru, Hans/Bhave, Ajaye Gajanan/Mittal, Neha/Feliu, Efrén/Faehnle, Maija (2014): "Mitigating and Adapting to Climate Change: Multi-Functional and Multi-Scale Assessment of Green Urban Infrastructure." In: Journal of Environmental Management 146, pp. 107-115.

Descola, Philippe. (1986): La Nature Domestique. Symbolisme et Praxis dans l'Ecologie des Achuar, Paris: Éditions de la Maison des Sciences de l'Homme.

Donoghue, Michael (1985): "A Critique of the Biological Species Concept and Recommendations for a Phylogenetic Alternative." In: Bryologist 88/3, pp. 172-181.

Drax Group plc. (2016): 5 Things you never knew about Forests. https://www.drax.com/sustainability/5-things-you-never-knew-about-forests/ (accessed April 21, 2020).

Drax Group plc. (2017a): How Wood Pellets are Revitalizing a Community. https://www.draxbiomass.com/wood-pellets-revitalizing-community/ (accessed April 21, 2020).

Drax Group plc. (2017b): What is a Working Forest? https://www.drax.com/sustainability/what-is-a-working-forest/ (accessed April 21, 2020).

Drax Group plc. (2017c): Active Management of Forests Increases Growth and Carbon Storage. https://www.drax.com/sustainability/active-management-forests-increases-growth-carbon-storage/ (accessed August 14, 2020).

Drax Group plc. (2020): Enabling a Zero Carbon, Lower Cost Energy Future: Annual Report and Accounts 2019. https://www.drax.com/wp-content/uploads/2020/0 3/Drax_AR2019_Web.pdf (accessed August 13, 2020).

Duffy, Rosaleen (2016): "War, by Conservation." In: Geoforum 69, pp. 238-248.

Dümpelmann, Sonja (2019): Seeing Trees. A History of Street Trees in New York City and Berlin, New Haven, CT: Yale University Press.

Edensor, Tim (2015): "The Gloomy City: Rethinking the Relationship between Light and Dark." In: Urban Studies 52/3, pp. 422-438.

Edensor, Tim (2017): "Seeing with Light and Landscape: A Walk around Stanton Moor." In: Landscape Research 42/6, pp. 616-633.

Edensor, Tim/Hughes, Rachel (2019): "Moving Through a Dappled World: The Aesthetics of Shade and Shadow in Place." In: Social & Cultural Geography. DOI: 10.1080/14649365.2019.1705994, pp.1-19.

EIA (2020): July 2020 Monthly Energy Review, US Energy Information Administration https://www.eia.gov/totalenergy/data/monthly/pdf/mer.pdf (accessed August 17, 2020).

Endersby, Jim (2008): Imperial Nature: Joseph Hooker and the Practices of Victorian Science, Chicago, IL: University of Chicago Press.

Ereshefsky, Marc (2000): The Poverty of the Linnaean Hierarchy: A Philosophical Study of Biological Taxonomy, Cambridge: Cambridge University Press.

Ernwein, Marion (2021): "Bringing Urban Parks to Life: The More-Than-Human Politics of Urban Ecological Work." In: Annals of the American Association of Geographers 111/2, pp. 559-576.

Ernwein, Marion (2020): "From Undead Commodities to Lively Labourers: (Re)Valuing Vegetal Life, Reclaiming the Power to Design-With Plants." In: Gandy, Matthew/Jasper, Sandra (eds.), The Botanical City, Berlin: Jovis, pp. 237-242.

Escobar, Arturo (1996): "Constructing Nature: Elements for a Poststructural Political Ecology." In Peet, Richard/Watts, Michael (eds.), Liberation Ecologies: Environment, Development, and Social Movements, London: Routledge, pp. 46-68.

Escobar, Arturo (2020): Pluriversal Politics: The Real and the Possible, Durham, NC: Duke University Press.

Estebanez, Jean/Porcher, Jocelyne/Douine, Justine (2017): "Travailler à Faire Semblant: Les Animaux au Cinéma." In: Ecologie et Politique 54, pp. 103-121.

Euromonitor (2016): Gardening Global Overview: Social, Sustainable and Smart, 2017. (www.euromonitor.com/gardening-global-overview-social-sustainable-and-smart/report (accessed October 18, 2018).

European Commission (2019): Brief on Biomass for Energy in the European Union, Brussels, Belgium: European Commission's Knowledge Centre for Bioeconomy.

European Union (2018): "Directive (EU) 2018/2001 of the European Parliament and of the Council of 11 December 2018 on the Promotion of the Use of Energy from

Renewable Sources (recast)." In: Official Journal of the European Union L328, pp. 82-209.

Evans-Pritchard, Edward E. (1969): The Nuer: A Description of the Modes of Livelihood and Political Institutions of a Nilotic people, Oxford: Oxford University Press.

Fairhead, James/Leach, Melissa/Scoones, Ian (2012): "Green Grabbing: A New Appropriation of Nature?" In: Journal of Peasant Studies 39/2, pp. 237-261.

FAO (2019) Eighth Session of the Governing Body, Rome, 11-16 November 2019. (http://www.fao.org/plant-treaty/eighth-governing-body/en).

Federici, Silvia (1975): Wages Against Housework, Bristol: Power of Women Collective/Falling Wall Press.

Federici, Silvia (1998): Caliban and the Witch: Women, the Body and Primitive Accumulation, Brooklyn, NY: Autonomedia.

Ferret, Carole (2014): "Towards an Anthropology of Action: From Pastoral Techniques to Modes of Action." In: Journal of Material Culture 19/3, pp. 279-302.

Findly, Ellison Banks (2002): "Borderline Beings: Plant Possibilities in Early Buddhism." In: Journal of the American Oriental Society 122/2, pp. 252-263.

Fine, Ben (2005): "From Actor-Network Theory to Political Economy." In: Capitalism Nature Socialism 16/4, pp. 91-108.

Fisher, Berenice/Tronto, Joan (1991). "Toward a Feminist Theory of Care." In: Emily Abel/Margaret Nelson (eds.), Circles of Care: Work and Identity in Women's Lives, Albany, NY: SUNY Press, pp. 36-54.

Fitzsimmons, Margaret (1989): "The Matter of Nature." In: Antipode 21/2, pp. 106-120.

Fleming, Jake (2017): "Toward Vegetal Political Ecology: Kyrgyzstan's Walnut–Fruit Forest and the Politics of Graftability." In: Geoforum 79, pp. 26-35.

Foster, John Bellamy (2000): Marx's Ecology: materialism and nature, New York, NY: Monthly Review Press.

Fredericks, Rosalind (2018): Garbage Citizenship: Vital Infrastructures of Labor in Dakar, Senegal, Durham, NC: Duke University Press.

Friedrich, Alexander (2017): "The Rise of Cryopower: Biopolitics in the Age of Cryogenic Life." In: Joanna Radin/Emma Kowal (eds.) Cryopolitics. Frozen Life in a Melting World, Cambridge, MA: The MIT Press, pp. 59-70.

Gaffin, Stuart/Rosenzweig, Cynthia/Kong, Angela (2012): "Adapting to Climate Change through Urban Green Infrastructure." In: Nature Climate Change 2, p. 704.

Gandy, Matthew (2002): Concrete and Clay: Reworking Nature in New York City, Cambridge, MA: The MIT Press.

Gandy, Matthew (2005): "Cyborg Urbanization: Complexity and Monstrosity in the Contemporary City." In: International Journal of Urban and Regional Research 29/1, pp. 26-49.

Gareau, Brian (2005): "We Have Never Been Human: Agential Nature, ANT, and Marxist Political Ecology." In: Capitalism Nature Socialism 16/4, pp. 127-140.

Gesing, Friederike (2016): Working with Nature in Aotearoa, New Zealand: An ethnography of coastal protection, Bielefeld: Transcript.

Gessert, George (1993): "Flowers of Human Presence: Effects of Esthetic Values on the Evolution of Ornamental Plants." In: Leonardo 26/1, pp. 37-44.

Gibson, Chris/Warren, Andrew (2020): "Keeping Time with Trees: Climate Change, Forest Resources, and Experimental Relations with the Future." In: Geoforum 108, pp. 325-337.

Gill, Rosalind/Pratt, Andy (2008): "In the Social Factory? Immaterial Labour, Precariousness and Cultural Work." In: Theory, Culture and Society 25/7-8, pp. 1-30.

Gill, Susannah/Handley, John F./Ennos, Roland/Pauleit, Stephan (2007): "Adapting Cities for Climate Change: The Role of the Green Infrastructure." Built Environment 33, pp. 115-133.

Ginn, Franklin (2014): "Sticky lives: Slugs, Detachment and More-than-Human Ethics in the Garden." In: Transactions of the Institute of British Geographers 39/4, pp. 532-544.

Ginn, Franklin (2016): Domestic Wild: Memory, nature and gardening in suburbia, London: Routledge.

Ginn, Franklin/Ascensão, Eduardo (2018): "Autonomy, erasure and persistence in the urban gardening commons." In: Antipode 50/4, pp. 929-952.

Giraud, Eva (2019): What Comes after Entanglement? Activism, Anthropocentrism, and an Ethics of Exclusion, Durham, NC: Duke University Press.

Glennie, Paul/Thrift, Nigel (2009): Shaping the Day: A History of Timekeeping in England and Wales 1300-1800, Oxford: Oxford University Press.

Goffman, Erving (2002[1959]): Front and back regions of everyday life. In: Highmore, Ben Ben, ed. *The Everyday Life Reader*, London: Routledge.

Gould, Carol C. (1981): Marx's Social Ontology: Individuality and Community in Marx's Theory of Social Reality, Cambridge, MA: The MIT Press.

Gourou, Pierre (1948): "La Civilisation du Végétal." In: Indonesië 5, pp. 385-396.

Greeley, William Buckhout (1925): "The Relation of Geography to Timber Supply." In: Economic Geography 1/1, pp. 1-14.

Green, Maia/Lawson, Victoria (2011): "Recentring Care: Interrogating the Commodification of Care." In: Social & Cultural Geography 12/6, pp. 639-654.

Greenhough, Beth (2014): "More-Than-Human Geographies." In: Roger Lee/Noel Castree/Rob Kitchin/Victoria Lawson/Anssi Paasi/Chris Philo/Sarah Radcliffe/Susan M. Roberts/Charles W.J. Withers (eds.) The SAGE Handbook of Human Geography, London/Thousand Oaks/New Delhi/Singapore: SAGE, pp. 94-119.

Gürakar, Esra Çeviker (2016): Politics of Favoritism in Public Procurement in Turkey: Reconfigurations of Dependency Networks in the AKP Era, New York, NY: Palgrave Pivot.

Hall, Matthew (2011): Plants as Persons: A Philosophical Botany, Albany, NY: SUNY Press.

Hallé, Francis (1999) In Praise of Plants, Cambridge: Timber Press.

Haraway, Donna (1997): Modest Witness@Second Millenium.Female Man© Meets OncoMouse™, New York, NY: Routledge.

Haraway, Donna (2003): The Companion Species Manifesto, Chicago, IL: Prickly Paradigm Press.

Haraway, Donna (2008): When Species Meet, Minneapolis, MN: University of Minnesota Press.

Haraway, Donna (2016): Staying with the Trouble: Making Kin in the Chthulucene, Durham, NC: Duke University Press.

Haraway, Donna/Gane, Nicolas. (2006). "When We Have Never Been Human, What Is to Be Done?: Interview with Donna Haraway." In: Theory, Culture & Society 23/7-8, pp. 135-158.

Harrison, Rodney (2017): "Freezing Seeds and Making Futures: Endangerment, Hope, Security, and Time in Agrobiodiversity Conservation Practices." In: Culture, Agriculture, Food and Environment: The Journal of Culture & Agriculture 39/2, pp. 80-89.

Hartigan, John Jr. (2017): Care of the Species: Races of Corn and the Science of Plant Biodiversity, Minneapolis, MN: University of Minnesota Press.

Hartigan, John Jr. (2019): "Plants as Ethnographic Subjects." In: Anthropology Today 35/2, pp. 1-2.

Harvey, David (1973): Social Justice and the City, Baltimore, MD: The Johns Hopkins University Press

Harvey, David (1989): The Condition of Postmodernity: An Inquiry into the Origins of Cultural Change, Oxford: Blackwell.

Harvey, David (1996): Justice, Nature & the Geography of Difference, Oxford: Blackwell.

Harvey, David (1999): The Limits to Capital: New Edition, London: Verso.

Harvey, David (2000): Spaces of Hope, Edinburgh: Edinburgh University Press.

Haudricourt, André-Georges (1962): "Domestication des Animaux, Culture des Plantes et Traitement d'Autrui." In: L'Homme 2/1, pp. 40-50.

Hawkes, Jack G./Maxted, Nigel/Ford-Lloyd, Brian V. (2012): The Ex Situ Conservation of Plant Genetic Resources, Berlin: Springer.

Hayden, Cori (2003): When Nature Goes Public: The Making and Unmaking of Bioprospecting in Mexico, Princeton, NJ: Princeton University Press.

Head, Lesley/Atchison, Jennifer/Phillips, Catherine/Buckingham, Kathleen (2014): "Vegetal Politics: Belonging, Practices and Places." In: Social & Cultural Geography 15/8, pp. 861-870.

Head, Lesley/Atchison, Jennifer/Gates, Alison (2012): Ingrained: A Human Bio-geography of Wheat, Surrey: Ashgate.

Head, Lesley/Atchison, Jennifer/Phillips, Catherine (2015): "The Distinctive Capacities of Plants: Re-Thinking Difference via Invasive Species." In: Transactions of the Institute of British Geographers 40/3, pp. 399-413.

Head, Lesley/Atchison, Jennifer/Phillips, Catherine/Buckingham, Kathleen (2016): Vegetal Politics: Belonging, Practices and Places, London: Routledge.

Head, Lesley/Muir, Pat (2004): "Nativeness, Invasiveness, and Nation in Australian Plants." In: Geographical Review 94/2, pp. 199-217.

Hearne, Dennis A. (1975): Trees for Darwin and Northern Australia, Canberra: Australian Government Publishing Service.

Helmreich, Stefan (2008): "Species of Biocapital." In: Science as Culture 17/4, pp. 463-478.

Herbert, Eugenia W. (2012): Flora's Empire: British Gardens in India, Philadelphia, PA: University of Pennsylvania Press.

Heyd, Thomas (2006): "Thinking Through Botanic Gardens." In: Environmental Values 15/2, pp. 197-212.

Heynen, Nick/Perkins, Harold (2005): "Scalar Dialectics in Green: Urban Private Property and the Contradictions of the Neoliberalization of Nature." In: Capitalism Nature Socialism 16/1, pp. 99-113.

Heynen, Nick/Perkins, Harold/Roy, Parama (2006): The Political Ecology of Uneven Urban Greenspace: The Role of Political Economy and Race and Ethnicity in Producing Environmental Inequality in Milwaukee. In: Urban Affairs Review 42/1, pp. 3-25.

Heynen, Nick/Robbins, Paul (2005): "The Neoliberalization of Nature: Governance, Privatization, Enclosure, and Valuation." In: Capitalism Nature Socialism 16/1, pp. 5-8.

Heynen, Nik (2006): "Green Urban Political Ecologies: Toward a Better Understanding of Inner-City Environmental Change." In: Environment and Planning A 38/3, pp. 399-416.

Heynen, Nik/Perkins, Harold A./Roy, Parama (2007): "Failing to Grow 'their' own Justice? The Co-Production of Racial/Gendered Labor and Milwaukee's Urban Forest." In: Urban Geography 28/8, pp. 732-54.

Hinchliffe, Steve (2008): "Reconstituting Nature Conservation: Towards a Careful Political Ecology." In: Geoforum 39/1, pp. 88-97.

Hinchliffe, Steve/Whatmore, Sarah (2006): "Living Cities: Towards a Politics of Conviviality." In: Science as Culture 15/2, pp. 123-138.

Hodges, Donald/Hartsell, Andrew/Brandeis, Consuelo/Brandeis, Tom/Bentley, James (2011): "Recession Effects on the Forests and Forest Products Industries of the South." In: Forest Products Journal 61/8, pp. 614-624.

Holling, Crawford Stanley/Gunderson, Lance (2002): "Resilience and Adaptive Cycles." In Holling, Crawford Stanley/Gunderson, Lance (eds.), Panarchy: Understanding Transformations in Human and Natural Systems, Washington, D.C.: Island Press, pp. 25-62.

Houle, Karen (2011): "Animal, Vegetable, Mineral: Ethics as Extension or Becoming?" In: Journal of Critical Animal Studies 9/1, pp. 89-116.

Hubbes, Martin (1999): "The American Elm and Dutch Elm Disease." In: The Forestry Chronicle 75/2, pp. 265-273.

Huber, Matthew (2018): "Resource Geographies I: Valuing Nature (Or Not)." In: Progress in Human Geography 42/1, pp. 148-159.

Hull, Matthew (2012): Government of Paper: The Materiality of Bureaucracy in Urban Pakistan, Berkeley, CA: University of California Press.

Hürriyet (2010): "Dünyanın en büyük 3. tohum gen bankası açıldı." https://www.hurriyet.com.tr/gundem/dunyanin-en-buyuk-3-tohum-gen-bankasi-acildi-13982679 (accessed December 17, 2020).

Ibáñez, Fernando/Wall, Luis/Fabra, Adriana (2017): "Starting Points in Plant-Bacteria Nitrogen-Fixing Symbioses: Intercellular Invasion of the Roots." In: Journal of Experimental Botany 68/8, pp. 1905-1918.

Ingold, Tim (1983): "The Architect and the Bee: Reflections on the Work of Animals and Men." In: Man 18/1, pp. 1-20.

Ingold, Tim (2000): The Perception of the Environment: Essays on Livelihood, Dwelling and Skill, London: Routledge.

Instone, Lesley (2009): "Northern Belongings: Frontiers, Fences, and Identities in Australia's Urban North." In: Environment and Planning A 41/4, pp. 827-841.

International Plant Protection Convention (2002): International Standards for Phytosanitary Measures #15: Guidelines for Regulating Wood Packaging Material in International Trade. Rome: Food and Agriculture Organization of the United Nations.

International Plant Protection Convention (2017): Explanatory Document for ISPM 15 (Regulation of Wood Packaging Material in International Trade), Rome: Food and Agriculture Organization of the United Nations.

Iqtidar, Humeira (2017): "How Long is Life? Neoliberalism and Islamic Piety." In: Critical Inquiry 43/4, pp. 790-812.

Jackson, Mark (2020): "On Decolonizing the Anthropocene: Disobedience via Plural Constitutions." In: Annals of the American Association of Geographers 111/3, pp. 698-708.

Jameson, Fredric (1991): Postmodernism, or, the Cultural Logic of Late Capitalism, Durham, NC: Duke University Press.

Johnson, Elizabeth R. (2017): "At the Limits of Species Being: Sensing the Anthropocene." In: South Atlantic Quarterly 116/2, pp. 275-292.

Jones, Owain/Cloke, Paul (2002): Tree Cultures: The Place of Trees and Trees in Their Place, Oxford: Berg.

Jongerden, Joost (2018): "Conquering the State and Subordinating Society under AKP Rule: A Kurdish Perspective on the Development of a New Autocracy in Turkey." In: Journal of Balkan and Near Eastern Studies 21/3, pp. 260-273.

Kallis, Giorgos/Swyngedouw, Erik (2018): "Do Bees Produce Value? A Conversation Between an Ecological Economist and a Marxist Geographer." In: Capitalism, Nature, Socialism 29/3, pp. 36-50.

Karapinar, Baris/Adaman, Fikret/Ozetan, Gokhan (2010): Rethinking Structural Reform in Turkish Agriculture: Beyond the World Bank's Strategy, New York, NY: Nova Science Publishers.

Kawa, Nicholas (2016): "How Religion, Race, and the Weedy Agency of Plants Shape Amazonian Home Gardens." In: Culture, Agriculture, Food and Environment 38/2, pp. 84-93.

Kay, Kelly/Kenney-Lazar, Miles (2017): "Value in Capitalist Natures: An Emerging Framework." In: Dialogues in Human Geography 7/3, pp. 295-309.

Keil, Roger (1995): "The Environmental Problematic in World Cities." In Knox, Paul/Taylor, Peter (eds.), World Cities in a World System, Cambridge: Cambridge University Press, pp. 280-297.

Keil, Roger (2003): "Urban Political Ecology." In: Urban Geography 24/8, pp. 723-738.

Keyder, Çağlar/Yenal, Zafer (2013): Bildiğimiz tarımın sonu: küresel iktidar ve köylülük. Istanbul: İletişim Yayınları.

Kimmerer, Robin Wall (2020): Braiding Sweetgrass: Indigenous Wisdom, Scientific Knowledge, and the Teachings of Plants, London: Penguin.

Kirksey, Eben (2015): "Species: A Praxiographic Study." In: Journal of the Royal Anthropological Institute 21/4, pp. 758-780.

Kirsch, Scott/Mitchell, Don (2004): "The Nature of Things: Dead Labor, Nonhuman Actors, and the Persistence of Marxism." In: Antipode 36/4, pp. 687-705.

Kleijn, David/Bommarco, Riccardo/Fijen, Thijs/Garibaldi, Lucas/Potts, Simon/van der Putten, Wim (2019): "Ecological intensification: Bridging the gap between science and practice." In: Trends in Ecology & Evolution 34/2, pp. 154-166.

Kloppenburg, Jack (2004): First the Seed: The Political Economy of Plant Biotechnology, 1492-2000, 2nd ed., Madison, WI: University of Wisconsin Press.

Knapp, Sandra (2019): "Are Humans Really Blind to Plants?" In: Plants, People, Planet 1/3, pp. 164-168.

Konrad, Heino/Kirisits, Thomas/Riegler, Markus/Halmschlager, Erhard/Stauffer, Christian (2002): "Genetic Evidence for Natural Hybridization between the Dutch Elm Disease Pathogens Ophiostoma novo-ulmi ssp. novo ulmi and O. novo-ulmi ssp. americana." In: Plant Pathology 51/1, pp. 78-84.

Kotsila, Panagiota/Anguelovski, Isabelle/Baró, Francesc/Langemeyer, Johannes/Sekulova, Filka/Connolly, James (2021): "Nature-Based Solutions as Discursive Tools and Contested Practices in Urban Nature's Neoliberalisation Process." In: Environment and Planning E: Nature and Space 4/2, pp. 252-274.

Krinsky, John/Simonet, Maud (2017): Who Cleans the Park? Public Work and Urban Governance in New York City, Chicago, IL: University of Chicago Press.

Krzywoszynska, Anna (2020): "Nonhuman Labor and the Making of Resources: Making Soils a Resource through Microbial Labor." In: Environmental Humanities 12/1, pp. 227-249.

Latour, Bruno (1986): "The Powers of Association." In Law, John (ed.), Power, Action, and Belief: A New Sociology of Knowledge, London: Routledge & Kegan Paul, pp. 264-280.

Latour, Bruno (1993): We Have Never Been Modern, New York, NY: Harvester Wheatsheaf.

Latour, Bruno (1994): "On Technical Mediation – Philosophy, Sociology, Genealogy." In: Common Knowledge 3/2, pp. 29-64.

Latour, Bruno (2004): Politics of Nature, Cambridge, MA: Harvard University Press.

Law, John (1994): Organizing Modernity, Oxford: Blackwell.

Lawford, Elliana (2016a): "Family of Darwin Golfer Killed by Falling Branch Plead for Similar Trees to be Chopped Down." In: ABC News, March 11, 2016. https://www.abc.net.au/news/2016-03-11/old-african-mahogany-trees-in-public-need-to-go-say-family/7241444 (accessed June 5, 2019).

Lawford, Elliana (2016b): "Death of Man Struck by Tree at Golf Course 'Preventable', NT Coroner Finds." In: ABC News, April 21, 2016. https://www.abc.net.au/news/2016-04-21/death-of-man-struck-by-tree-branch-preventable-says-coroner/7345302 (accessed 6 June, 2020).

Lawhon, Mary/Ernstson, Henrik/Silver, Jonathan (2014): "Provincializing Urban Political Ecology: Towards a Situated UPE through African Urbanism." In: Antipode 46/2, pp. 497-516.

Lawler, Eva (2018): "More Jobs, Cooler City: Another Step for Cavenagh Street, Civic and State Square Projects." Minister for Infrastructure, Planning and Logistics, NT Government. Media Release, November 20, 2018. http://newsroom.nt.gov.au/mediaRelease/28405 (accessed February 14, 2020).

Lea, Tess (2014): Darwin, Sydney: New South.

Lewis-Jones, Kay E (2019): "Holding the Wild in the Seed: Place, Escape and Liminality at the Millennium Seed Bank Partnership." In: Anthropology Today 35/2, pp. 3-7.

Li, Tania (2014): "What is Land? Assembling a Resource for Global Investment." In: Transactions of the Institute of British Geographers 39/4, pp. 589-602.

Lowe, Celia (2006): Wild Profusion: Biodiversity Conservation in an Indonesian Archipelago, Information Series, Princeton, NJ: Princeton University Press.

Luke, Timothy (2003): "Global Cities vs. 'global cities:' Rethinking Contemporary Urbanism and Public Ecology." In: Studies in Political Economy 70/1, pp. 11-33.

Malinowski, Bronislaw (1978 [1935]): Coral Gardens and Their Magic: A Study of the Methods of Tilling the Soil and of Agricultural Rites in the Trobriand Islands, New York, NY: Dover.

Mancuso, Stefano (2018): The Revolutionary Genius of Plants: A New Understanding of Plant Intelligence and Behavior, New York, NY: Atria.

Marder, Michael (2012): "Plant Intentionality and the Phenomenological Framework of Plant Intelligence." In: Plant Signaling & Behavior 7/11, pp. 1365-1372.

Marder, Michael (2013): Plant-Thinking: A Philosophy of Vegetal Life, New York, NY: Columbia University Press.

Margulies, Jared D./Bersaglio, Brock (2018): "Furthering Post-Human Political Ecologies." In: Geoforum 94, pp. 103-106.

Margulies, Jared/Bullough, Leigh-Anne/Hinsley, Amy/Ingram, Daniel/Cowell, Carly/Goettsch, Barbara/Klitgård, Bente/Lavorgna, Anita/Sinovas, Pablo/Phelps, Jacob (2019): "Illegal Wildlife Trade and the Persistence of 'Plant Blindness'." In: Plants, People, Planet 1/3, pp. 173-182.

Marx, Karl (1976 [1867]): Capital: A Critique of Political Economy, Vol. 1, Translated by B Fowkes, New York, NY: Penguin.

Marx, Karl (1982 [1867]): Capital: A Critique of Political Economy, Vol. 1, Harmondsworth: Penguin.

Marx, Karl (1988 [1844]): Economic and Philosophic Manuscripts of 1844, Translated by Martin Milligan, Amherst: Prometheus Books, pp. 13-168.

Marx, Karl (1993 [1939]): Grundrisse: Foundations of the Critique of Political Economy, London: Penguin.

McCracken, Donal (1997): Gardens of Empire, London: Leicester University Press.

Meeker, Natania/Szabari, Antonia (2020) : Radical Botany : Plants and Speculative Fiction, New York : Fordham.

Meyer, Peter/DeOreo, William (1999): Residential End Uses of Water, Tampa, FL: AWWA Research Foundation and American Water Works Association.

Mini, Caroline/Hogue, Terri/Pincetl, Stephanie (2014): "Estimation of Residential Outdoor Water Use in Los Angeles, California." In: Landscape and Urban Planning 127, pp. 124-135.

Mitchell, A.G., Brasier, Clive (1994): "Contrasting Structure of European and North American Populations of Ophiostoma ulmi." In: Mycological Research 98/5, pp. 576-582.

Mitchell, Timothy (2011): Carbon Democracy: Political Power in the Age of Oil, London: Verso.

Moll, Gary (1995): "Urban Forestry: A National Initiative." In Bradley, Gordon (ed.), Urban Forest Landscapes: Integrating Multidisciplinary Perspectives, Seattle, WA: University of Washington Press, pp. 12-16.

Moore, Jason (2015): Capitalism in the Web of Life: Ecology and the Accumulation of Capital, London: Verso.

Moore, Jason W. (2018): "The Capitalocene Part II: Accumulation by Appropriation and the Centrality of Unpaid Work/Energy." In: The Journal of Peasant Studies 45/2, pp. 237-279.

Munn, Nancy D. (1992): "The Cultural Anthropology of Time: A Critical Essay." In: Annual Review of Anthropology 21/1, pp. 93-123.

Murdoch, Jonathan (1995): "Actor-Networks and the Evolution of Economic Forms: Combining Description and Explanation in Theories of Regulation, Flexible Specialization, and Networks." In: Environment and Planning A 27/5, pp. 731-757.

Murdoch, Jonathan (1997): "Towards a Geography of Heterogeneous Associations." In: Progress in Human Geography 21/3, pp. 321-337.

Murdoch, Jonathan (1998): "The Spaces of Actor-Network Theory." In: Geoforum 29/4, pp. 357-374.

Murdoch, Jonathan (2001): "Ecologising Sociology: Actor-Network Theory, Co-construction and the Problem of Human Exemptionalism." In: Sociology 35/1, pp. 111-133.

Murphy, Michelle (2015): "Unsettling Care: Troubling Transnational Itineraries of Care in Feminist Health Practices." In: Social Studies of Science 45/5, pp. 717-737.

Musharraf, Pervez (2006): In the Line of Fire: A Memoir. New York, NY: Simon & Schuster.

Mustafa, Daanish (2005): "The Production of an Urban Hazardscape in Pakistan: Modernity, Vulnerability and the Range of Choice." In: Annals of the Association of American Geographers 95/3, pp. 566-586.

Mustafa, Daanish/Smucker Tom/Ginn, Franklin/Johns, Rebecca/Connelly, Shanon (2010): "Xeriscape People and the Cultural Politics of Turf-Grass Transformation." Environment and Planning D: Society and Space 28/4, pp. 600-617.

Myers, Natasha (2015): "Amplifying the Gaps between Climate Science and Forest Policy: The Write2Know Project and Participatory Dissent." In: Canada Watch Fall 2015, pp. 18-21.

Myers, Natasha (2015): "Conversations on Plant Sensing: Notes from the Field." In: NatureCulture 3, pp. 35-66.

Myers, Natasha (2016): "Photosynthesis." In: Lexicon for an Anthropocene Yet Unseen, Cultural Anthropology (https://culanth.org/fieldsights/photosynthesis). Last Accessed December 4, 2020.

Myers, Natasha (2018): "How to Grow Livable Worlds: Ten Not-So-Easy Steps." In: Oliver Smith, Kerry (ed.) The World to Come, Gainsville, FL: Harn Museum of Art, pp. 53-63.

Narotzky, Susana (2018): "Rethinking the Concept of Labour." In: Journal of the Royal Anthropological Institute 24/S1, pp. 29-43.

Nealon, Jeffrey (2016): Plant Theory: Biopower and Vegetable Life, Stanford, CA: Stanford University Press.

Needham, Joseph/Gwei-Djen, Lu/Hsing-Tsung, Huang (1986): Science and Civilisation in China. Volume 6, Biology and biological technology. Part 1 Botany, Cambridge: Cambridge University Press.

Nield, Lawrence (2018): "Requiem or Renewal? This is how a Tropical City like Darwin can Regain its Cool." In: The Conversation, October 22, 2018. Accessed: 17 July, 2020. (https://theconversation.com/requiem-or-renewal-this-is-how-a-tropical-city-like-darwin-can-regain-its-cool-102839).

Niklas, Karl (2016): Plant Evolution: An Introduction to the History of Life, Chicago, IL: University of Chicago Press.

Nikles, D. Garth (2006): "The Domestication of African Mahogany (*Khaya senegalensis*) in Northern Australia." In: Australian Forestry 69/1, pp. 68-69.

Nowak, David/Dwyer, John (2007): "Understanding the Benefits and Costs of Urban Ecosystems." In Kuser, John (ed.), Urban and Community Forestry in the Northeast, Dordrecht: Springer, pp. 25-46.

NT News (2018): "Time to Ditch Problem Trees." In: NT News, March 21, 2018. https://www.ntnews.com.au/news/opinion/time-to-ditch-problem-trees/news-story/be705f1eb14f8abf8f965b4a4b4177f0 (accessed October 29, 2020).

O'Connor, James (1996): "The Second Contradiction of Capitalism." In Benton, Ted (ed.), The Greening of Marxism, New York, NY: Guilford Press, pp. 197-221.

Oswalt, Christopher/Cooper, Jason/Brockway, Dale/Brooks, Horace/Walker, Joan/Connor, Kristina/Oswalt, Sonja/Conner, Roger (2012): History and current condition of longleaf pine in the Southern United States. Gen. Tech. Rep. SRS–166, Asheville, NC: U.S. Department of Agriculture Forest Service, Southern Research Station.

Oswalt, Sonja/Smith, Brad (2014): U.S. Forest Resource Facts and Historical Trends. FS–1036, Washington, D.C.: U.S. Department of Agriculture, Forest Service.

Oswalt, Sonja/Smith, Brad/Miles, Patrick/Pugh, Scott (2019): Forest Resources of the United States, 2017: A Technical Document Supporting the Forest Service 2020 RPA Assessment, Gen. Tech. Rep. WO-97, Washington, D.C.: U.S. Department of Agriculture, Forest Service.

Palin, Megan (2015): "Post-Cyclone Plantings, Now Wreaking Havoc." In: NT News, January 13, 2015. https://www.ntnews.com.au/news/postcyclone-plantings-now-wreaking-havoc/news-story/e48ba77981b0ca10cf011fa9359e5caf (accessed October 29, 2020).

Palmer, James (2021): "Putting Forests to Work? Enrolling Vegetal Labor in the Socioecological Fix of Bioenergy Resource Making." In: Annals of the American Association of Geographers 111/1, pp. 141-156.

Parreñas, Juno Salazar (2018): Decolonizing Extinction: The Work of Care in Orangutan Rehabilitation. Durham, NC: Duke University Press.

Parry, Bronwyn (2004): Trading the Genome: Investigating the Commodification of Bio-Information, New York, NY: Columbia University Press.

Pavord, Anna (1999): The Tulip: The Story of a Flower that has Made Men Mad, London: Bloomsbury.

Paxson, Heather (2018): "The Naturalization of Nature as Working." In: Cultural Anthropology. Online.

Peace, Tom (1960): "The Status and Development of Elm Disease in Britain." In: Forestry Commission Bulletin 33, pp. 1-44.

Peck, Jamie/Tickell, Adam (1994): "Jungle Law Breaks Out: Neoliberalism and Global-Local Disorder." In: Area 26/4, pp. 317-326.

Peck, Jamie/Tickell, Adam (2002): "Neoliberalizing Space." In Brenner, Neil/Theodore, Nik (eds.), Spaces of Neoliberalism: Urban Restructuring in North America and Western Europe, Oxford, Blackwell, pp. 33-57.

Peltola, Taru/Tuomisaari, Johanna (2015): "Making a Difference: Forest Biodiversity, Affective Capacities, and the Micro-Politics of Expert Fieldwork." In: Geoforum 64, pp. 1-11.

Peres, Sara (2019): "Seed Banking as Cryopower: A Cryopolitical Account of the Work of the International Board of Plant Genetic Resources, 1973–1984." In: Culture, Agriculture, Food and Environment: The Journal of Culture & Agriculture 41/2, pp. 76-86.

Perkins, Harold A. (2006): "Manifestations of Contradiction: Lakes within the Production/Consumption Dialectic." In: Antipode 38/1, pp. 128-149.

Perkins, Harold A. (2007): "Ecologies of Actor-Networks and (non)-Social Labor Within the Urban Political Economies of Nature." In: Geoforum 38/6, pp. 1152-62.

Perkins, Harold/Heynen, Nik/Wilson, Joe (2004): "Inequitable Access to Urban Reforestation: The Impact of Urban Political Economy on Housing Tenure and Urban Forests." In: Cities 21/4, pp. 291-299.

Phillips, Catherine/Atchison, Jennifer (2020): "Seeing the Trees for the (Urban) Forest: More-than-human Geographies and Urban Greening." In: Australian Geographer 5/2, pp. 155-168.

Philo, Chris/Wilbert, Chris (2000): Animal Spaces, Beastly Spaces, London: Routledge.

Pimental, David (2007): "Environmental and Economic Costs of Managing Vertebrate Species Invasions into the United States." In: Managing Vertebrate Invasive Species 38, pp. 1-8.

Pipe, Nicholas/Brasier, Clive/Buck, K (2000): "Evolutionary Relationships of the Dutch Elm Disease Fungus Ophiostoma novo-ulmi to Other Ophiostoma Species Investigated by Restriction Fragment Length Polymorphism Analysis of the rDNA Region." In: Journal of Phytopathology 148/9-10, pp. 533-539.

Plumwood, Val (2008): "Shadow Places and the Politics of Dwelling." In: Australian Humanities Review 44, pp. 139-50.

Polanyi, Karl (1944): The Great Transformation, New York, NY: Farrar & Rinehart.

Pollan, Michael (2001): The Botany of Desire: A Plant's-Eye View of the World, New York, NY: Random House.

Pollan, Michael (2013): "The Intelligent Plant: Scientists Debate a New Way of Understanding Flora." In: The New Yorker, December 23, 2013.

Porcher, Jocelyne (2014): "The Work of Animals: A Challenge for Social Sciences." In: Humanimalia: A Journal of Human/Animal Interface Studies 6/1.

Porcher, Jocelyne (2015): "Animal Work." In: The Oxford Handbook of Animal Studies. Oxford: Oxford University Press.

Porcher, Jocelyne (2017): "Elmo et Paro (R), Pourquoi l'un Travaille et l'Autre pas, et ce que ça Change." In: Ecologie et Politique 54, pp. 17-34.

Porcher, Jocelyne/Estebanez, Jean (eds.) (2019): Animal Labor: A New Perspective on Human-Animal Relations, Bielefeld: Transcript.

Postone, Moishe (1993): Time, Labor, and Social Domination: A Reinterpretation of Marx's Critical Theory, Cambridge: Cambridge University Press.

Powers, Richard (2018): The Overstory, London: WW Norton & Company.

Prance, Ghillean (2000): "The Conservation of Botanical Diversity." In: Jack G. Hawkes/Nigel Maxted/Brian V. Ford-Lloyd (2012), The Ex Situ Conservation of Plant Genetic Resources, Berlin: Springer, pp. 3-14.

Prudham, Scott (2003): "Taming Trees: Capital, Science, and Nature in Pacific Slope Tree Improvement." In: Annals of the American Association of Geographers 93/3, pp. 636-656.

Prudham, Scott (2005): Knock on Wood: Nature as Commodity in Douglas-Fir Country. New York, NY: Routledge.

Puig de la Bellacasa, Maria (2011): "Matters of Care in Technoscience: Assembling Neglected Things." In: Social Studies of Science 41/1, pp. 85-106.

Puig de la Bellacasa, Maria (2017): Matters of Care: Speculative Ethics in More than Human Worlds, Minneapolis, MN: University of Minnesota Press.

Radin, Joanna/Kowal, Emma (2017): "Introduction: The Politics of Low Temperature." In: Joanna Radin/Emma Kowal (eds.) Cryopolitics: Frozen Life in a Melting World, Cambridge, MA: The MIT Press, pp. 3-25.

Rajan, Kaushik Sunder (2006): Biocapital: The Constitution of Postgenomic Life, Durham, NC: Duke University Press.

Rajan, Kaushik Sunder (ed.) (2012): Lively Capital: Biotechnologies, Ethics, and Governance in Global Markets, Durham, NC: Duke University Press.

Rambelli, Fabio (2001): Vegetal Buddhas: Ideological Effects of Japanese Buddhist Doctrines on the Salvation of Inanimate Beings, Kyoto: Scuola Italiana di Studi sull'Asia Orientale.

Reice, Seth (1994): "Nonequilibrium Determinants of Biological Community Structure: Biological Communities are Always Recovering from the Last Disturbance. Disturbance and Heterogeneity, not Equilibrium, Generate Biodiversity." In: American Scientist 82/5, pp. 424-435.

Riddell, William (2017): "Aspects of Breeding Ecology and Diet of the Brahminy Kite 'Haliastur indus' over two Breeding Seasons in Darwin, Northern Territory." In: Australian Field Ornithology 34, p. 116

Rival, Laura (1998): The Social Life of Trees: Anthropological Perspectives on Tree Symbolism, Oxford: Berg.

Roa-Rodríguez, Carolina/van Dooren, Thom (2008): "Shifting Common Spaces of Plant Genetic Resources in the International Regulation of Property." In: The Journal of World Intellectual Property 11/3, pp. 176-202.

Robbins, Paul (1998): "Paper Forests: Imagining and Deploying Exogenous Ecologies in Arid India." In: Geoforum 29/1, pp. 69-86.

Robbins, Paul (2001): "Tracking Invasive Land Covers in India, or Why Our Landscapes Have Never Been Modern." In: Annals of the Association of American Geographers 91/4, pp. 637-659.

Robbins, Paul (2004a): "Culture and Politics of Invasive Species." In: Geographical Review 94/2, pp. iii-iv.

Robbins, Paul (2004b): "Comparing Invasive Networks: Cultural and Political Biographies of Invasive Species." In: Geographical Review 94/2, pp. 139-156.

Robbins, Paul (2006): Lawn people: How Grasses, Weeds and Chemicals Make Us Who We Are, Philadelphia, PA: Temple University Press.

Robbins, Paul/Fraser, Alistair (2003): "A Forest of Contradictions: Producing the Landscapes of the Scottish Highlands." In: Antipode 35/1, pp. 95-118

Robertson, Morgan/Wainwright, Joel (2013): "The Value of Nature to the State." In: Annals of the American Association of Geographers 103/4, pp. 890-905.

Roosth, Sophia. (2018) "Virus, Coal, and Seed: Subcutaneous Life in the Polar North." Los Angeles Review of Books. https://lareviewofbooks.org/article/virus-coal-seed-subcutaneous-life-polar-north (accessed August 18, 2020).

Rots, Aike (2017): Shinto, Nature and Ideology in Contemporary Japan: Making Sacred Forests, London: Bloomsbury.

Rudy, Alan (2005): "On ANT and Relational Materialisms." In: Capital Nature Socialism 16/4, pp. 109-125.

Rudy, Alan/Gareau, Brian (2005): "Actor-Network Theory, Marxist Economics, and Marxist Political Ecology." In: Capitalism Nature Socialism 16/4, pp. 85-90.

Sanders, Dawn (2019): „Standing in the Shadows of Plants." In: Plants People Planet 1/3, pp. 130-138.

Santamouris, Mattheos/Haddad, Shamila/ Ulpiani, Giulia/Fox, Jonathan/Paolini, Ricardo/Synnefa, Afroditi/Fiorito, Francesco/Garshasbi, Samira (2018): *Heat Mitigation Program. Darwin Northern Territory* Final Report. Sydney, Australia, University of New South Wales.

Schiebinger, Londa (2004): Plants and Empire, Cambridge, MA: Harvard University Press.

Schlarbaum, Scott/Hebard, Frederick/Spaine, Pauline/Kamalay, Joseph (1997): "Three American Tragedies: Chestnut Blight, Butternut Canker, and Dutch Elm Disease." In Britton, Kerry (ed.), Exotic Pests of Eastern Forests Conference Proceedings, Nashville, TN: Exotic Pest Plant Council, pp. 45-54.

Schmidt, Markus/Meinhart, Camillo (2009): Diverseeds: Plant Genetic Resources for Food and Agriculture. Documentary, News, 2009. (http://www.imdb.com/title/tt1512771).

Schreiber, Lawrence/Peacock, John (1979): Dutch Elm Disease and its Control, Washington, D.C.: Government Printing Office.

Schulthies, Becky (2019): "Partitioning, Phytocommunicability and Plant Pieties." In: Anthropology Today 35/2, pp. 8-12.

Schulze, Ernst-Detlef/Körner, Christian/Law, Beverly/Haberl, Helmut/Luyssaert, Sebastiaan (2012): "Large-Scale Bioenergy from Additional Harvest of Forest Biomass is Neither Sustainable Nor Greenhouse Gas Neutral." In: GCB Bioenergy 4/6, pp. 611-616.

Scott, James (1998): Seeing like a State: How Certain Schemes to Improve the Human Condition Have Failed, New Haven, CT: Yale University Press.

Searchinger, Timothy/Beringer, Tim/Holtsmark, Bjart/Kammen, Daniel/Lambin, Eric/Lucht, Wolfgang/Raven, Peter/van Ypersele, Jan-Pascal (2018): "Europe's Renewable Energy Directive Poised to Harm Global Forests." In: Nature Communications 9/3741, pp. 1-4.

Sherald, James (1982): Dutch Elm Disease and its Management. U.S. Department of Agriculture Forest Service, Washington, D.C.: Government Printing Office.

Shirane, Haruo (2013): Japan and the Culture of the Four Seasons: Nature, Literature, and the Arts, New York, NY: Columbia University Press.

Shukin, Nicole (2009): Animal Capital: Rendering Life in Biopolitical Times, Minneapolis, MN: University of Minnesota Press.

Siddiqa, Ayesha (2017): Military Inc.: Inside Pakistan's Military Economy, London: Pluto.

Simone, AbdouMaliq (2004): "People as Infrastructure: Intersecting Fragments in Johannesburg." In: Public Culture 16/3, pp. 407-429.

Simonet, Maud (2018): Travail Gratuit: La Nouvelle Exploitation? Paris: Textuel.

Smith, N. (2007): "Nature as Accumulation Strategy." In: Socialist Register 43.

Smith, Neil (1984): Uneven Development: Nature, Capital and the Production of Space, Oxford: Blackwell.

Springmann, Marco/Wiebe, Keith/Mason-D'Croz, Daniel/ Sulser, Timothy/Rayner, Mike/ Scarborough, Peter (2018): "Health and Nutritional Aspects of Sustainable Diet Strategies and their Association with Environmental Impacts: A Global Modelling Analysis with Country-Level Detail." In: The Lancet Planetary Health 2/10, pp. 451-461.

Sprugel, Douglas (1991): "Disturbance, Equilibrium, and Environmental Variability: What is 'Natural' Vegetation in a Changing Environment?" In: Biological Conservation 58/1, pp. 1-18.

Srinivasan, Krithika (2014): "Caring for the Collective: Biopower and Agential Subjectification in Wildlife Conservation." In: Environment and Planning D: Society and Space 32/3, pp. 501-517.

Stépanoff, Charles/Vigne, Jean-Denis (eds.) (2018): Hybrid Communities: Biosocial Approaches to Domestication and Other Trans-Species Relationships, London: Routledge.

Strathern, Marilyn (2001): "The Patent and the Malanggan." In: Pinney, Christopher/Thomas, Nicholas (eds.), Beyond Aesthetics: Art and the Technologies of Enchantment, London: Routledge, pp. 259-86.

Strebel, Ignaz (2011): "The Living Building: Towards a Geography of Maintenance Work." In: Social & Cultural Geography 12/3, pp. 243-62.

Sundberg, Juanita. (2014): "Decolonizing Posthumanist Geographies." In: Cultural Geographies 21, pp. 33–47.

Swyngedouw, Erik (1996): "The City as a Hybrid: On Nature, Society and Cyborg Urbanization." In: Capitalism Nature Socialism 7/2, pp. 65-80.

Swyngedouw, Erik (2005): "Dispossessing H2O: The Contested Terrain of Water Privatization." In: Capitalism Nature Socialism 16/1, pp. 81-98.

Swyngedouw, Erik/Heynen, Nik (2003): "Urban Political Ecology, Justice, and the Politics of Scale." In: Antipode 35/5, pp. 898-918.

Talbot, Ian (2012): Pakistan: A New History, London: Hurst & Company.

Tamminen, Sakari (2019): Biogenetic Paradoxes of the Nation: Finncattle, Apples, and Other Genetic-Resource Puzzles, Durham, NC: Duke University Press.

Tamminen, Sakari/Brown, Nik (2011): "Nativitas: Capitalizing Genetic Nationhood." In: New Genetics and Society 30/1, pp. 73-99.

The Huntington (no date): International Succulent Introductions Plant Introductions of the Huntington Botanical Gardens. http://media.huntington.org/ISI/catalogintro.html (accessed June 28, 2020).

Thomas, Keith. (1983): Man and the Natural World: Changing Attitudes in England, 1500-1800, New York, NY: Viking.

Thompson, Edward P. (1967): "Time, Work-Discipline, and Industrial Capitalism." In: Past & Present 38, pp. 56-97.

Thompson, Jesse (2018a): "Hospitalisations Increase and Asphalt Hits 60 Degrees without Darwin Heat Mitigation Strategy." In: ABC News, September 18,

2018. https://www.abc.net.au/news/2018-09-19/hospitalisations-spike-asphalt
-hits-60c-on-hot-darwin-days/10246398 (accessed February 14, 2020).

Thompson, Jesse (2018b): "Wood Sculptor Makes Public Art out of Trees Downed in Darwin by Cyclone Marcus." In: ABC News, March 22, 2018. https://www.abc.net.au/news/2018-03-22/darwin-artist-takes-chainsaw -to-fallen-trees-from-cyclone-marcus/9575276 (accessed June 19, 2019).

Thummarukudy, Muralee (2012): "Waste: Disaster Waste Management: An Overview." In: Rajib Shaw/Phong Tran (eds.), Environment Disaster Linkages (Community, Environment and Disaster Risk Management, Vol. 9), Bingley: Emerald, pp. 195-218.

Todd, Zoe (2016): "An Indigenous Feminist's Take on the Ontological Turn: 'Ontology' is Just Another Word for Colonialism." In: Journal of Historical Sociology 29/1, pp. 4-22.

Tsing, Anna (2018): "A Multispecies Ontological Turn?" In: Omura Keiichi/Otsuki Grant Jun/Satsuka Shiho/Morita Atsuro (eds.), The World Multiple: The Quotidian Politics of Knowing and Generating Entangled Worlds, New York, NY: Routledge, pp. 233-246.

Tsing, Anna L. (2015): The Mushroom at the End of the World: On the Possibility of Life in Capitalist Ruins, Princeton, NJ: Princeton University Press.

Turner, Ellie (2016): "So Many Should Have Done so Much More." In: NT News, March 12, 2016. https://www.ntnews.com.au/news/northern-territory/so-ma ny-should-have-done-so-much-more/news-story/03734ee01a9a40a6eb185ab19 23cf642 (accessed June 5, 2019).

Ulin, Robert C. (1996): Vintages and Traditions: An Ethnohistory of Southwest French Wine Cooperatives, Washington, D.C.: Smithsonian Institution Press.

United States National Arboretum, Agricultural Research Service (1995): Ulmus americana Cultivars "Valley Forge" and "New Harmony." U.S. National Arboretum, Cultivar Release, Floral and Nursery Plants Research Unit, 1.

USDA Foreign Agricultural Service (2019): Global Agricultural Information Network Report: EU Biofuels Annual 2019, GAIN Report Number NL9022.

Van der Sommen, Frans J./Pearson, Diane M./Boggs, Guy S. (2018): "Analysis of the Interrelationship between Houses, Trees and Damage in a Cyclone Affected City: Can Landscape Design and Planning Utilising Trees Minimise Cyclone Impact?" In: International Journal of Disaster Risk Reduction 28, pp. 701-710.

van der Veen, Marijke (2014) "The Materiality of Plants: Plant-People Entanglements." In: World Archaeology 46/5, pp. 799-812.

van Dooren, Thom (2009): "Banking Seed: Use and Value in the Conservation of Agricultural Diversity." In: Science as Culture 18/4, pp. 373-95.

van Dooren, Thom (2014): Flightways: Life and Loss at the Edge of Extinction, New York, NY: Columbia University Press.

van Dooren, Thom/Kirksey, Eben/Münster, Ursula (2016): "Multispecies Studies: Cultivating Arts of Attentiveness." In: Environmental Humanities 8/1, pp. 1-23.

Vandermeer, Jeff (2014): The Southern Reach Trilogy, FSG Originals.

Vanovac, Neda (2018): "Cyclone Marcus: Recovery Payments Available for Some Residents, Council Considers Removing Mahoganies." In: ABC News, March 20, 2018. https://www.abc.net.au/news/2018-03-20/cyclone-marcus-darwin-resid ents-back-work-looming-threat-storm/9565912 (accessed October 19, 2020).

Wadiwel, Dinesh (2018): "Chicken Harvesting Machine: Animal Labor, Resistance, and the Time of Production." In: South Atlantic Quarterly 117/3, pp. 527-549.

Wakefield, Stephanie (2020): "Making Nature into Infrastructure: The Construction of Oysters as a Risk Management Solution in New York City." In: Environment and Planning E: Nature and Space 3/3, pp. 761-785.

Wakita, Osamu (1999): Osaka, the Merchants' Capital of Early Modern Japan, Ithaca and London: Cornell University Press.

Walker, George R. (2010): "A Review of the Impact of Cyclone Tracy on Building Regulations and Insurance." In: Australian Meteorological and Oceanographic Journal 60/3, pp. 199-206.

Walker, Peter (2005): "Political Ecology: Where is the Ecology?" In: Progress in Human Geography 29/1, pp. 73-82.

Walters, Keith J. (1978): "The Reconstruction of Darwin after Cyclone Tracy." In: Disasters 2/1, pp. 59-68.

Wandersee, James/Schussler, Elisabeth (1999): "Preventing Plant Blindness." In: The American Biology Teacher 61/2, pp. 84-86.

Warren, Charles (2007): "Perspectives on the 'Alien' versus 'Native' Species Debate: A Critique of Concepts, Language, and Practice." In: Progress in Human Geography 31/1, pp. 427-446.

Wear, David/Greis, John (2012): The Southern Forest Futures Project: Summary Report. General Technical Report SRS-168, Asheville, NC: USDA Forest Service Southern Research Station.

Webber, Joan/Brasier, Clive (1984): "The Transmission of Dutch Elm Disease: A Study of the Processes Involved." In Anderson, Jonathan/Rayner, Alan/Walton, David (eds.), Invertebrate-Microbial Interactions, Cambridge, Cambridge University Press, pp. 271-306.

Weeks, Kathi (2007): "Life Within and Against Work: Affective Labor, Feminist Critique, and Post-Fordist Politics." In: Ephemera 7/1, pp. 233-249.

Weeks, Kathi (2011): The Problem with Work: Feminism, Marxism, Antiwork Politics, and Postwork Imaginaries. Durham, NC: Duke University Press.

West, Brad (2000): "Mythologising a Natural Disaster in Post-Industrial Australia: The Incorporation of Cyclone Tracy within Australian National Identity." In: Journal of Australian Studies 24/66, pp. 197-204.

Westengen, Ola Tveitereid/Skarbø, Kristine/Hunduma Mulesa, Teshome/Berg, Trygve (2018): "Access to Genes: Linkages between Genebanks and Farmers' Seed Systems." In: Food Security 10/1, pp. 9-25.

Wesley, Frances/Carpenter, Stephen/Brock, William/Holling, Crawford Stanley/Gunderson, Lance (2002): "Why Systems of People and Nature are Not Just Social and Ecological Systems." In Holling, Crawford Stanley/Gunderson, Lance (eds.), Panarchy: Understanding Transformations in Human and Natural Systems, Washington, D.C.: Island Press, pp. 103-119.

Whatmore, Sarah (2002): Hybrid Geographies: Natures Cultures Spaces, London: Sage Publications.

Whatmore, Sarah (2004): "Humanism's Excess: Some Thoughts on the 'Post-Human'ist Agenda." In: Environment and Planning A 36/8, pp. 1360-1363.

Williams, Matt (2018): "Stubborn Darwin Will Never be Defeated." In: NT News, March 17, 2018, https://www.ntnews.com.au/news/northern-territory/stubborn-darwin-will-never-be-defeated/news-story/5e121ab0cafdbd27e015876bb433 6310 (accessed June 5, 2019).

Williams, Mike (1989): Americans and Their Forests: A Historical Geography, Cambridge: Cambridge University Press.

Wolch, Jennifer (1996): "Zoöpolis." Capitalism Nature Socialism 7/2, pp. 21-48.

Wolch, Jennifer/Pincetl, Stephanie/Pulido, Laura (2002): "Urban Nature and the Nature of Urbanism." In Dear, Michael (ed.), From Chicago to L.A.: Making Sense of Urban Theory, Thousand Oaks, CA: Sage Publications, pp. 367-402.

Zeder, Melinda (2015): "Core Questions in Domestication Research." In: Proceedings of the National Academy of Sciences of the United States of America 112/11, pp. 3191-3198.

Zimmerer, Karl/Young, Kenneth (eds.) (1998): Nature's Geography: New Lessons for Conservation in Developing Countries, Madison, WI: University of Wisconsin Press.

Zwar, Will (2018a): "Council to Decide Whether to Clear more than 800 'Unsuitable' Trees throughout Darwin." In: NT News, July 16, 2018, https://www.ntnews.com.au/lifestyle/arboreal-cleansing-provides-darwin-with-opportunity/news-story/274328af a36c1bf2a67o68d132o23d54 (accessed June 5, 2019).

Zwar, Will (2018b): "Darwin Council Wants to Cover Half of the CBD with a Natural Tree Canopy." In: NT News, November 20, 2018, https://www.ntnews.com.au/news/northern-territory/darwin-council-wants-to-cover-half-of-the-cbd-with-a-natural-tree-canopy/news-story/befca4279dc16b5a48661f8ac18a3b6ef (accessed June 5, 2019).

Social Sciences

kollektiv orangotango+ (ed.)
This Is Not an Atlas
A Global Collection of Counter-Cartographies
2018, 352 p., hardcover, col. ill.
34,99 € (DE), 978-3-8376-4519-4
E-Book: free available, ISBN 978-3-8394-4519-8

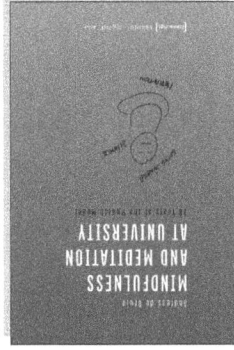

Gabriele Dietze, Julia Roth (eds.)
Right-Wing Populism and Gender
European Perspectives and Beyond
April 2020, 286 p., pb., ill.
35,00 € (DE), 978-3-8376-4980-2
E-Book: 34,99 € (DE), ISBN 978-3-8394-4980-6

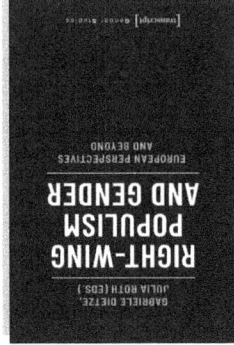

Mozilla Foundation
Internet Health Report 2019
2019, 118 p., pb., ill.
19,99 € (DE), 978-3-8376-4946-8
E-Book: free available, ISBN 978-3-8394-4946-2

Social Sciences

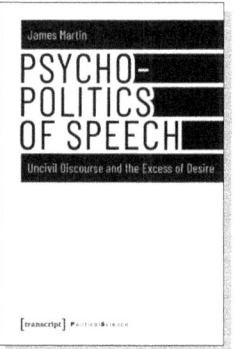

James Martin
Psychopolitics of Speech
Uncivil Discourse and the Excess of Desire

2019, 186 p., hardcover
79,99 € (DE), 978-3-8376-3919-3
E-Book:
PDF: 79,99 € (DE), ISBN 978-3-8394-3919-7

Michael Bray
Powers of the Mind
Mental and Manual Labor
in the Contemporary Political Crisis

2019, 208 p., hardcover
99,99 € (DE), 978-3-8376-4147-9
E-Book:
PDF: 99,99 € (DE), ISBN 978-3-8394-4147-3

Ernst Mohr
The Production of Consumer Society
Cultural-Economic Principles of Distinction

April 2021, 340 p., pb., ill.
39,00 € (DE), 978-3-8376-5703-6
E-Book: available as free open access publication
PDF: ISBN 978-3-8394-5703-0

**All print, e-book and open access versions of the titles in our list
are available in our online shop www.transcript-publishing.com**

GPSR Authorized Representative: Easy Access System Europe, Mustamäe tee
50, 10621 Tallinn, Estonia, gpsr.requests@easproject.com